IRELAND'S LEGENDS AND MYTHS

DÁNIEL FUIL

CONTENTS

"Ní neart go cur le chéile."
(Nee nyart guh kur leh khay-luh)
"There is no strength without unity."

— ANCIENT IRISH WISDOM

INTRODUCTION

Ireland is a land steeped in stories, where myth and history weave together to create a tapestry of wonder, bravery, and magic. From the echoing halls of ancient kings to the mystical forests where heroes were forged, these tales have been passed down through generations, preserving the heart of Irish culture and imagination.

This book invites you on a journey through Ireland's most beloved legends and myths while immersing you in the beauty of the Irish language, Gaeilge. By blending storytelling with basic Irish vocabulary, we aim to create a unique experience where readers can both enjoy these timeless tales and connect with the language and culture of Éire (Ay-rah), Ireland. The stories are written in English, but you will find Irish words woven seamlessly into the narrative, each accompanied by pronunciation and translation. This bilingual approach allows you to explore Irish mythology while learning key Gaeilge terms naturally. Whether you are new to Irish or seeking to deepen your understanding, these tales provide a magical and educational journey.

To enhance your experience, pay attention to the integrated vocabulary and pronunciation guides, which will help you connect with the rhythm and sounds of Gaeilge. Embrace the cultural notes included in each story, offering insights into Ireland's history, traditions, and the enduring significance of its mythology. Enjoy the blend of humor, tragedy, and heroism that defines Irish storytelling. These themes reflect the wit, resilience, and spirit of the Irish people.

This collection is more than a book of myths; it is an invitation to step into the world of Ireland's legendary heroes, gods, and magical realms. May these stories bring you closer to the heart of Irish culture, where every word and legend is a thread in the vibrant fabric of our heritage. Go n-éirí an bóthar leat (Guh nye-ree on boh-har lat)—May the road rise to meet you—as you embark on this journey through the myths and magic of Ireland.

CHAPTER 1

HOUND OF ULSTER

Cú Chulainn (Coo Hull-un) is one of the most celebrated figures in Irish mythology, a symbol of courage, strength, and destiny. His story comes from the Ulster Cycle, a collection of ancient tales that recount the deeds of the warriors and kings of northern Ireland, known as Ulaidh (Ul-uh, Ulster). Cú Chulainn is said to be a demigod, son of the Irish god Lugh and Deichtire, a mortal who was sister of the king of Ulster. Cú Chulainn's legend begins not as a mighty warrior, but as a boy named Sétanta (Shay-tan-tah), full of curiosity and fearlessness.

This story follows Sétanta's journey from a clever and bold child to the hero known as the Hound of Ulster. Through his quick thinking and unmatched bravery, he earns his name and place in history. Along the way, we'll encounter cluiche iomána (kluh-ka ih-moh-nah, a hurling match), laochra (lay-kh-ruh, warriors), and the draíocht (dree-ocht, magic) that weaves through the myths of Ireland.

Prepare to enter a world of fierce battles, ancient feuds, and heroic deeds as we trace the beginnings of Cú Chulainn's incredible story. Let this tale bring you closer to the heart of Irish culture, where myth and language meet to create something timeless.

The Hound of Ulster

Long before he became known as Cú Chulainn (Coo Hull-un, meaning the Hound of Culann), the legendary hero was simply Sétanta (Shay-tan-tah), a spirited boy with dreams as vast as the green hills of his homeland. Born in the dúiche (doo-hah, territory) of Ulster, Sétanta stood out from an early age. While other boys played games or shirked their chores, Sétanta was driven by a relentless energy and a desire to prove himself.

Even as a child, Sétanta possessed remarkable neart (nyart, strength) and scil (skil, skill). He could outrun the fastest hounds and hurl a sleá (shlah, spear) farther than any adult. He was clever, too—always thinking three steps ahead in any game or challenge. Though small for his age, he carried himself with the confidence of a laoch (lay-ukh, hero) in the making.

Sétanta's greatest aspiration was to join the Fianna (fee-ah-nah, warriors) of Ulster, the most renowned band of warriors in Ireland. He idolized their courage, their skill in battle, and their loyalty to the rí (ree, king). When he wasn't practicing with his makeshift weapons or wrestling with older boys, he was pestering his father for tales of their bravery. His father, a minor chieftain, often said, "Someday, my boy, the bards will sing of your deeds."

But Sétanta wasn't content to wait for "someday." One afternoon, while playing iománaíocht (ih-muh-nee-ukht, hurling) with a group of older boys, Sétanta's cleverness shone through. The older boys underestimated him, laughing at his smaller size and trying to push him out of the game. But Sétanta, quick as a gé (gay, goose) on the water, used his agility and wits to outmaneuver them. He darted past their defenses, striking the ball cleanly into the cúl (kool, goal) time and time again.

As the boys watched in awe, their laughter turned to cheers. One of them exclaimed, "This lad is as fierce as a madra rua (mah-drah roo-ah, fox) and twice as cunning!" From that day on, the older boys treated Sétanta as their equal, if not their superior.

Despite his victories, Sétanta's ambitions didn't stop with besting his peers. He wanted to prove himself to the warriors of

Ulster, the Fir Uladh (fir ul-ah, Men of Ulster), who gathered at the great hall of King Conchobar (Kawn-kho-bar). "I'll show them I belong," he vowed one night, staring at the stars above his ríocht (ree-uhkt, kingdom). Little did he know, his chance to prove himself would come sooner than he expected—and in a way no one could have imagined.

One fateful day, Sétanta was invited by King Conchobar (Kawn-kho-bar), ruler of Ulster, to attend a grand féasta (fay-sta, feast) at the home of Culann (Coo-lawn), the renowned blacksmith. Culann's ceárta (kyar-ta, forge) was famed across the land for its finely crafted weapons and tools, and his hospitality was equally legendary. Warriors, nobles, and bards gathered there to feast and tell tales, and Sétanta was eager to join them.

Before the gathering, Conchobar stopped by the field where Sétanta was engrossed in a game of iománaíocht (ih-muh-nee-ukht, hurling). "Come with me, boy," the king called out, his voice carrying across the field.

"I'll follow shortly," Sétanta replied, gripping his camán (kah-mawn, hurling stick). "I just need to finish this game." Conchobar smiled, knowing Sétanta's determination well, and continued on to Culann's forge.

As twilight settled over the hills, Sétanta made his way to the ceárta (kyar-ta, forge). The sounds of music and laughter spilled from the feast, and the glow of torches illuminated the path. But just as he neared the entrance, a low growl stopped him in his tracks. From the shadows emerged Culann's madra faire (mah-drah fwar-eh, guard dog), a massive beast with sharp teeth bared and eyes glowing like embers. Trained to protect the forge and its master, the dog charged at Sétanta, ready to attack.

Without hesitation, Sétanta raised his camán and hurled his sliotar (shlit-er, hurling ball) with incredible force. The ball struck the dog with precision, and before the beast could recover, Sétanta lunged forward, grappling it with his bare hands. In a display of strength and skill far beyond his years, he subdued the dog, killing it in self-defense.

The commotion brought Culann and the guests rushing out of the ceárta. The sight of the lifeless guard dog and the boy standing over it stunned them into silence. Culann's face darkened with grief and anger. "That dog was not just my protector," he said, his voice heavy with emotion. "It was my companion. Who will guard my forge now?"

Sétanta stepped forward, his young face solemn. "I will take its place," he declared, his voice steady despite the murmurs of disbelief from the crowd. "Until you can train a new madra faire, I will guard your forge as fiercely as that dog did."

Culann studied the boy for a moment, his anger giving way to admiration. "You are no ordinary child," he said. "From this day forth, you shall be known as Cú Chulainn (Coo Hull-un, Hound of Culann)."

The crowd erupted into cheers, and even Conchobar nodded with approval. Sétanta's vow not only soothed Culann's grief but also marked the boy's transition into something greater. He was no longer just Sétanta; he was now Cú Chulainn, a name that would echo through the ages.

This moment at the ceárta was a turning point for Sétanta, cementing his path toward heroism. By standing up to the guard dog and taking responsibility for his actions, he demonstrated not only courage but also onóir (un-ore, honor). It was here, under the watchful eyes of Ulster's finest, that the boy began his journey to becoming one of Ireland's greatest legends.

Cú Chulainn's (Coo Hull-un) first great challenge came not long after he earned his name. Word of his courage and skill spread quickly, and soon, Ulster's oireachtas (ur-ok-tas, assembly) declared that the boy would be allowed to join their ranks as a warrior. Though he was still young, his determination and talent had already earned him respect among Ulster's finest.

One day, news arrived that an enemy warrior from Connacht (Kawn-oct), a land often at odds with Ulster, had crossed into its borders, threatening the peace. This warrior, Fer Baeth (Fair Bah-hah), was infamous for his brute strength, cunning tactics, and merciless nature in battle. His presence sent a ripple of unease through Ulster, and the warriors of the Red Branch Knights began to prepare for a swift and decisive response.

In the great hall of Emain Macha (Eh-mon Mah-khah), the warriors gathered to plan their defense. The air was thick with tension as Conchobar (Kawn-kho-bar), king of Ulster, listened to reports of Fer Baeth's destruction. Then, before anyone could propose a strategy, a clear, steady voice cut through the murmurs.

"Let me face him," said Cú Chulainn, his voice calm but resolute.

All heads turned to the young warrior, who stood at the center of the hall, his hands resting on the hilt of his spear. There was no hesitation in his tone, no doubt in his expression. He was ready.

The older warriors exchanged uneasy glances. Despite Cú Chulainn's recent victories, he was still so young, barely more than a boy. Could he truly face a seasoned fighter like Fer Baeth and hope to survive?

"Cú Chulainn," one of the older knights began cautiously, "this is no small test. Fer Baeth is a warrior of great strength and cruelty. It would be wiser to face him as one of many, rather than alone."

But Cú Chulainn's eyes blazed with determination. "I am the Hound of Culann," he said, his voice unwavering. "I have sworn to protect this tír (teer, land) and its people. Let me prove my loyalty and my strength."

Conchobar, seated in his high chair at the head of the hall, watched the boy closely. He saw not the rashness of youth, but the unshakable resolve of a true warrior. He nodded slowly, silencing the murmurs of dissent with a raised hand.

"If you believe you can defeat him, Cú Chulainn," Conchobar said, his tone steady, "then the honor is yours. But remember this: Ulster's strength lies not in one warrior but in the unity of its people. Fight with courage, but fight wisely."

A murmur of approval spread through the hall, though some still looked uneasy. Cú Chulainn bowed his head in respect to his king, then turned and strode from the hall to prepare for the coming battle. As he left, his childhood friend Láeg (Layg), who served as his loyal charioteer, hurried to his side.

"You're truly going to face Fer Baeth alone?" Láeg asked, his voice a mix of admiration and concern.

"I am," Cú Chulainn replied, gripping the shaft of his spear. "For if I cannot protect this ríocht (ree-uhkt, kingdom) on my own, how can I call myself its champion?"

And so, with the weight of Ulster's hopes upon him, Cú Chulainn prepared for his first true test as a warrior. Little did he know, this would be the battle that would etch his name into the annals of legend forever.

As the sun set over the hills, Cú Chulainn rode out to face Fer Baeth alone. The enemy warrior stood tall and imposing, his claíomh (klee-uv, sword) glinting in the fading light. "Is this who they've sent to face me?" Fer Baeth sneered, laughing at the sight of the young boy.

Cú Chulainn tightened his grip on his sleá (shlah, spear). "You'll find me more than enough," he replied, his voice steady.

The battle began with Fer Baeth charging forward, his sword raised high. But Cú Chulainn was faster. He sidestepped the attack with ease, his movements sharp and precise. Using his agility to his advantage, he launched his sleá (shlah, spear), striking Fer Baeth's shield and forcing him to stagger back.

Fer Baeth roared in anger, swinging wildly in an attempt to overpower the boy. But Cú Chulainn remained calm, using his smaller size and speed to outmaneuver his opponent. He darted around Fer Baeth, landing precise blows with his ga (gah, spear) and wearing the larger man down.

At last, the moment came. Cú Chulainn feinted to one side, drawing Fer Baeth off balance, and then struck with all his might. His spear pierced the enemy's armor, and Fer Baeth fell to the ground, defeated.

The warriors of Ulster, watching from a distance, erupted into cheers. Cú Chulainn stood over his fallen opponent, not with arrogance, but with the quiet confidence of a true warrior. He had proven himself in single combat, defending his homeland and earning the respect of even the most seasoned fighters.

This victory marked the beginning of Cú Chulainn's rise to fame. Though he was still young, his neart (nyart, strength), misneach (mish-nakh, courage), and lúth (loo, agility) were undeniable. From that day on, he was not just a boy with a name; he was a force to be reckoned with, a warrior destined for greatness.

With his first victory behind him, as Cú Chulainn (Coo Hull-un, Hound of Culann), returned to Emain Macha (Eh-min Mah-kha), the stronghold of Ulster, where the warriors of the Craobh Rua (Kreev Roo-ah, Red Branch) awaited him. The assembly of warriors erupted in cheers as he entered the hall, his sleá slung across his back and his eyes alight with triumph.

Conchobar (Kawn-kho-bar), king of Ulster, rose from his seat at the head of the halla (hall-ah, hall). "Today, a great victory has been won," he declared, his voice ringing out over the gathered warriors. "Not by an army, but by one who shows the courage, skill, and heart of a true warrior. Cú Chulainn, you have proven yourself worthy."

The mood in the hall grew solemn as Conchobar beckoned Cú Chulainn forward. At the center of the room stood a great stone altar, adorned with symbols of Ulster's strength: a sword, a shield, and a sleá. It was here that warriors swore their oaths, pledging their lives to the protection of their people and their land.

Cú Chulainn stepped forward, kneeling before the altar. Conchobar placed a hand on his shoulder, his expression filled with pride. "Cú Chulainn," he said, "do you swear to uphold the honor of Ulster, to protect its people, and to fight for its freedom with every breath you take?"

Cú Chulainn met the king's gaze. "I swear it," he replied, his voice steady and unwavering. "I will defend Ulster with my neart (nyart, strength), my misneach (mish-nakh, courage), and my dílseacht (deel-shakt, loyalty)."

As Cú Chulainn spoke the words, a cheer rose from the warriors of the Red Branch. They stepped forward, one by one, placing their hands over their hearts in a gesture of solidarity. By taking this oath, Cú Chulainn was no longer just a boy; he was one of them—a warrior of Ulster, bound by honor and loyalty.

To mark the occasion, Conchobar handed Cú Chulainn a claíomh (klee-uv, sword), its blade gleaming in the torchlight. "This sword is yours," he said. "May it serve you well in the battles to come."

The ceremony ended with a great feast. The warriors of Ulster raised their cups, toasting Cú Chulainn and recounting his first great victory. But amid the celebration, a sense of anticipation hung in the air. The boy who had bested Fer Baeth (Fair Bah-hah) would soon face far greater challenges. His journey as a hero had only just begun.

As Cú Chulainn sat among his newfound brothers, he felt the weight of his oath settle upon him. He was no longer Sétanta, the clever and fearless boy. He was Cú Chulainn, the Hound of Ulster, sworn to defend his land and his people. His path was set, and his destiny awaited.

In the years to come, his name would echo across the land, etched into the legends of Ireland forever.

Sin é (Shin ay) That's it, The End.

The tale of Cú Chulainn was part of the Réicshe Uladh (Rayk-sheh Ull-ah, Ulster Cycle), one of the great cycles of Irish mythology. These stories, rooted in the oral tradition of ancient Ireland, are centered around the kingdom of Ulster and its legendary warriors. Themes of heroism, loyalty, and personal sacrifice run deeply through these tales, reflecting the values of early Irish society.

The name Cú Chulainn (Coo Hull-un) meant "Hound of Culann." In ancient Ireland, a hound symbolized loyalty, strength, and protection—qualities deeply revered in warriors. By taking on this name, Cú Chulainn not only acknowledged his actions but embraced the responsibility they brought, forever tying his identity to his vow of loyalty and service.

Names and titles in Irish mythology often carried significant meaning, serving as markers of identity and destiny. The act of earning one's name, as Cú Chulainn did, reflected the importance of deeds and honor in defining a person's place in society.

The story of Cú Chulainn reflected the core values of ancient Irish culture. Warriors were expected to protect their land, demonstrate unwavering courage, and uphold their oaths. In return, they were celebrated as heroes, their names preserved in songs and stories. Loyalty to kin and community was paramount, and honor often meant putting the needs of others above one's own.

Cú Chulainn's oath to serve as a protector of Ulster highlighted the societal expectation that warriors would dedicate their lives to their people. His heroic deeds exemplified how individual strength and bravery could inspire collective unity and pride.

This tale, like many others in Irish mythology, resonates with universal themes of resilience, sacrifice, and the pursuit of justice, making it timeless in its appeal. Cú Chulainn's journey is not just the story of one hero—it reflects the values and spirit that defines Ireland's cultural heritage.

CHAPTER 2

CHILDREN OF LIR

The *Children of Lir* is one of Ireland's most treasured legends, a timeless tale woven with themes of love, loss, and resilience. At its heart lies Lir, a nobleman whose greatest joy is his four cherished children. Their bond brings light and harmony to their lives—until jealousy and betrayal unleash a powerful curse that changes their fate forever.

This is a story of unwavering family ties, the enduring strength of love, and the courage to persevere through even the darkest of trials. It's a tale that has echoed through Irish folklore for generations.

The Children of Lir

Long ago, in a time of kings and magic, there lived a nobleman named Lir, who ruled over a beautiful ríocht (ree-uhkt, kingdom). His lands stretched across rolling green hills and sparkling lakes, and his home was a place of peace and joy. The heart of Lir's happiness was his four children: Fionnuala (fyun-oo-lah, white shoulder), Aodh (ee, fire), Fiachra (fee-uh-krah, raven), and Conn (kahn, chief).

They were not only the light of his life but also beloved by all who met them.

Fionnuala, the eldest, was wise beyond her years, with a gentle spirit that calmed any quarrel. Aodh, the fiery one, was full of courage and energy, always leading the group into adventures. Fiachra, with his thoughtful nature, loved the quiet beauty of the world around him. And Conn, the youngest, was full of curiosity, constantly asking questions about the stars, the rivers, and the land. Together, they brought laughter and life to their father's hall.

The children were inseparable. Whether exploring the quiet shores of a nearby loch (lock, lake) or running through the forests, they did everything together. Their bond was as unshakable as the mountains of Ireland. Lir often watched them with pride, knowing that their love for one another was his greatest treasure.

Lir's ríocht (ree-uhkt, kingdom) was as beautiful as a poem sung by a file (fil-eh, poet). Rolling hills stretched as far as the eye could see, blanketed in lush green féar (fay-er, grass) that seemed to shimmer under the sun. Silver srutháin (sruh-hawn, streams) wove their way through the landscape, feeding into deep, crystal-clear locha (lock-ah, lakes) that reflected the skies above. The air was always filled with the sounds of éanacha (ay-nah-kah, birds) singing and the gentle rustling of leaves, creating a melody that seemed to echo the peace of Lir's realm.

At the heart of the ríocht stood Lir's home, a grand halla (hall-ah, hall) built from stone and timber. Its walls were strong, but its interior was warm and welcoming, with roaring tinte (chin-teh, fires) and the scent of fresh arán (ah-rawn, bread) and wildflowers. It was a place where guests were always treated with cairdeas (kar-jass, kindness), and where laughter was as common as the morning dew.

The greatest joy of the ríocht, however, was Lir's children. Their bond brought light to the darkest days. Fionnuala's wisdom made her the natural leader among the siblings, and she cared for her brothers with a gentle lámh (lahv, hand). Aodh's boundless fuinneamh (fwin-yiv, energy) inspired games and adventures that filled the hall with shrieks of delight. Fiachra's quiet machnamh (mock-niv, thoughtfulness) brought balance to their group, while Conn's endless fiosracht (fis-rokht, curiosity) ensured there was never a dull moment.

Their days were spent exploring their father's tailte (tahl-teh, lands), running barefoot through wildflower-filled machairí (mah-kah-ree, meadows) and swimming in the cool waters of the locha. They built droichid (drik-id, bridges) from fallen logs and skipped smooth stones across the water, their laughter echoing in the air. In the evenings, they gathered by the tinteán (chin-chawn, hearth), where they listened to tales of ancient laochra (lay-kh-rah, heroes) and great catha (kah-hah, battles). Lir often joined them, his deep voice weaving stories of courage and draíocht (dree-ocht, magic) that made their eyes grow wide with wonder.

The people of Lir's ríocht adored the children. Villagers would smile as they passed, offering baskets of ripe caora (kay-rah, berries) or freshly baked arán donn (ah-rawn dunn, brown bread). "Blessed are we," they would say, "to have such joy in our land." The children, in turn, brought cineáltas (kin-all-tas, kindness) to all they met, their laughter as much a gift as their father's cosaint (cuss-int, protection).

Yet, even in this paradise, shadows can grow. Unseen by the children, jealousy stirred in the heart of Lir's new wife, Aoife (ee-fah). Watching the grá (graw, love) Lir poured upon his children, she felt bitterness rise within her. Day by day, her éad (ay-ed, envy) deepened, twisting her thoughts. She watched as the children played, their laughter a melody that stung her heart. Her smiles became forced, her words less warm, until her bitterness grew into a dark plean (plan, plan) that would change the ríocht forever.

The peace of Lir's ríocht began to wane as the shadows of éad (ay-ed, envy) took root in the heart of his new wife, Aoife (ee-fah). She was áilleacht (aw-lokt, beautiful) and cliste (klish-teh, clever), but her heart was not cineálta (kin-all-ta, kind). From the moment she entered Lir's halla, she felt herself an strainséir (stran-shayr, outsider) to the grá (graw, love) that surrounded the children. No matter how hard she tried, she could not win the cairdeas (kar-jass, affection) of Fionnuala (fyun-oo-lah, white shoulder), Aodh (ee, fire), Fiachra (fee-uh-krah, raven), and Conn (kahn, chief). Their bond with each other and their father was neamhbhriste (nyav-vris-teh, unbreakable), and this wounded Aoife's bród (brohd, pride).

Day by day, her éad grew. She watched as Lir laughed with his children, his aghaidh (ah-giv, face) filled with joy. She listened as their voices echoed through the halla, their áthas (aw-hass, happiness) a constant reminder of her own loneliness. Envy, like a dark síol (shee-uhl, seed), began to consume her thoughts. She convinced herself that she would never have Lir's heart as long as the children were in his saol (sayl, life).

One maidin (mah-jin, morning), Aoife made her decision. She called for the children, suggesting they take a journey together to visit her muintir (mwin-cheer, family). "A change of radharc (rah-yark, scenery) will be good for all of us," she said with a meangadh (mang-ah, smile), her voice sweet and reassuring. The children, trusting and eager for adventure, agreed without hesitation.

As their carbad (kar-bahd, chariot) rolled through the tuath (too-ah, countryside), they sang songs and laughed, oblivious to Aoife's dark intentions. They passed sparkling locha (lock-ah, lakes) and crossed rolling cnoca (knock-ah, hills), their spirits as light as the néalta (nayl-tah, clouds) above. But when they reached a quiet stretch of land near the shores of a great loch, Aoife's demeanor changed. Her laughter ceased, and her gaze grew cold.

She ordered the carbad to stop and led the children to the water's edge. There, under the shade of ancient daracha (dah-rah-kah, oak trees), she raised her hands and began to chant. Her voice echoed with power as she called upon draíocht dorcha (dree-ocht dur-uh-ka, dark magic) to carry out her will.

The children looked at her in confusion, their trust slowly dissolving into eagla (ah-glah, fear). Before they could run, Aoife's spell was complete. A brilliant solas (suh-lass, light) surrounded them, and when it faded, Fionnuala, Aodh, Fiachra, and Conn were no longer human. They had become ealaí (al-uh-ee, swans), their feathers white as sneachta (shnak-ta, snow) and their eyes filled with sorrow.

Aoife stepped back, admiring her work. "You shall live as ealaí for nine hundred years," she declared, her voice devoid of trua (true-ah, pity). "Three hundred years on this loch, three hundred on the stormy waters of the Sea of Moyle, and three hundred more on the Western Lakes. Only the sound of cloig (klog, church bells) will set you free."

The children cried out in despair, their voices now the mournful cries of swans. Fionnuala, her brave heart unbroken, swam close to her brothers. "Do not despair," she said, her voice soft yet steady. "As long as we are together, we will endure this curse."

Aoife, satisfied with her work, returned to Lir's halla. But when she arrived, ciontacht (kint-acht, guilt) began to weigh on her. She confessed her actions to Lir, expecting maithiúnas (mah-hoo-nas, forgiveness). Instead, she faced his fearg (farr-ug, wrath). Enraged by her feall (fyal, betrayal), Lir banished her from the ríocht, cursing her to wander the talamh (tall-uv, land) in shame for the rest of her days.

The children, now swans, remained near their father's lands, their cries of sorrow echoing across the uisce (ish-keh, waters). Though they had lost their human forms, their bond as siblings remained láidir (law-jeer, strong). Together, they would face the centuries of hardship that lay ahead, clinging to the hope that one day, they would be free.

The children of Lir, now ealaí (al-uh-ee, swans), drifted across the still waters of the loch, their graceful forms shimmering in the sunlight. Though their bodies had changed, their voices remained, carrying the sorrow of their plight in mournful songs that echoed across the water. Travelers who passed by would stop and listen, captivated by the haunting beauty of their music, unaware of the trua (true-ah, tragedy) that had befallen them.

The first three hundred years on the lake near their father's ríocht were both a comfort and a sorrow. They stayed close to the dúiche (doo-hah, homeland) they had once known, hoping to catch a glimpse of Lir. Sometimes, as the grian (gree-an, sun) set, they saw their father walking along the shores, his shoulders bent under the weight of his grief. He would call out their names, and though they longed to respond, their voices could only produce cries of longing.

Fionnuala (fyun-oo-lah, white shoulder), ever the protector, guided her brothers through their new reality. She taught them to navigate the loch, to find bia (bee-ah, food), and to stay together no matter what. Aodh (ee, fire) kept their spirits alive with his fiery determination, often leading playful chases across the water to distract his siblings from their sadness. Fiachra (fee-uh-krah, raven) remained the thoughtful one, finding solace in the quiet beauty of their surroundings, while Conn (kahn, chief), the youngest, clung to his siblings for neart (nyart, strength) and comfort.

As the years passed, the children adapted to their swan forms, but their hearts ached for the lives they had lost. They missed running through the machairí (mah-kah-ree, meadows), the warmth of their father's barróg (bar-ohg, embrace), and the joy of sharing stories by the tinteán (chin-chawn, hearth). They clung to Fionnuala's words: "As long as we are together, we can endure anything."

After three centuries, the curse forced them to leave the lake. They flew to the wild and stormy Sea of Moyle, a cold and unforgiving expanse of water between Ireland and Scotland. Here, the tonnta (tuhn-tah, waves) were fierce, and the winds howled like a banshee (bahn-shee, spirit). The siblings huddled together for warmth, their feathers battered by relentless stoirm (stur-im, storms).

The Sea of Moyle tested their resolve. Days turned into nights of endless cold, and bia (bee-ah, food) was scarce. Fionnuala spread her wings to shield her brothers from the biting winds, whispering words of misneach (mish-nahk, courage). Aodh braved the storms to scout for calmer waters, while Fiachra and Conn leaned on their older siblings, their strength waning under the harsh conditions.

Despite the trials, their love for one another never faltered. On the darkest nights, they sang songs of their father's ríocht, of the green hills and peaceful locha they once knew. Their songs carried their dóchas (doh-khass, hope), a fragile thread of light in an otherwise dark existence.

Finally, after another three hundred years, the curse drew them to the Western Lakes. The waters here were gentler, the winds softer. For the first time in centuries, they found some semblance of suaimhneas (soo-iv-ness, peace). They swam under clear skies, their reflections in the still water a reminder of the bond that had kept them strong.

Though their spirits were weary and their feathers worn, the siblings remained together. They had survived stoirmí (stur-mee, storms), hunger, and centuries of solitude, their love unbroken by the curse. Fionnuala often reminded her brothers, "Our time is not yet done, but it will come. One day, we will hear the sound that will free us."

As the final years of the curse passed, the siblings waited in quiet anticipation. Though their lives had been marked by caillteanas (kahl-cheh-nass, loss), they knew they had endured because of each other. Their story became part of the talamh (tall-uv, land), whispered among travelers who claimed to have heard the swans' sorrowful songs.

Would their saoradh (seer-uh, freedom) ever come? The children of Lir, weary but hopeful, clung to the promise of a new fáinne geal an lae (fawn-yeh gyal an lay, dawn).

After nine hundred years of wandering Ireland's uisce (ish-keh, waters), the children of Lir had endured stoirmí (stur-mee, storms), uaigneas (oo-ig-ness, solitude), and brón (brohn, sorrow). Their feathers, once pristine, were now weathered from centuries of hardship. Still, they remained together, their bond láidir (law-jeer, strong) as ever. On the Western Lakes, they often gazed toward the fáinne geal an lae (fawn-yeh gyal an lay, bright dawn), hoping for the sound that would finally set them free.

One quiet morning, as the ceo (kyo, mist) lifted from the water, a faint yet unfamiliar sound reached their ears. It was unlike the cries of the éanacha (ay-nah-kah, birds) or the rustling of the crainn (krah-n, trees) in the breeze. It was soft, steady, and warm—the ringing of cloig (klog, church bells). The siblings froze, their hearts trembling with dóchas (doh-khass, hope).

"It is the sound," Fionnuala whispered, her voice a mixture of awe and relief. "The sound that will break the curse."

With renewed neart (nyart, strength), the siblings lifted themselves from the loch and flew toward the source of the bells. Their wings, though heavy with age, carried them across the sky as the sound grew louder. As they approached the talamh (tall-uv, land), they saw a small séipéal (shay-peel, chapel) nestled among the cnoca (knock-ah, hills). A sagart (sah-gart, priest) stood outside, ringing the bell to call the faithful to urnaí (ur-nee, prayer).

The children landed on the féar (fay-er, grass), their swan forms trembling as the draíocht (dree-ocht, magic) that had bound them began to unravel. A radiant solas (suh-lass, light) surrounded them, growing brighter with every toll of the bell. Slowly, their feathers gave way to human craiceann (krak-enn, skin), and their wings became arms. After nine hundred years, Fionnuala (fyun-oo-lah, white shoulder), Aodh (ee, fire), Fiachra (fee-uh-krah, raven), and Conn (kahn, chief) were human once more.

Though free of the curse, the siblings were no longer the vibrant leanaí (lah-nye, children) they had once been. Time had taken its toll, and they stood as frail, elderly figures, their faces etched with both cumha (koo-ah, sorrow) and resilience. Yet their grá (graw, love) for one another remained unchanged.

The sagart (sah-gart, priest), astonished by what he had witnessed, approached them. "You are no ordinary travelers," he said. "Who are you, and what míorúilt (meer-oolt, miracle) has brought you here?"

Fionnuala stepped forward, her voice soft but steady. "We are the children of Lir, cursed to live as ealaí (al-uh-ee, swans) for nine hundred years. Your bells have set us free, and we are buíoch (bwee-ock, grateful) beyond words."

The priest invited them into the chapel, where he prayed over them and gave them dídean (dee-jun, shelter). Though their time as humans would be short, the siblings were at suaimhneas (soo-iv-ness, peace). Together, they shared their story with the priest, ensuring that it would live on in Ireland's seanchas (shan-khas, folklore).

In their final days, the children of Lir remained together, just as they had through every stoirm and hardship. Their story became a siombail (shim-bill, symbol) of grá, resilience, and the enduring power of family. Travelers who visited the chapel swore they could still hear the faint echoes of their songs on the gaoth (gwee, wind), a reminder of the swans who had endured centuries of sorrow and found freedom in the sound of church bells.

The story of the children of Lir spread across Ireland, carried by travelers, sagairt (sah-gart, priests), and scéalaithe (shkay-lah-heh, storytellers) who had heard their tale. Their lives, marked by unimaginable cruatán (kroo-ah-tawn, trials), became a siombail (shim-bill, symbol) of the enduring bonds of clann (klawn, family) and the resilience of the human spirit. In every corner of the talamh (tall-uv, land), their amhráin (ow-rawn, songs) were remembered, their brón (brohn, sorrow) honored, and their misneach (mish-nahk, courage) celebrated.

The séipéal (shay-peel, chapel) where they found their freedom became a place of quiet oilithreacht (ull-ih-racht, pilgrimage). Visitors would come to stand where Fionnuala, Aodh, Fiachra, and Conn had stood, imagining the moment when the ealaí (al-uh-ee, swans) became human once more. Locals whispered that on maidineacha ceoiche (mah-jin-ah-kah kyo-ih-kheh, misty mornings), when the waters of the nearby loch were still, the echoes of the children's amhráin (ow-rawn, songs) could still be heard, carried on the gaoth (gwee, wind) like a beannacht (ban-ockt, blessing).

Their story became part of Ireland's seanchas (shan-khas, folklore), told by tinteán (chin-chawn, firesides) and in classrooms, passed down from generation to generation. It was more than a tale of brón and draíocht (dree-ocht, magic); it was a lesson in grá (graw, love), dílseacht (deel-shakt, loyalty), and the neart (nyart, strength) that comes from aontacht (ayn-tacht, unity). The children of Lir reminded all who heard their story that, no matter the dúshláin (doo-shlaw-in, trials) one faces, the bonds of clann and grá can endure even the darkest of times.

Even today, the children's tale is woven into the fíodóireacht (fee-oh-door-acht, fabric) of Ireland's féiniúlacht (fayn-yoo-lacht, identity). Their amhráin, their misneach, and their dóchas (doh-khass, hope) continue to inspire those who hear their story, reminding them of the draíocht and resilience that live within Ireland's cnoca (knock-ah, hills), locha (lock-ah, lakes), and hearts.

The children of Lir, now immortalized in scéalta (shkayl-tah, story) and ceol (kyohl, song), will forever remain a part of Ireland—a testament to the unyielding power of grá.

Sin é (Shin ay) That's it, The End.

This story is one of Ireland's most enduring legends, steeped in themes of transformation, resilience, and familial love. Part of the Mythological Cycle, it reflects the Irish people's deep connection to nature and their reverence for the bonds of family. This tale also embodies the sorrow of exile and the enduring hope for freedom—universal themes that resonate across cultures.

Names and titles in Irish mythology, such as Fionnuala (fyun-oo-lah, white shoulder) and Aodh (ee, fire), often carry symbolic weight. These names reflect the characters' attributes or their roles in the story, adding depth to their identities. The swans themselves symbolize grace and purity, and their transformation into these creatures represents a poignant blend of beauty and tragedy.

The concept of draíocht (dree-ocht, magic) in Irish mythology is not just about spells and enchantments but is deeply intertwined with the natural world. The draíocht dorcha (dree-ocht dur-kha, dark magic) used by Aoife to curse the children serves as a reminder of the duality of magic in Irish lore—it can both destroy and redeem.

Irish mythology frequently portrays the importance of oaths and the consequences of breaking them. Lir's unwavering love for his children and their mutual loyalty exemplify the values of honor, kinship, and endurance. Stories like this one teach lessons about the strength found in aontacht (ayn-tacht, unity) and the dóchas (doh-khass, hope) that sustain us through the darkest times.

CHAPTER 3

BATTLE OF MOYTURA

In the heart of Ireland's ancient past lies the tale of the *Battle of Moytura* (Moy-choo-rah), a story that captures the eternal struggle between light and darkness, resilience and oppression. At its core are the Tuatha Dé Danann (Too-ah-hah Day Dah-nahn), the godlike protectors of Ireland, renowned for their wisdom, skill, and draíocht (dree-ocht, magic). These champions of creativity and justice stood against the Fomorians (Foh-mor-ee-ans), a race of dark giants led by the fearsome Balor (Bah-lur), whose deadly eye symbolized chaos and destruction.

This tale begins in a time of oppression, when the Fomorians demanded cruel tributes from the people of Ireland, casting a shadow of fear over the land. Yet, amid this darkness, hope flickered. Nuada (Noo-ah-dah), the noble leader of the Tuatha Dé Danann, rose to rally his people. Though wounded in an earlier battle, he reclaimed his kingship with a silver arm forged by divine magic. Under his guidance and the brilliance of the young warrior Lugh (Loo), the Tuatha Dé Danann prepared to face their greatest challenge.

On the sacred plains of Moytura, the forces of light and dark clashed in a battle that would define the destiny of Ireland.

Through courage, sacrifice, and unyielding unity, the Tuatha Dé Danann fought not just for themselves, but for the freedom of their people and the enduring balance of the land.

This is more than a story of war—it is a tale of resilience, heroism, and the unbreakable spirit of a people. As you read, you'll journey through the vibrant world of Irish mythology, where magic and fate intertwine with the values of justice, honor, and community. Prepare to step onto the battlefield of Moytura and witness the power of light triumphing over darkness.

The Battle of Moytura

In the ancient days of Ireland, the Tuatha Dé Danann (Too-ah-ha Day Dan-an, people of the goddess Danu) stood as protectors of the land, revered for their strength, wisdom, and mastery of draíocht (dree-ocht, magic). Yet, even their greatness faced a dire threat. Across the seas, the Fomorians (Foh-mor-ee-ans), a race of towering giants, rose to power. Led by Balor (Bah-lur), a monstrous being whose single eye unleashed destruction with a mere glance, the Fomorians sought to dominate Ireland. Their rule brought misery, as they demanded cruel tributes from the people, choking the land in fear and oppression.

Amid this darkness, Nuada (Noo-ah-dah), the noble king of the Tuatha Dé Danann, emerged as a beacon of hope. His courage in battle was unmatched, and his leadership inspired loyalty. But even the mightiest could falter.

During an earlier conflict with the Fomorians, Nuada lost his arm in combat. According to the laws of his people, no king with a physical blemish could remain on the throne. Nuada was forced to step down, and in his place rose Bres (Brehss), a half-Fomorian ruler.

At first, there was dóchas (doh-khass, hope) that Bres might bridge the divide between the two peoples. Instead, his reign deepened the wound. Bres proved a harsh and greedy ruler, favoring his Fomorian kin and enforcing burdensome tributes on the Tuatha Dé

Danann. Under his rule, the people suffered greatly, and the once-proud warriors of the Tuatha Dé Danann longed for a return to justice.

Nuada, though deposed, had not given up hope. Dian Cécht (Dee-ahn Kay-acht), the Tuatha Dé Danann's healer, crafted a marvel of draíocht: a silver arm that moved as naturally as flesh. Restored to wholeness, Nuada reclaimed his rightful place as king, rallying his people with a renewed spirit of defiance. The Tuatha Dé Danann began to prepare for war, determined to drive the Fomorians from their land.

The battleground was chosen—the sacred plain of Moytura (Moy-choo-rah). Here, the forces of light and dark would collide in a battle that would shape the destiny of Ireland. The Tuatha Dé Danann gathered their warriors, weapons, and spells, uniting under Nuada's leadership. Among them stood not only seasoned fighters but also druids, healers, and bards, each lending their strength to the cause. As the storm of conflict loomed, dóchas (doh-khass, hope) burned brightly in the hearts of the Tuatha Dé Danann, ready to reclaim their land and their freedom.

The stage was set for a battle unlike any other, where strength, courage, and the enduring power of draíocht would decide the fate of Ireland.

The Fomorians, towering giants of chaos and destruction, loomed over the horizon, their presence casting a shadow across Ireland. At their helm stood Balor (Bah-lur), a fearsome giant whose single eye radiated a deadly power. The eye, hidden beneath a heavy lid, could only be opened with the help of his servants, but once revealed, it unleashed a beam of destruction capable of leveling armies. It was said that nothing could withstand Balor's gaze—his eye was a symbol of darkness itself, a force that consumed all in its path.

As news of the Fomorian army's approach spread, fear gripped the land. Their warriors, clad in iron and wielding brutal weapons, were as relentless as the seas from which they had come. They marched with the intent to crush the Tuatha Dé Danann and solidify their rule over Ireland. But the Tuatha Dé Danann, led by Nuada (Noo-ah-dah), refused to yield. On the sacred plain of Moytura (Moy-choo-rah), the stage was set for a battle that would determine the future of the island.

In this dark hour, a beacon of hope arrived in the form of Lugh (Loo), a young warrior with extraordinary gifts. Known as Lugh Lámhfhada (Loo Lahv-ah-dah, Lugh of the Long Arm), he was a master of all arts—warfare, poetry, healing, and more. Legends spoke of his unmatched skill and divine lineage, marking him as a figure of destiny. When Lugh arrived at Nuada's court, he was met with skepticism. How could one so young be the answer to their plight?

Lugh stepped forward with confidence, declaring his talents. "I bring the skills of a warrior, a healer, a bard, and a craftsman. Let me serve the Tuatha Dé Danann," he said.

The warriors murmured, but Nuada saw something in the young man's eyes—a spark of greatness. To test his worth, Nuada set him a challenge: to prove his mastery in combat.

Lugh's demonstration left no doubt. With unmatched agility and precision, he bested the court's finest warriors. His words, as a bard, inspired hope; his strategies, as a tactician, promised victory. Nuada, recognizing Lugh's potential, granted him command of the Tuatha Dé Danann's forces, declaring, "You shall lead us to Moytura."

With Lugh at the helm, preparations for the battle intensified. Warriors honed their skills, druids wove protective spells, and craftsmen forged weapons imbued with draíocht (dree-ocht, magic). Among their arsenal was the Claíomh Solais (Klee-uv Soh-lish, Sword of Light), said to strike with the force of a thunderbolt, and the Lúireach Lán Ghlas (Loor-yahkh Lawn Ghlahs, Full Green Breastplate), which shielded its wearer from harm.

As the day of the battle approached, the Tuatha Dé Danann gathered their allies and drew strength from their shared purpose. Under the leadership of Lugh, they prepared to face Balor and his

Fomorian forces. On the plains of Moytura, light and darkness would collide in a struggle that would echo through the ages.

The battle of Moytura (Moy-choo-rah) unfolded beneath a brooding sky, the air thick with tension and the promise of conflict. The Tuatha Dé Danann, shining in their enchanted armor, stood like a beacon of dóchas against the oppressive shadow of the Fomorians. Each warrior carried a weapon imbued with draíocht (dree-ocht, magic), forged in preparation for this very moment. Druids murmured incantations, their voices weaving unseen shields of protection, while healers tended to the wounded even before the first strike. Their unity and determination filled the air, a sharp contrast to the chaotic and fearsome presence of their opponents.

The Fomorians advanced like an unrelenting tide, their towering forms casting long shadows over the battlefield. At their forefront loomed Balor (Bah-lur), the embodiment of destruction, his single, deadly eye concealed beneath a heavy lid. Each step of the monstrous army sent tremors through the ground, their roars like the rumble of an impending storm. Their iron-clad warriors and monstrous beasts exuded raw power, their sheer numbers threatening to overwhelm the Tuatha Dé Danann.

When the first clash came, it erupted in a cacophony of metal against metal, battle cries, and the crackling hum of magical energy. The Tuatha Dé Danann moved with precision, their warriors forming a fluid and cohesive force, each step guided by the strategic mind of their leader, Lugh. The young champion, with his golden hair gleaming like the sun, commanded the battlefield with both courage and skill. By his side, Nuada (Noo-ah-dah), the Silver-Handed King, fought with unmatched ferocity, the Claíomh Solais (Klee-uv Soh-lish, Sword of Light) flashing like lightning as it cut through the Fomorian ranks.

The Fomorians, relying on brute strength and overwhelming numbers, pressed forward without relent. Balor, towering above his army, barked orders that shook the earth. The battlefield seemed to hold its breath as his servants began the grim task of lifting the lid that concealed his terrible eye. When Balor's gaze was unleashed, a devastating beam of energy surged forth, scorching the earth and tearing through the Tuatha Dé Danann's ranks. Screams echoed across the plain as warriors fell, their shields and spells unable to withstand the overwhelming force of Balor's power.

But the Tuatha Dé Danann were not easily broken. Their druids redoubled their efforts, casting counterspells and shrouding their warriors in protective wards. Healers worked tirelessly to save the wounded, their hands glowing with the light of draíocht. Through the chaos, Lugh emerged as a symbol of resilience. With his sling in hand, he wove through the battlefield, inspiring his people to press on despite the odds.

At last, the moment came when Lugh stood face-to-face with Balor, the dark giant whose eye had wrought so much destruction. Balor's laughter rumbled like distant thunder. "You think you, a mere boy, can defeat me?" he sneered, his voice dripping with contempt.

Lugh, unshaken, met his gaze. "I am more than you see," he replied, his voice steady. Drawing a stone imbued with draíocht, he loaded his sling and took aim. With a mighty release, the stone shot through the air like a comet. It struck Balor's eye with unerring precision, shattering it in an explosion of blinding light. Balor's roar of agony echoed across Moytura as he collapsed, his immense form crashing to the ground.

With Balor defeated, the Fomorian forces faltered. Leaderless and demoralized, they scattered in disarray, their once-mighty army reduced to chaos. The Tuatha Dé Danann seized the opportunity, pressing forward with renewed vigor. Their cries of victory filled the air as they drove the Fomorians from the battlefield.

When the dust settled, Moytura, once a site of sorrow and oppression, became a symbol of liberation. The warriors of the Tuatha Dé Danann, though bloodied and battered, stood victorious. They had faced the darkness and triumphed, their unity and courage shining as brightly as the enchanted weapons they carried.

Ireland was free, and the legacy of the Tuatha Dé Danann was cemented in the annals of myth. The fall of Balor marked not just the end of a tyrant but the triumph of light over darkness, hope over despair. At the center of this victory stood Lugh, whose heroism and determination ensured his place among the greatest champions of Irish legend.

The battlefield at Moytura (Moy-choo-rah) lay quiet in the aftermath of the fierce struggle. The once-vibrant plain was now marked by the scars of war—trampled grass, broken weapons, and the lifeless forms of warriors from both sides. Though the Tuatha Dé Danann emerged victorious, their triumph came at a cost.

Among the fallen was Nuada (Noo-ah-dah), the Silver-Handed King. He had fought valiantly, wielding the Claíomh Solais (Klee-uv Soh-lish, Sword of Light) until his final breath. It was his leadership and bravery that had steadied the Tuatha Dé Danann through their darkest hours, and his sacrifice would never be forgotten. Lugh (Loo), still weary from his confrontation with Balor (Bah-lur), knelt beside Nuada's body, vowing to honor his legacy by leading with the same strength and wisdom.

As the remaining warriors gathered, their druids performed ancient rites over the fallen. Prayers of gratitude and blessings were spoken, the air filled with the soft cadence of Gaeilge (Gwel-gah, Irish). Cairns were built to mark the graves of the warriors, their spirits commended to the Otherworld with reverence and grá (graw, love). Each stone placed upon the burial mounds was a testament to their misneach (mish-nakh, courage) and sacrifice.

Despite their losses, a sense of renewal filled the Tuatha Dé Danann. The oppressive shadow of the Fomorians (Foh-mor-ee-ans) had lifted, and the land of Ireland seemed to breathe freely once more. The people of Ireland, once burdened by cruel tributes, would now enjoy peace and prosperity under the guidance of their victorious protectors.

In a solemn ceremony, Lugh was declared the new leader of the Tuatha Dé Danann. Standing tall, with the light of the sun catching his golden hair, he embodied hope and renewal. His mastery of every art and skill, combined with his unwavering bravery, made him the ideal leader to guide the Tuatha Dé Danann into a brighter future.

Under Lugh's leadership, the Tuatha Dé Danann began the work of healing the land. The scars of battle faded, replaced by fields of green and blooming flowers. Music and laughter returned to the halls of Ireland, the people united in celebration of their hard-won freedom.

The story of the battle at Moytura became a legend, passed down through generations. It was not just a tale of triumph over darkness but a reminder of the strength found in unity, the resilience of the human spirit, and the sacrifices made for the greater good.

As the sun set over Moytura, its golden light bathed the cairns of the fallen, casting a warm glow over the resting place of heroes. Ireland had been reclaimed, and the legacy of the Tuatha Dé Danann would endure, inspiring hope and courage in the hearts of its people forever.

Sin é (Shin ay) That's it, The End.

The tale of the Battle of Moytura holds a central place in Irish mythology, symbolizing the eternal struggle between light and darkness, creativity and destruction, order and chaos. At the heart of this story are the Tuatha Dé Danann (Too-ah-hah Day Dah-nahn), who embody resilience, ingenuity, and the pursuit of justice. They are more than warriors; they are champions of creativity, wisdom, and harmony, striving to protect their land and people from the oppressive rule of the Fomorians (Foh-mor-ee-ans).

Balor, with his deadly eye that destroys everything in its gaze, represents the raw, destructive power of unchecked chaos. His defeat at the hands of Lugh, a hero of unmatched skill and ingenuity, reflects the triumph of light, order, and renewal over darkness and despair. Lugh's victory is not just a personal achievement; it is a symbolic act that restores balance and peace to Ireland.

The setting of Moytura (Moy-choo-rah), a sacred plain, underscores the themes of transformation and renewal. It serves as the battleground where justice is reclaimed, sacrifices are honored, and the resilience of the Tuatha Dé Danann leads to a brighter future. In Irish mythology, such locations often carry deep cultural resonance, acting as spaces where history and myth intertwine to create a sense of shared identity and purpose.

This story is deeply rooted in the values of ancient Irish society. Justice, honor, and loyalty are paramount, as is the belief in the collective strength of the community. The Tuatha Dé Danann, united by their shared purpose and mutual trust, reflect the importance of working together to overcome even the most formidable challenges.

Magic, fate, and heroism weave through the narrative, adding layers of complexity to the tale. The use of enchanted weapons, like the Claíomh Solais (Klee-uv Soh-lish, Sword of Light), and the influence of prophecy emphasize the interplay between destiny and human action in Irish mythology. These elements enrich the story, making it both a gripping legend and a profound exploration of universal themes.

The Battle of Moytura is not just a tale of gods and giants; it is a timeless story of resilience, sacrifice, and the unyielding hope for a better world. It continues to resonate, reminding us of the enduring power of courage, creativity, and the unity of a people determined to protect what they hold dear.

CHAPTER 4

SALMON OF KNOWLEDGE

The tale of *Fionn MacCumhaill (Fee-un Mac-Coo-ill) and the Salmon of Knowledge* is a cornerstone of Irish mythology, cherished for its blend of destiny, wisdom, and adventure. It follows the story of a boy on the path to greatness, whose life takes a transformative turn through an unexpected twist of fate. At its heart, the legend explores the power of mentorship and the value of knowledge, all set against the vibrant backdrop of Ireland's ancient landscapes. Before rising as the famed leader of the Fianna (Fee-ah-nah), Fionn's remarkable journey began by the banks of the River Boyne (Bine), where his destiny changed forever.

The Salmon of Knowledge

Long ago in Ireland, a land of heroes, magic, and timeless myths, a boy destined for greatness was born. Fionn MacCumhaill (Fee-uhn Mac-Coo-ill), who would one day become one of Ireland's most celebrated warriors, began life under a shadow of danger. His father, Cumhall (Coo-ill), was a fearless leader and champion of his people, but his life ended in battle before Fionn's birth. To protect her child from Cumhall's enemies, Fionn's mother, Muirne (Mur-neh), made a heart-wrenching decision.

Fionn was sent deep into the forests of Ireland, entrusted to Bodhmall (Bow-vawl), Cumhall's sister and a wise druidess, and Líath Lúachra (Lee-ah Loo-uh-krah), a fierce warrior. Together, these two women raised him in secrecy, ensuring his survival and preparing him for the challenges that lay ahead.

In the forest, Fionn grew up surrounded by the whispers of nature and the teachings of his guardians. The towering trees became his fortress, and the murmuring streams his guide. Bodhmall and Líath Lúachra taught him everything he needed to survive in the wild. From Bodhmall, he learned the secrets of draíocht (dree-ocht, magic), how to read the stars, and the songs of the wind. Líath Lúachra trained him in the art of combat, her movements swift and precise as she demonstrated the way of the spear and shield.

Fionn became adept at tracking deer through the féar (fayr, grass) and moving silently like a shadow. His days were filled with training, but his nights were filled with wonder. As the fire crackled and the grian (gree-an, sun) set behind the hills, he would listen to tales of Cumhall's bravery. "He was a man of honor," Bodhmall would say, her voice soft with pride. "And you, Fionn, are his legacy."

Though he was safe in the forest, Fionn often gazed beyond the trees, wondering about the world his father had defended. He felt a growing longing to honor Cumhall's name and reclaim his place among Ireland's heroes.

As Fionn grew older, his skills sharpened. He became a hunter, a strategist, and a warrior. His sharp mind matched his physical prow-ess, and his guardians marveled at how quickly he learned. "You'll be more than a warrior," Líath Lúachra told him. "You'll be a leader."

One day, Fionn stumbled upon a forgotten dún (doon, strong-hold) hidden in the forest. Its crumbling walls and moss-covered stones whispered stories of battles fought long ago. Standing there,

Fionn felt a connection to his father's past, as if Cumhall's spirit was urging him forward. It was then that Fionn decided he could no longer remain hidden. He had a destiny to fulfill.

When the day came for Fionn to leave the forest, Bodhmall and Líath Lúachra prepared him for his journey. Bodhmall gave him a seoid draíochta (show-id dree-ocht-ah, magical charm) to protect him from harm. Líath Lúachra handed him a finely crafted sleá (shlah, spear), its tip gleaming like the first light of dawn. "Go with courage," she said. "And remember, you carry not just your father's legacy, but your own."

Fionn embraced his guardians, thanking them for their care and wisdom. Then, with the forest at his back, he stepped into the open world. He would face unknown challenges, but his heart burned with purpose. He was not just Cumhall's son—he was Fionn MacCumhaill, ready to carve his own legend into the annals of Irish history.

The journey of Fionn MacCumhaill had begun.

Fionn's journey led him to the banks of the River Boyne (Bine), its waters shimmering under the afternoon sun. Here, he encountered a man unlike any he had met before. Finegas (Fin-eh-gass), a revered poet and seer, was known throughout Ireland for his vast knowledge and devotion to the pursuit of wisdom.

Finegas had spent years by the river, seeking the legendary Bradán Feasa (Brah-dawn Fassa, Salmon of Knowledge). This mystical fish was said to have consumed nine sacred hazelnuts that fell into the water from the trees above, granting it all the wisdom of the world. It was foretold that whoever ate the salmon would inherit its knowledge, a gift that Finegas had long sought.

Fionn approached Finegas, his curiosity piqued by the poet's reputation and dedication. "I have heard of you," Fionn said, bowing respectfully. "Teach me your wisdom, and I will help you in your quest."

The poet regarded the young warrior with a thoughtful expression. Finegas saw not just eagerness but a quiet determination in Fionn's eyes. "Very well," he said. "You may stay and learn, but know that true wisdom is not easily earned. It requires patience, dedication, and an open heart."

From that day, Fionn became Finegas's apprentice. He gathered wood for the fire, helped repair the fishing nets, and listened intently to the poet's tales. By the riverbank, Finegas told him the story of the Bradán Feasa, its wisdom described as a treasure greater than gold or jewels. "It is not merely knowledge," Finegas said, "but the understanding of how to live well, to lead, and to inspire."

Days turned into weeks as Fionn and Finegas worked together, casting lines into the water and keeping watch for the salmon. Finegas shared the lore of the River Boyne, explaining how the sacred hazelnuts carried the essence of eagna (ag-nah, wisdom). He also recounted tales of Ireland's heroes, teaching Fionn about courage, justice, and the importance of humility.

Fionn absorbed these lessons eagerly, his sharp mind capturing every word. Finegas marveled at how quickly the boy grasped complex ideas, and their bond deepened. They often sat by the fire in the evenings, the poet weaving tales of Ireland's past while Fionn listened with rapt attention.

Despite their efforts, the salmon remained elusive. Still, Fionn remained patient, his respect for Finegas and his pursuit of wisdom growing with each passing day. Together, they embodied a shared belief: that wisdom was worth every sacrifice, and its pursuit was a journey as meaningful as the destination.

One crisp morning, after weeks of patient watching and waiting, Finegas finally reeled in the Bradán Feasa (Brah-dawn Fassa, Salmon of Knowledge). The fish glimmered in the sunlight, its scales iridescent as though touched by magic. Finegas's eyes widened with joy, and he lifted the salmon reverently from the water. "At last," he said, his voice trembling, "the wisdom of the world is within reach."

Returning to their small camp by the River Boyne, Finegas set about preparing for the long-awaited moment. "Fionn," he said, his tone serious, "this is no ordinary task. You must cook the salmon carefully, ensuring it remains perfect. But under no circumstances are you to taste even a single morsel. Do you understand?"

Fionn nodded solemnly. "I will not fail you," he promised, taking the salmon and setting it over the fire.

As the salmon cooked, Fionn tended to it with care, turning it over the flames and ensuring it was evenly done. The smell of the roasting fish filled the air, rich and tantalizing. Watching the fire dance, Fionn thought of the stories Finegas had told him about the salmon's sacred wisdom, its power to guide and inspire.

Suddenly, a blister formed on the fish's skin, bubbling up from the heat. Without thinking, Fionn pressed it down with his thumb, and the scalding juice burned him. Instinctively, he placed his thumb in his mouth to ease the pain.

In that moment, a flood of knowledge coursed through him. His mind expanded with insights he couldn't fully comprehend but instinctively understood. It was as though the mysteries of the world—past, present, and future—had unfolded before him.

When Finegas returned, he noticed a change in Fionn. The boy's eyes seemed brighter, his posture more assured. "What has happened?" Finegas asked, his voice heavy with suspicion.

Fionn hesitated, unsure of how to explain. Finally, he admitted, "As I cooked the salmon, its juice burned my thumb. I put it in my mouth without thinking, and now I feel... different."

Finegas was silent for a moment, his expression unreadable. Then, he let out a long sigh and smiled gently. "It seems the salmon's wisdom was not meant for me after all," he said. "It was always destined for you, Fionn."

Though Finegas had spent years pursuing the salmon, he bore no resentment. Instead, he encouraged Fionn to embrace his newfound gift. "Wisdom is not a treasure to hoard," he said, "but a light to guide others. Use it well, for Ireland will one day look to you as a leader."

From that day forward, Fionn carried the wisdom of the Bradán Feasa within him. Whenever he needed guidance, he would press his thumb to his mouth, unlocking the boundless knowledge granted by the salmon. This moment marked the beginning of his transformation from a clever boy to a legendary hero, destined to lead and inspire.

Fionn awoke the day after tasting the Bradán Feasa (Brah-dawn Fassa, Salmon of Knowledge) feeling profoundly different. The world seemed sharper, every detail imbued with meaning. He understood things he had never been taught, as if the secrets of life had been whispered to him in his sleep. Sitting by the River Boyne (Bine), he gazed at the flowing water and felt its rhythm echoing the cycles of life. The weight of his gift settled upon him—not a burden, but a responsibility.

Finegas watched him with a mix of pride and sadness. "You have been chosen, Fionn," the poet said. "This wisdom is not an end but a beginning. Your path is clear now—you must seek out the Fianna (Fee-ah-nah), the great band of warriors who protect Ireland. They will need a leader, and I have no doubt that leader is you."

Though their time together had been brief, Finegas had grown fond of the boy who had worked so diligently by his side. Now, he stood by the riverbank, offering his final words of advice. "Remember, wisdom is not enough on its own," he said. "It must be paired with courage and integrity. The Fianna are more than warriors— they are protectors of Ireland's people and its honor. Lead with your heart as well as your mind."

Fionn nodded, his eyes bright with determination. "I will not forget what you've taught me," he said. "Your guidance has prepared me for this journey."

As Fionn turned to leave, Finegas called out one last time. "The people will tell tales of you, Fionn MacCumhaill," he said. "But never let their stories define you. Be the hero they need, not the one they expect."

With Finegas's blessing, Fionn began his journey to join the Fianna. The road ahead was uncertain, but his newfound wisdom gave him confidence. Along the way, he encountered obstacles that tested not only his strength but his insight.

In one village, a farmer lamented a herd of cattle that refused to cross a river. Fionn, observing the animals, noticed they hesitated at a slippery patch of rocks near the water's edge. He guided them safely across by scattering straw over the stones, earning the farmer's gratitude.

In another town, Fionn came upon a group of travelers arguing over how to share a narrow bridge. Instead of taking sides, Fionn proposed a simple solution: each group would cross halfway and switch at the center. His cleverness left the travelers in awe, and word of the young man with both strength and wisdom began to spread.

As he approached the Fianna's stronghold, Fionn felt the weight of his destiny pressing upon him. He was no longer just a boy raised in the forests—he was Fionn MacCumhaill, bearer of the Salmon's wisdom and heir to a legacy of greatness. The trials ahead would be daunting, but his resolve was unshakable. Guided by his wisdom, his courage, and the lessons of those who had shaped him, Fionn was ready to face whatever lay ahead.

Ireland awaited its hero, and Fionn was prepared to answer the call.

Fionn's journey led him to the Fianna (Fee-ah-nah), Ireland's most elite band of warriors. They were renowned for their bravery, loyalty, and strength, and joining their ranks required more than just skill in combat—it demanded intelligence, integrity, and an unwavering commitment to protect the land and its people. Fionn approached their leader, Goll MacMorna (Gull Mock-Moor-nah), and declared his intent to join.

Goll regarded the young man with skepticism. "What makes you believe you're worthy of the Fianna?" he asked, his tone challenging.

Fionn met his gaze, his voice steady. "I bring not only strength but wisdom," he said. "I will prove my worth through deeds, not words."

The Fianna set Fionn a series of grueling trials. He hunted wild boar in the thickest forests, outwitted enemies in tactical challenges, and demonstrated unmatched skill in battle. But it wasn't just his physical prowess that impressed them—it was his ability to think clearly under pressure, to find solutions where others saw only problems.

In one test, Fionn led a group of warriors through a treacherous mountain pass, devising a plan to outmaneuver an ambush by using the terrain to their advantage. His leadership turned a potential disaster into a decisive victory.

The final trial came when the Fianna faced a threat to Tara (Tarah), the seat of the High Kings of Ireland. A powerful raider had laid siege to the sacred site, and Goll tasked Fionn with defending it. Using both strategy and courage, Fionn not only repelled the attack but captured the raider, securing peace for Tara.

Impressed by his wisdom and bravery, the Fianna welcomed Fionn as one of their own. In time, his reputation grew, and he rose to become their leader. Under his guidance, the Fianna thrived, their unity and strength unmatched.

Fionn's wisdom, gifted by the Salmon of Knowledge, became his greatest asset as a leader. It allowed him to see beyond the heat of battle, to anticipate dangers before they arose, and to make decisions that balanced justice and compassion. He led the Fianna through countless trials, from defending Ireland against invaders to settling disputes among rival clans.

One of his most famous acts of leadership came during a great famine. With resources dwindling, tensions rose among the people. Fionn mediated the conflict with fairness and foresight, ensuring that food was distributed equitably and that alliances were strengthened rather than fractured.

His wisdom also extended to nurturing the next generation. Fionn trained young warriors, passing down the lessons he had learned, not only in combat but in character. He taught them that strength without wisdom was a danger, and that true leadership came from serving others.

Sin é (Shin ay) That's it, The End.

The story of Fionn MacCumhaill and the Salmon of Knowledge is one of Ireland's most cherished legends, passed down through generations and woven into the Fiannaíocht (Fee-ah-nee-ucht), or Fenian Cycle, a cornerstone of Irish mythology. It is a tale that celebrates wisdom, courage, and destiny, capturing the imagination of all who hear it.

At its heart, this legend reflects the Irish reverence for wisdom as the highest virtue, surpassing strength or wealth. The Salmon of Knowledge, imbued with the power of sacred hazelnuts, symbolizes the connection between knowledge and nature, with the hazel tree standing as a sacred emblem in Irish lore. Fionn's accidental taste of the salmon's wisdom suggests that destiny often reveals itself in unexpected ways, a recurring theme in Irish mythology.

Fionn's journey, guided by the mentorship of Finegas (Fin-eh-gass), underscores the cultural value placed on learning and guidance. Finegas, despite his lifelong pursuit of the salmon, willingly accepts that the wisdom was meant for Fionn. This selflessness highlights the esteemed role of teachers and storytellers in shaping Ireland's heroes.

The transformation of Fionn from a hidden child to the leader of the Fianna (Fee-ah-nah), Ireland's legendary band of warriors, is not just a personal triumph but a reflection of the enduring themes of loyalty and courage found throughout the Fiannaíocht. His rise to greatness illustrates how wisdom, tempered with bravery and integrity, can guide not only an individual but an entire community.

The tale of the Salmon of Knowledge is more than a myth—it is a timeless lesson. It teaches that true power lies not in physical might but in the clarity and insight that wisdom provides. Through Fionn MacCumhaill, the wisdom of the salmon fulfilled its purpose, shaping not just one life but the destiny of a people. His legacy, carried in the stories told around firesides and bardic halls, reminds us of the enduring connection between Ireland's heroes, its natural world, and the timeless pursuit of knowledge.

CHAPTER 5

SWORD OF NUADA

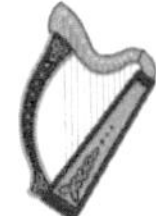

In the time of the Tuatha Dé Danann (Too-ah-hah Day Dan-an, People of the Goddess Danu), a king's strength was not only measured by his courage but also by the symbols of his leadership. Among these was the Claíomh Solais (Klee-uv Soh-lish, Sword of Light), a weapon of extraordinary power that guaranteed victory to its wielder. This sword, gleaming with an otherworldly brilliance, was not merely a tool of war—it was a symbol of justice and the divine right to rule.

This is the story of *Nuada (Noo-ah-dah) and the Sword of Light*, the noble king of the Tuatha Dé Danann, whose reign was tested by both loss and resilience. From his fall as king after a grievous injury to his triumphant return with a silver arm crafted through magic, Nuada's tale weaves themes of sacrifice, leadership, and the enduring strength of a people united. Set in the mystical landscapes of ancient Ireland, this legend shines as brightly as the Claíomh Solais itself.

The Sword of Nuada

Nuada (Noo-ah-dah), the first king of the Tuatha Dé Danann (Too-ah-hah Day Dan-an, People of the Goddess Danu), rose to power with a vision of justice and unity for his people. When the Tuatha Dé Danann arrived in Ireland, they brought with them four treasures of immense power, each symbolizing their connection to magic, wisdom, and strength. Among these treasures was the Claíomh Solais (Klee-uv Soh-lish, Sword of Light), a gleaming weapon that ensured victory to its bearer and became the embodiment of rightful leadership.

Nuada was chosen as king not only for his courage but also for his fairness and dedication to his people. In the early days of his reign, he wielded the Claíomh Solais to defend his kingdom against threats, most notably the Fomorians (Foh-mor-ee-ans), a race of shadowy giants who sought to dominate Ireland. The Fomorians were known for their immense strength and ruthless tactics, spreading fear wherever they went.

In one of his earliest battles, Nuada faced a mighty Fomorian champion who towered over the battlefield like a stormcloud. With the Claíomh Solais in his hands, Nuada led his warriors into the fray. The sword seemed to hum with power, its light cutting through the darkness as if the very sun fought alongside him. With a single, precise strike, Nuada felled the champion, scattering the Fomorian forces and securing a hard-won victory for his people.

This triumph solidified Nuada's role as a protector and leader. Stories of his bravery and the sword's brilliance spread across the land, inspiring loyalty among his people and fear among his enemies. The Claíomh Solais was no ordinary weapon—it was a beacon of hope, a symbol that justice would prevail even in the darkest of times.

However, the sword was also a heavy burden. To wield it was to bear the weight of leadership, knowing that every victory came at a cost. For Nuada, the Claíomh Solais was not just a tool of war but a reminder of his duty to his people and the sacrifices required to protect them.

As the Tuatha Dé Danann flourished under Nuada's reign, the Fomorian threat continued to linger on the horizon. The clash between these two forces was inevitable, and Nuada knew that his strength, wisdom, and the power of the Claíomh Solais would soon be tested like never before.

Nuada (Noo-ah-dah), once hailed as an invincible leader, faced a turning point during a fierce battle against the Fomorians (Foh-mor-ee-ans). The shadowy giants had returned, seeking to reclaim the land they believed was theirs. Nuada, wielding the Claíomh Solais (Klee-uv Soh-lish, Sword of Light), led his warriors with unmatched valor. But even kings are not immune to fate.

In the heart of the conflict, Nuada confronted a fearsome Fomorian warrior, towering and relentless. The clash between them was the stuff of legend, with the sword's radiant light clashing against the brute force of the Fomorian's massive blade. Though Nuada fought with unparalleled skill, the battle turned when the Fomorian struck a devastating blow, severing Nuada's arm. The Claíomh Solais fell from his grasp, its light momentarily dimmed as the battlefield erupted in chaos.

The Tuatha Dé Danann managed to drive the Fomorians back, but the cost was great. Their beloved king had been gravely wounded, and under the ancient laws of their people, a king of the Tuatha Dé Danann must be physically perfect. Though Nuada's spirit remained strong, his body no longer met the requirements of kingship.

The decision to abdicate weighed heavily on Nuada. As he relinquished the throne and the Claíomh Solais, the burden of leadership passed to Bres (Brehss), a half-Fomorian known for his striking beauty and cunning mind. At first, some among the Tuatha Dé Danann hoped that Bres's mixed heritage might forge peace between their people and the Fomorians. Yet others felt unease, fearing that Bres's loyalty to his Fomorian kin might outweigh his duty to the Tuatha Dé Danann.

For Nuada, the transition was bittersweet. His warriors and druids mourned the loss of a king whose courage had guided them through countless trials. The sight of the Claíomh Solais in Bres's hands was a sharp reminder of the life Nuada had been forced to leave behind. Though physically diminished, Nuada's heart burned with a quiet resolve. He vowed to continue serving his people, even if not as their king.

Bres's rule began with promises of prosperity, but Nuada watched from the shadows as his people grew uneasy under their new leader. The Tuatha Dé Danann, once united in strength and hope, began to feel the strain of Bres's growing favoritism toward the Fomorians. Tributes were demanded, resources drained, and the spirit of the Tuatha Dé Danann dimmed.

As Nuada adapted to his new reality, he resolved not to let his injury define him. With the help of the Tuatha Dé Danann's greatest healer, Dian Cécht (Dee-ahn Kay-acht), Nuada sought a way to reclaim his place among his people. The road ahead was uncertain, but Nuada's courage remained unshaken, his mind already turning toward the possibility of renewal and redemption.

Under Bres's (Brehss) reign, the Tuatha Dé Danann faced a bleak and trying time. What had begun with hope for a harmonious rule quickly turned into discontent. Bres, favoring his Fomorian kin, imposed heavy tributes on the Tuatha Dé Danann, demanding their wealth, labor, and resources. Warriors once proud of their freedom were reduced to servitude, and the people's joy turned to bitterness. The once-vibrant halls of their kingdom grew quiet, their songs replaced by whispers of despair.

Nuada (Noo-ah-dah), watching from the sidelines, felt the weight of his people's suffering. Though no longer their king, he remained their champion at heart. The sight of the Tuatha Dé Danann bowed under Bres's unjust rule kindled a fire within him. He resolved to reclaim his throne—not for personal glory, but to restore the honor and dignity of his people.

It was then that Dian Cécht (Dee-ahn Kay-acht), the Tuatha Dé Danann's master healer, offered Nuada a path to redemption. Known for his unmatched skill and knowledge of draíocht (dree-ocht, magic), Dian Cécht proposed crafting a solution to Nuada's injury—a silver arm that would not only restore his physical form but also his right to rule.

The process was painstaking. Using ancient magic and the finest materials, Dian Cécht forged a limb of gleaming silver, intricate in its craftsmanship and powerful in its design. When the arm was complete, Nuada stood before his people, the light of the Claíomh Solais (Klee-uv Soh-lish, Sword of Light) once again reflected in his hand. The silver arm moved with the fluidity of life itself, a testament to the brilliance of Dian Cécht's skill.

With his newfound strength, Nuada returned to the court of the Tuatha Dé Danann. Bres, confident in his control, did not expect the former king to challenge his rule. But when Nuada entered the great hall, the warriors and druids who had once served under him rose to their feet. Their cheers echoed through the chamber, a resounding declaration that their true king had returned.

Nuada's reinstatement was swift and unanimous. The Claíomh Solais, which had dimmed under Bres's unworthy hand, blazed once more in Nuada's grasp. Bres, exposed for his tyranny and favoritism, was forced to relinquish the throne. Stripped of power, he fled to the Fomorians, vowing revenge against the Tuatha Dé Danann.

With Nuada restored as their leader, the Tuatha Dé Danann reclaimed their pride and unity. The silver arm, a symbol of resilience and renewal, reminded all who saw it that even in the face of loss, greatness could be regained. Under Nuada's guidance, the Tuatha Dé Danann prepared themselves for the challenges to come, knowing that the Fomorians would not let this victory go unanswered.

The Fomorians, enraged by the loss of their hold over the Tuatha Dé Danann, gathered their forces for an all-out assault. Their leader, Balor (Bah-lur), a giant of unparalleled strength and malice, marched at their helm, his single deadly eye concealed beneath a heavy lid. It was said that one gaze from Balor's eye could decimate an entire army, reducing all it saw to ash and ruin. The stakes for the Tuatha Dé Danann had never been higher—this battle would determine the fate of Ireland.

Nuada (Noo-ah-dah), now restored to his rightful place as king, stood tall before his people. Clad in shining armor and wielding the Claíomh Solais (Klee-uv Soh-lish, Sword of Light), he embodied hope and resilience. His silver arm caught the sunlight, glinting like a beacon, a reminder of the trials he had endured and the strength he had reclaimed. The Tuatha Dé Danann, inspired by their king's courage, rallied under his leadership, their determination burning brighter than their fear.

On the sacred plains of Moytura (Moy-choo-rah), the two armies met in a thunderous clash. The earth trembled beneath the weight of the Fomorian giants, their monstrous roars echoing through the air. The Tuatha Dé Danann, smaller in number but fierce in spirit, moved with precision and agility. Druids wove protective spells, while warriors fought with unwavering resolve. At the heart of the battle was Nuada, his strikes with the Claíomh Solais cutting through the chaos like flashes of lightning.

Balor, watching from the rear, unleashed his deadly gaze. With the help of his servants, the lid of his eye was lifted, and a beam of destruction swept across the battlefield. The Tuatha Dé Danann scrambled to evade its path, their druids chanting frantically to shield their forces. Despite their efforts, the power of Balor's eye was devastating, leaving a swath of destruction in its wake.

Nuada knew that the battle could not be won without confronting Balor directly. With the Claíomh Solais in hand, he charged through the fray, carving a path toward the Fomorian leader. His warriors followed, their courage bolstered by his presence. When he reached Balor, Nuada stood firm, his silver arm raised high. Balor laughed, his voice a deep rumble that shook the ground.

"Do you think your little sword can match the power of my gaze?" Balor sneered, his massive form looming over Nuada.

With a roar, Nuada leapt forward, striking at Balor with all his strength. The Claíomh Solais shone with a brilliance that rivaled the sun, its blade connecting with Balor's eye just as it began to open. A blinding light erupted, illuminating the battlefield as Balor let out a deafening roar. The power of the sword shattered the eye's destructive force, turning it back upon Balor himself. The Fomorian leader fell, his immense body crashing to the ground like a toppled mountain.

The Fomorian forces, stunned by the loss of their leader, faltered. Seizing the moment, the Tuatha Dé Danann pressed forward, driving their enemies from the field. Victory was within their grasp.

But triumph came at a cost. Nuada, having spent every ounce of his strength in the fight, collapsed amidst the chaos. His warriors rushed to his side, but it was clear that the strain of the battle had taken its toll. With his final breaths, Nuada smiled, knowing that he had fulfilled his duty. The Tuatha Dé Danann had reclaimed their freedom, and the future of Ireland was secure.

As the battle subsided, the warriors of the Tuatha Dé Danann gathered to honor their fallen king. The Claíomh Solais, its blade still glowing faintly, was laid to rest beside him, a symbol of his sacrifice and the enduring strength of his people. Nuada's legacy would live on, a shining example of leadership, courage, and the ultimate price of victory.

Long after the battle of Moytura (Moy-choo-rah) ended and the Fomorians (Foh-mor-ee-ans) were driven from Ireland, the tale of Nuada (Noo-ah-dah) and the Claíomh Solais (Klee-uv Soh-lish, Sword of Light) lived on. It was a story told around hearths and in the halls of bards, a story of courage, sacrifice, and the true cost of leadership. Nuada's name became synonymous with justice and resilience, his life a shining example of what it meant to lead with honor.

The Tuatha Dé Danann (Too-ah-hah Day Dan-an) laid their fallen king to rest with great reverence. On the plains of Moytura, where his final victory had secured freedom for his people, they built a grand cairn to mark his resting place. Stones were carried from across the land, each placed with care and whispered prayers.

The cairn stood not only as a monument to Nuada but also as a symbol of the unity and strength of the Tuatha Dé Danann.

Beside Nuada, they placed the Claíomh Solais. The sword that had turned the tide of battle was now at rest, its glow softened but its legacy undiminished. Though the Tuatha Dé Danann recognized the power of the sword, they understood its deeper meaning. It was not just a weapon; it was a beacon of justice and a reminder of the responsibility borne by those who wield power.

The Claíomh Solais was revered as one of the four treasures of the Tuatha Dé Danann, alongside the Lia Fáil (Lee-ah Fawl, Stone of Destiny), the Cauldron of the Dagda (Kawl-drun uhv the Dahg-dah), and the Spear of Lugh (Spear uhv Loo). Each treasure embodied a virtue: the sword represented the unwavering justice and strength of a true ruler. Generations of leaders would look to these treasures for inspiration, their stories shaping the ideals of kingship and governance.

As the centuries passed, the tale of Nuada and his sword was woven into the cultural fabric of Ireland. It reminded the people of the values that defined their ancestors: courage in the face of overwhelming odds, the resilience to endure hardship, and the selflessness to sacrifice for the greater good. Nuada's story, passed down through the ages, inspired countless heroes and leaders, its lessons as relevant in times of peace as they were in moments of struggle.

The cairn of Nuada became a place of pilgrimage, where bards would sing of his deeds and chieftains would come to reflect on the weight of leadership. The land around Moytura grew lush and vibrant, as if nourished by the memory of its greatest king. The story of Nuada and the Claíomh Solais served as a guiding light for the Tuatha Dé Danann and for all who cherished the ideals of justice and unity.

In Irish mythology, the legacy of Nuada shines brightly, a reminder that true leadership is not about wielding power but about serving one's people with wisdom and integrity. His story, like the eternal glow of the Claíomh Solais, continues to illuminate the path for those who seek to uphold justice and protect the bonds that unite their community.

Sin é (Shin ay) That's it, The End.

The tale of Nuada and the Claíomh Solais (Klee-uv Soh-lish, Sword of Light) is a cornerstone of Irish mythology, capturing the spirit of the Tuatha Dé Danann (Too-ah-hah Day Dan-an, People of the Goddess Danu) and their enduring legacy. Through Nuada's journey, the story reveals timeless themes of resilience, justice, and the trials of leadership—values cherished by ancient Ireland.

The Claíomh Solais was one of the four sacred treasures brought to Ireland by the Tuatha Dé Danann, each representing virtues essential to leadership and balance. Alongside the Spear of Lugh, a symbol of victory; the Lia Fáil (Lee-ah Fawl, Stone of Destiny), affirming rightful kingship; and the Cauldron of the Dagda (Kawl-drun of the Dahg-dah), a source of abundance and renewal, the Claíomh Solais stood as a symbol of justice and strength. Together, these treasures embodied the ideals of ruler-ship, demanding that leaders serve with honor and integrity.

Nuada (Noo-ah-dah), known as the silver-handed king, exempli-fies justice and resilience in the face of adversity. His leadership reflects fairness and unwavering commitment to his people, even when it came at great personal cost. Nuada's story serves as a powerful reminder that true strength comes not from perfection but from the determination to overcome challenges. His silver arm, forged by Dian Cécht (Dee-ahn Kay-acht), symbolizes his adapt-ability and the redefinition of what it means to lead.

Nuada's loss of his arm in battle and his forced abdication underscore the ancient Irish value of physical wholeness in rulers. Yet his eventual return, equipped with his silver arm, transforms this narrative, showing that leadership is about courage, resilience, and selflessness. His journey emphasizes that a ruler's duty is to protect and uplift their people, even in the face of personal hardship.

Leadership in Irish mythology is often portrayed as a heavy responsibility. Rulers like Nuada were expected to embody fairness, bravery, and a deep sense of service. His willingness to sacrifice for his people demonstrates that the essence of leadership lies not in power but in the ability to unite and inspire. Nuada's story remains a cultural touchstone, illustrating the ideals of justice, community, and the pursuit of the greater good.

The legend of Nuada and the Claíomh Solais transcends its mythological origins, offering lessons that resonate today. It reminds us that adversity can lead to growth, that leadership requires compassion and sacrifice, and that justice is the ultimate goal of those destined to wield power. Nuada's tale continues to shine as a beacon of resilience, fairness, and unity in the rich tapestry of Irish culture.

CHAPTER 6

COMING OF THE MILESIANS

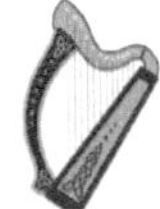

In the mists of Ireland's ancient past, the Tuatha Dé Danann (Too-ah-hah Day Dan-an, People of the Goddess Danu) descended upon the island. Shrouded in mystery, these godlike beings arrived not by ship, but through clouds that rolled across the land like a whisper from another world. With them, they brought draíocht (dree-ocht, magic), a force that shaped the hills and rivers of Ireland, imbuing the land with a sense of wonder and power.

The Tuatha Dé Danann were not mere mortals; they were warriors, poets, healers, and craftsmen whose lives blended seamlessly with the mystical. Their treasures—like the Claíomh Solais (Klee-uv Soh-lish, Sword of Light) and the Lia Fáil (Lee-ah Fawl, Stone of Destiny)—were said to hold immense power, symbols of the wisdom and strength they embodied. Under their rule, Ireland flourished. The land became a beacon of prosperity, its fields lush, its skies alive with magic, and its people thriving under the guidance of these extraordinary beings.

Yet, their reign would not last unchallenged. Across the seas, another people, the Milesians (Meel-ee-shuns), prepared to stake their claim to the island. Descendants of Míl Espáine (Meel Es-pawn-

49

ya), they were driven by destiny and ambition. They brought with them a different kind of power—not one of magic, but of resilience, strategy, and the unyielding belief that Ireland was meant to be theirs.

The Tuatha Dé Danann and the Milesians stood at the edge of myth and history, their collision destined to reshape Ireland forever. One people ruled through draíocht and divine connection to the land, while the other relied on determination and mortal ingenuity. Their meeting would mark the end of one era and the beginning of another, blending the realms of gods and men into a single story of transformation, legacy, and the enduring spirit of Ireland.

Thus begins the tale of the Tuatha Dé Danann and the coming of the Milesians, a story of magic and mortals, of triumph and loss, and of the threads that weave Ireland's ancient past into its enduring present.

The Tuatha Dé Danann (Too-ah-hah Day Dan-an, People of the Goddess Danu) were not like any people Ireland had ever seen. When they arrived on the shores of the island, they brought with them not just their warriors and leaders but a power that seemed to flow from the very earth and sky. Their arrival was shrouded in mystery, as they descended upon the land in a great, magical mist that cloaked their movements. To the people of Ireland, they appeared almost godlike, their mastery of draíocht (dree-ocht, magic) unmatched by any mortal force.

At that time, Ireland was ruled by the Fir Bolg (Fear Bol-ugh), a resilient and resourceful people who had claimed the island as their own. But the Tuatha Dé Danann, with their wisdom and strength, sought to bring a new era to the land. Conflict was inevitable. The First Battle of Moytura would decide who would rule Ireland.

The battle was fierce, stretching across the open plains of Moytura. The warriors of the Fir Bolg fought with great courage, but they were no match for the skill and magic of the Tuatha Dé Danann. Leading the charge was Nuada (Noo-ah-dah), the noble king of the Tuatha Dé Danann. His leadership inspired his people, and his bravery in battle became legendary. Though the Fir Bolg fought valiantly, they were ultimately defeated, and the Tuatha Dé Danann assumed control of the island.

With the Fir Bolg defeated, the Tuatha Dé Danann set about reshaping Ireland in their image, bringing with them the treasures of their four great cities—Falias, Gorias, Murias, and Finias. These cities, said to exist beyond the mortal realm, were steeped in ancient magic and wisdom, and each contributed a treasure that embodied a key virtue of leadership. These treasures became the foundation of the Tuatha Dé Danann's reign and the symbols of their power.

From Falias came the Lia Fáil (Lee-ah Fawl, Stone of Destiny), a sacred stone that was said to cry out beneath the feet of the rightful king, ensuring that only the worthy could rule. From Gorias came the Spear of Lugh, a weapon of unparalleled precision that never missed its mark and guaranteed victory to its wielder. From Murias came the Cauldron of Dagda (Kawl-drun of Dahg-dah), an enchanted vessel that never ran empty, providing sustenance to all who gathered around it. From Finias came the Claíomh Solais (Klee-uv Soh-lish, Sword of Light), a blade that could cut through any darkness, symbolizing justice and strength.

These treasures, infused with the magic of their creators, reflected the ideals of rulership and the unity that the Tuatha Dé Danann brought to Ireland, solidifying their legacy as divine leaders of the land.

With these treasures, the Tuatha Dé Danann ushered in a golden age for Ireland. Under their rule, the land flourished. Fields were lush and green, rivers teemed with life, and the people lived in harmony. Their mastery of magic allowed them to blend the natural world with the supernatural, creating a realm where creativity and wisdom thrived.

Nuada ruled with fairness, ensuring that justice was upheld and the needs of the people were met. The Tuatha Dé Danann's deep connection to the land and its magic gave them a profound respect for balance, ensuring that their reign was one of harmony and prosperity. Ireland became a place where both the mundane and the mystical coexisted, each enhancing the other.

But as their power grew, so too did the challenges they faced. The Tuatha Dé Danann knew their golden age would not last forever. Far beyond the seas, new forces were stirring. The Milesians (Meel-ee-shuns), descendants of Míl Espáine (Meel Es-pawn-ya), sought their own destiny in Ireland. Their arrival would mark the beginning of a new chapter in the island's history, one filled with conflict, change, and the blending of myth and reality.

For now, though, Ireland thrived under the Tuatha Dé Danann, their magic and wisdom leaving an indelible mark on the land they had claimed as their own. Their story, and the treasures they brought, would echo through the ages as symbols of resilience, creativity, and the enduring spirit of the Irish people.

Generations after the Tuatha Dé Danann (Too-ah-hah Day Danan, People of the Goddess Danu) claimed Ireland as their home, another wave of settlers appeared on the horizon. These were the Milesians (Meel-ee-shuns), descendants of Míl Espáine (Meel Es-pawn-ya), a great leader from Spain. Unlike the Tuatha Dé Danann, the Milesians were human, but they were no ordinary mortals. They were bold explorers and skilled warriors, and they believed that their lineage and destiny gave them the right to rule Ireland.

When their ships first appeared off the coast, the Tuatha Dé Danann watched with suspicion. They had ruled Ireland for centuries, their magic and wisdom shaping the land into a realm of beauty and harmony. To them, Ireland was more than a home—it was sacred, given to them by divine right. They would not give it up without a fight.

The Milesians, too, believed they were destined to claim the land. Their leader, Amergin (Ah-mur-gin), was not just a warrior but also a poet and druid. His words carried a power of their own, weaving together wisdom and persuasion. As the Milesians approached the shores, Amergin invoked the spirits of Ireland in verse, calling upon the land, sea, and sky to witness their arrival.

Their landing was met with immediate resistance. The Tuatha Dé Danann, determined to protect their home, summoned their draíocht (dree-ocht, magic) to create storms that lashed at the invaders' ships. Waves rose like mountains, winds screamed through the rigging, and the skies darkened as the Milesians struggled to stay afloat. The Tuatha Dé Danann believed they had driven the newcomers away.

But Amergin stepped forward, standing at the prow of his ship. As the storm raged around them, he raised his voice, chanting a poem of power and reverence:

"I am the wind that blows across the sea,
I am the wave of the ocean,
I am the stag of seven tines,
I am the hawk upon the cliff,
I am the sun, a bright spark of fire..."

Amergin's words were not merely poetic; they carried a force that resonated with the very essence of the land. The storms began to calm, the waves grew still, and the sky lightened. The Milesians, guided by their leader's wisdom, pressed forward, reaching the shores of Ireland.

The Tuatha Dé Danann, realizing the Milesians would not be so easily defeated, prepared to meet them on the battlefield. Their warriors and druids gathered, determined to defend their claim to the land. Yet, even as conflict brewed, the Milesians' respect for Ireland's natural and spiritual beauty was undeniable. Amergin's poetry, steeped in reverence for the land, hinted at a different kind of conquest—one not based solely on power but on connection and understanding.

The arrival of the Milesians marked the beginning of a great struggle. It was not merely a battle of arms but a clash of ideals: the mystical, divine right of the Tuatha Dé Danann versus the mortal determination and poetic wisdom of the Milesians. Amergin's ability to calm the storms showed that even in the face of magic, words and understanding held great power.

As the Milesians set foot on the soil of Ireland, they knew the real challenge lay ahead. The Tuatha Dé Danann, with their mastery of draíocht and their unwavering bond with the land, would not yield easily. For both sides, Ireland was more than a prize —it was a legacy, a destiny worth fighting for. The stage was set for a confrontation that would shape the future of the island and echo through its myths for generations.

The air was charged with tension as the Milesians prepared to face the Tuatha Dé Danann in a decisive battle for control of Ireland. The lush plains and mist-shrouded hills, which had thrived under the magical reign of the Tuatha Dé Danann, now became the stage for a confrontation that would determine the fate of the land.

The Tuatha Dé Danann summoned their full powers, calling upon draíocht to protect their ríocht (ree-uhkt, kingdom). Enchanted mists rolled across the land, obscuring the Milesians' path and sowing confusion in their ranks. The Tuatha Dé Danann's warriors, armed with the legendary treasures of their four great cities—Falias, Gorias, Murias, and Finias—stood ready to defend their homeland. The Claíomh Solais (Klee-uv Soh-lish, Sword of Light) gleamed in the hands of their champions, a symbol of justice and divine protection.

But the Milesians were no ordinary invaders. Led by Amergin (Ah-mur-gin), a poet, druid, and warrior, they had come not just with swords and shields but with reverence for the land and its mystical heritage. Amergin's wisdom guided their steps, and his eloquence inspired unity among his people. Before the battle, Amergin stood before the mist-covered plains and recited an invocation to Ireland itself, a poem that called upon the land's essence to grant them safe passage:

> "I am the wind on the sea,
> I am the wave of the ocean,
> I am the bull of seven battles..."

As Amergin spoke, the mists began to lift, revealing the beauty of the land and the determination of the Tuatha Dé Danann. The Milesians advanced, their resolve unshaken by the magical barriers set before them.

The clash of the two peoples was fierce and unforgettable. The Tuatha Dé Danann unleashed spells of great power, bending the elements to their will. Thunder roared, lightning streaked across the sky, and the earth itself seemed to tremble under the weight of their draíocht. Yet the Milesians, guided by Amergin's wisdom and strategy, pressed on with unwavering courage.

The turning point came when Amergin proposed a truce, appealing to the Tuatha Dé Danann's sense of justice and honor. He suggested that the island be divided, with the world above the ground belonging to the Milesians and the world below, the sídhe (shee, fairy mounds), becoming the realm of the Tuatha Dé Danann. It was a compromise born not of conquest but of mutual respect for the land and its spirits.

Though reluctant, the Tuatha Dé Danann accepted the terms. They retreated into the sídhe, withdrawing from the mortal world but remaining ever-present as guardians of Ireland's magic and spirit. In their new form as the aos sí (ays shee, the fairies or otherworldly beings), they continued to shape the land and inspire its people, though from the shadows.

The Milesians, now rulers of Ireland's surface, honored the legacy of the Tuatha Dé Danann by preserving their stories and respecting the sanctity of the fairy mounds. The battle had ended, but the tale of the Tuatha Dé Danann and their transformation into the aos sí lived on, becoming a cornerstone of Irish mythology and a reminder of the deep connection between the land, its people, and its magic.

Though the Tuatha Dé Danann retreated into the sídhe (shee, fairy mounds), their story was far from over. Their transformation into the aos sí (ays shee, otherworldly beings) marked not a defeat, but a reimagining of their role as protectors of the land. No longer rulers in the mortal sense, they became guardians of Ireland's spirit and magic, watching over the island from the shadows of the Otherworld.

The aos sí took their place in the collective memory of Ireland, woven into the landscape itself. The hills, mounds, and forests became sacred places, thought to be doorways to their hidden realm. Farmers left offerings at these sites, and travelers tread carefully near the sídhe, respecting the unseen presence of the Tuatha Dé Danann. These beings, once warriors and rulers, now represented Ireland's connection to the mystical and eternal, embodying the land's resilience and beauty.

For the Milesians, their victory was more than a conquest—it was a new beginning. Descended from Míl Espáine (Meel Es-pawn-ya), their arrival and success symbolized the transition from a divine age to an age of mortal kingship. Their leaders were not only warriors but also stewards of the land, tasked with balancing the legacy of the Tuatha Dé Danann with the needs of their people.

Under the Milesians, Ireland entered a new chapter. The traditions and values passed down from the Tuatha Dé Danann continued to shape the culture. The land's magic, though no longer openly wielded, remained alive in its stories, poetry, and deep reverence for the natural world. The Milesians honored the sídhe as sacred, ensuring that the bond between the mortal world and the Otherworld would never be broken.

The tale of the Tuatha Dé Danann and the Milesians became a cornerstone of Irish identity. It bridged myth and history, illustrating the enduring values of respect, resilience, and harmony with the land. As the Tuatha Dé Danann continued their silent vigil from the sídhe, their story lived on in the hearts of the Irish people, a testament to the unbroken connection between the land, its guardians, and its rulers.

Their legacy reminds us that even in transformation, their influence endures, echoing through the hills and rivers of Ireland, where the aos sí are said to dwell, keeping watch over their beloved home.

Sin é (Shin ay) That's it, The End.

The story of the Tuatha Dé Danann (Too-ah-hah Day Dan-an, People of the Goddess Danu) and the Milesians (Meel-es-awn-ya) blended myth and history, offering a profound reflection of Ireland's cultural identity. It bridged the divine and the mortal, combining the magical origins of the land with the human journey of leadership and transformation. Through themes of resilience, connection to the land, and the sacred balance between the seen and unseen, this tale captured the essence of Irish heritage.

The transition from the Tuatha Dé Danann to the Milesians represented a shift from Ireland's divine and mystical beginnings to its mortal rulers. The Tuatha Dé Danann symbolized the island's spiritual and magical roots, while the Milesians marked the emergence of a human legacy. This duality reflected Ireland's evolving identity, where the mythical and the historical coexisted. The story emphasized the importance of honoring one's past while forging a new future, a theme that resonated deeply with the Irish sense of continuity and cultural pride.

The Claíomh Solais (Klee-uv Soh-lish, Sword of Light), Spear of Lugh, Cauldron of Dagda, and Lia Fáil (Lee-ah Fawl, Stone of Destiny) were not merely artifacts of legend—they embodied the virtues essential to leadership: justice, courage, abundance, and rightful authority. These treasures guided the Tuatha Dé Danann and were inherited symbolically by the Milesians. They represented the responsibilities of rulers to serve their people with wisdom and integrity, values that remained central to Irish culture.

When the Tuatha Dé Danann retreated into the sídhe (shee, fairy mounds), they became the aos sí (ays shee, otherworldly beings), guardians of Ireland's spiritual essence. Their transition reflected the enduring Irish belief in the unseen forces that shaped and protected the land. The aos sí symbolized the balance between humanity and nature, reminding people that the land was both a resource and a sacred trust. This reverence for the mystical aspects of the natural world remained a cornerstone of Irish folklore and identity.

Amergin, the poet and leader of the Milesians, exemplified the

Irish reverence for creativity and eloquence. His poetry calmed storms and claimed Ireland not just physically but spiritually, illustrating the belief that words carried transformative power. In Irish tradition, poets and bards were revered as visionaries who could influence reality. Amergin's role highlighted the importance of wisdom, connection to the land, and the creative spirit in shaping leadership and belonging.

CHAPTER 7

DEIRDRE OF THE SORROWS

This is the story of Deirdre, the beautiful child of fate, whose life became a poignant tale of love, loyalty, and the unyielding grip of prophecy. Through her journey, you will uncover the power of fate and the timeless struggle between personal desires and the expectations placed upon us. Along the way, you'll learn some key Irish words to deepen your connection to this legendary tale.

Let us step into the world of Deirdre and the kingdom of Ulster, where beauty and tragedy are intertwined like threads in an ancient tapestry.

Deirdre of Sorrows

In the green hills of Ulster, where the air hums with the whispers of ancient songs, a prophecy was spoken that would change the course of a kingdom. Deirdre (Deer-drah), a child of extraordinary beauty, was destined for greatness—but not without sorrow. Even before her first cry echoed through the valleys, the druid Cathbad (Kah-thahd) foretold her fate: Deirdre would grow to be so beautiful that men would fight and kingdoms would crumble for her, bringing ruin to Ulster.

To prevent this ominous future, King Conchobar (Kawn-kho-bar), ruler of Ulster, made a fateful decision. He claimed Deirdre as his bride, determined to keep her under his control and avoid the calamity foretold. But destiny, as the druids would remind us, is not so easily tamed.

From the moment Deirdre (Deer-drah) was born, her life was shaped by a prophecy that cast a long shadow over the kingdom of Ulster. To prevent the foretold ruin, King Conchobar (Kawn-kho-bar) decreed that she would be raised in seclusion, hidden away from the eyes of the world until she was old enough to become his queen.

In a quiet forest glade, Deirdre grew up under the watchful care of her nursemaid, Leborcham (Leh-bore-kahm). Her days were peaceful but lonely, filled with the rustling of leaves, the songs of birds, and the stories her nursemaid told of the grand halls and brave warriors beyond the trees. Though she was shielded from the dangers of the outside world, the walls around her felt like a cage.

As the years passed, Deirdre's beauty blossomed, just as the prophecy had foretold. But with her beauty came a longing—a desire to see the world beyond the forest and to make her own choices. This yearning grew stronger until the day her fate was forever changed.

While walking through the woods, Deirdre came across Naoise (Nee-sha), a warrior of the Red Branch Knights. He stood tall and strong, his presence filling the air with a quiet confidence. Their eyes met, and in that fleeting moment, a spark ignited between them. Deirdre felt something she had never known before: love.

Naoise, too, was struck by Deirdre's radiance and the strength in her gaze. Though he knew the risk of pursuing her, he could not deny the connection he felt. Their love was forbidden, tied as Deirdre was to Conchobar's claim, yet it bloomed in defiance of the prophecy that sought to dictate their lives.

With her heart set on freedom, Deirdre made a bold decision.

She would not allow herself to be bound by Conchobar's will or the weight of fate. She and Naoise would follow their hearts, even if it meant challenging the might of the king himself.

Thus began their journey, a tale of love and rebellion that would echo through the ages, a story of two souls determined to forge their own destiny in the face of insurmountable odds.

Deirdre (Deer-drah) and Naoise (Nee-sha), bound by love and defiance, knew their decision to flee Ulster would set the kingdom aflame. Their love, pure and unyielding, had become a threat to the power and pride of King Conchobar (Kawn-kho-bar). The risk was great, but their longing for freedom was greater still.

Under the cover of darkness, the lovers prepared their escape. Naoise called upon his loyal brothers, Ardan (Ard-awn) and Ainle (An-leh), fierce warriors of the Red Branch Knights, to aid them. Though bound by loyalty to Ulster, the brothers could not abandon Naoise in his time of need. They swore to protect him and Deirdre, even if it meant defying their king.

Together, they stole away from the forests of Ulster, their path lit only by the stars above. Every step was fraught with danger, but Deirdre's courage never wavered. She clung to Naoise's hand, her heart pounding not with fear but with determination. They crossed rivers and scaled rocky hills, driven by the hope of a life beyond the reach of Conchobar's grasp.

At last, they reached the coast, where a small boat awaited them. The sea stretched wide and dark before them, a vast unknown. For Deirdre, it was both a symbol of freedom and a reminder of the uncertainty ahead. As they pushed off into the waves, the wind caught their sails, carrying them toward Scotland— a land of new beginnings and, they hoped, refuge.

Their journey across the sea was grueling. The waves tossed their small vessel like a leaf in the wind, and the cold bit at their skin. Yet through it all, Deirdre and Naoise found solace in each other's presence. Naoise's brothers sang songs of bravery and love to keep their spirits high, their voices rising above the roar of the ocean.

When they finally reached the shores of Scotland, a new chapter of their lives began. Far from the halls of Ulster, they found peace in the rolling green hills and quiet glens. Naoise and his brothers built a home, and for a time, they lived simply and happily. Deirdre, free from the shadow of Conchobar's claim, felt her heart lighten.

Yet, the prophecy lingered like a storm cloud on the horizon. Conchobar, driven by a mix of vengeance and obsession, could not let Deirdre go. To him, she was not just a woman but a symbol of his power and control. News of the lovers' escape spread across the land, and Conchobar's anger burned hotter with each passing day.

He sent emissaries to Scotland, bearing messages of supposed forgiveness and reconciliation. They spoke of peace, urging Naoise and Deirdre to return to Ulster under the king's protection. But Naoise and his brothers knew better than to trust the words of a man so consumed by pride.

Despite the fleeting happiness they found in their Scottish haven, the lovers could not escape the long reach of Conchobar's wrath. The king's pursuit, relentless and cunning, crept ever closer, threatening to unravel the fragile joy they had built.

Through it all, Deirdre and Naoise's love only deepened. Each stolen moment of laughter, each quiet night under the stars, became a treasure in the face of uncertainty. They vowed to stand together, no matter what fate had in store, their bond unbroken by fear or despair.

Their journey across the sea was a testament to their defiance, a leap of faith against the tide of destiny. But as the shadow of Ulster grew nearer, they knew the peace they had found could not last forever. Their love, like the prophecy, was destined to shape the fate of kingdoms.

The peace Deirdre and Naoise (Nee-sha) had found in Scotland was fragile, overshadowed by the looming threat of Conchobar (Kawn-kho-bar). The king's relentless obsession with reclaiming Deirdre and restoring his pride consumed him. His spies had long since discovered the lovers' haven, and Conchobar's cunning mind devised a plan steeped in deceit.

He sent envoys to Scotland bearing messages of reconciliation. These emissaries spoke of the king's remorse, his desire to mend the rift and welcome the lovers back to Ulster with honor and safety. The promises were sweet, but their words carried a hidden venom.

When the message reached Naoise and his brothers, skepticism gripped them. Ardan (Ard-awn) and Ainle (An-leh) urged caution, but Conchobar's offer was tantalizing. The prospect of returning home, of living without fear, tempted even the wary. Naoise, ever the brave and hopeful, believed in the possibility of suaimhneas (soo-iv-ness, peace).

Deirdre, however, felt a chill in her heart. The words of the emissaries were too smooth, their assurances too perfect. The whispers of prophecy rang louder in her mind. "It is a trap," she told Naoise, her voice laced with unease. Yet, her love for him and her concern for his brothers left her torn. Against her better judgment, she agreed to return.

The journey back to Ulster was somber. The land that once felt like home now seemed unfamiliar, its rolling hills and ancient woods shadowed by an ominous weight. As they neared Emain Macha, the seat of Conchobar's power, Deirdre's unease deepened. The king greeted them with open arms, his face a mask of warmth, but his eyes betrayed a cold, calculating hunger.

At first, Conchobar's promises seemed genuine. He hosted a grand feast in their honor, and the hall was filled with laughter and song. But Deirdre could not ignore the tension that hummed beneath the surface. The warriors of Ulster watched her too closely, and Conchobar's smile never quite reached his eyes.

It was during the height of the revelry that the betrayal unfolded. Naoise and his brothers were separated from Deirdre under the guise of an urgent council with the king. Moments later, the clash of steel echoed through the halls. Deirdre's heart sank as she realized the trap had been sprung.

She ran through the corridors, her voice calling out for Naoise, but the guards blocked her path. When she finally reached the courtyard, it was too late. Naoise lay lifeless on the cold stone, his brothers fallen beside him. The prophecy had been fulfilled—Deirdre's beauty had brought ruin to Ulster, and her love had been wrenched away in an act of treachery.

Deirdre fell to her knees, her cries piercing the night. Conchobar stood nearby, his expression one of triumph mixed with something darker—regret, perhaps, or the hollow realization that his obsession had cost him more than he could ever admit.

For Deirdre, there was no solace, no comfort to be found. Her heart shattered as she gazed upon Naoise, the man who had loved her so fiercely, who had defied fate itself for her. The light in her eyes dimmed, and with it, her will to endure.

Thus, the sorrow foretold by the druid Cathbad (Kah-thahd) came to pass, and the kingdom of Ulster was forever marked by the tragedy of Deirdre and Naoise. It was a story of love, betrayal, and the unrelenting grip of fate—one that would be whispered through the ages, a haunting reminder of the cost of obsession and the fragility of hope.

The halls of Emain Macha were steeped in silence following the bloodshed. Deirdre (Deer-drah), the woman whose beauty had inspired songs and sparked war, was now a shadow of herself. Her grief was immeasurable, a weight that pressed against her chest with every breath she took. Naoise (Nee-sha), her great love, was gone, and the world felt hollow in his absence.

Conchobar (Kawn-kho-bar), emboldened by his victory, sought to claim Deirdre as his own. He approached her, speaking of the future they could have together, as if the love she had shared with Naoise could be erased with his words. To him, Deirdre was a prize, a symbol of his power, a beauty to adorn his court.

But Deirdre's eyes, once filled with life and warmth, now burned with defiance. "You may have taken Naoise from me," she said, her voice steady despite the storm within her, "but you will never possess me. I am no man's trophy, least of all yours."

Her rejection stung Conchobar more deeply than any blade. His obsession with her had driven his actions, yet he found no satisfaction in his triumph. Deirdre, unbroken in spirit, stood before him as a reminder of his failure to control her heart.

Days turned into weeks, and Deirdre's sorrow grew. The world held no joy for her without Naoise by her side. She was watched constantly, Conchobar fearful she might escape or seek revenge. But Deirdre had no thoughts of vengeance—her only desire was to reunite with Naoise, even if it meant leaving the world behind.

In one version of her tale, Deirdre was forced into Conchobar's chariot, bound for a new life as his queen. As they traveled, she gazed upon the land she once loved, now tainted by the memory of betrayal and loss. When the chariot reached a high cliff, Deirdre saw her chance. Without hesitation, she flung herself into the void below, choosing death over a life ruled by Conchobar.

In another telling, Deirdre's sorrow consumed her entirely. She withdrew from the world, refusing food and drink, her grief carving deeper lines into her face with each passing day. One morning, her guards found her lifeless, her body still but her expression peaceful, as though she had found Naoise in her dreams and followed him to the otherworld.

Deirdre's death marked the final chapter in a story that had begun with a prophecy. It was a victory not for Conchobar, but for love and fate—forces beyond the control of any king. Her sacrifice ensured that her heart would remain her own, untamed by tyranny.

In Ulster, her name became a legend. Poets sang of her beauty, her bravery, and her undying love for Naoise. The people mourned her as a symbol of the tragic cost of pride and obsession. Though her life was brief, Deirdre's story endured, a poignant reminder of the power of love and the enduring struggle for freedom in the face of oppression.

And so, Deirdre, the beautiful child of fate, lives on in the hearts of those who hear her tale. In her defiance, she triumphed, and in her sorrow, she became eternal.

Long after Deirdre's (Deer-drah) tragic death, her story lived on, whispered across the hills of Ulster and sung by bards at roaring fires. It became more than a tale of love and loss—it became a reflection of Ireland's soul, embodying themes of courage, defiance, and the price of unchecked power.

In the wake of her passing, the people of Ulster mourned not only for Deirdre and Naoise (Nee-sha) but for the kingdom itself, fractured by the consequences of Conchobar's (Kawn-kho-bar) obsession. The king, though victorious in claiming Deirdre's life, was left hollow. His reign bore the stain of betrayal, and his name became a warning against the perils of pride and tyranny.

Deirdre's name, however, became a symbol of unyielding love and the enduring struggle for freedom. Bards, the keepers of Ireland's history and culture, wove her story into the fabric of the Ulster Cycle, the epic collection of tales that celebrated the heroism and tragedies of ancient Ireland. They sang of her beauty that rivaled the dawn, her love for Naoise that defied fate, and her sorrow that brought kings to their knees.

In their songs, Deirdre was not just a tragic figure but a heroine who chose love and freedom over submission. Her defiance of Conchobar, even in the face of overwhelming power, resonated deeply with the Irish spirit—a people who had long cherished their independence and identity despite countless challenges.

Poems like Deirdre's Lament captured the depth of her grief and the eternal bond she shared with Naoise. Her voice, through the words of the bards, became immortal:

> "Were it I alone to suffer,
> And Naoise spared this pain,
> But now the light has left my life,
> And I shall not see it again."

The lessons of Deirdre's story reached beyond Ulster's borders. It warned rulers against the dangers of obsession and control, reminding them that love and freedom cannot be possessed. For ordinary people, it offered a bittersweet dóchas (doh-khass, hope)

—that even in the face of tragedy, love remains the most powerful force, worth any price.

As centuries passed, Deirdre's tale was told and retold, evolving with each generation but always preserving its core truths. Her name became synonymous with beauty, bravery, and sacrifice. The land of Ulster, where she once walked, bore the echoes of her sorrow and strength.

Even today, the story of Deirdre endures, a testament to the timeless nature of her legacy. It reminds us that, though life may be fleeting and love may often end in heartbreak, both are worth fighting for. Deirdre's spirit lives on, a guiding star in Ireland's rich tapestry of legends, forever teaching the world that true freedom lies not in what we possess but in the courage to follow our hearts.

Sin é (Shin ay) That's it, The End

Prophecies are a cornerstone of Irish mythology, acting as both warnings and catalysts for the actions of heroes and heroines. In Deirdre's (Deer-drah) tale, the prophecy foretold by the druid Cathbad (Kah-thahd) looms over her entire life. Rather than averting disaster, the prophecy seems to drive the choices of those involved, ensuring its tragic fulfillment. This reflects a recurring theme in Irish lore: that fate is inescapable, and attempts to defy it often hasten its realization. Deirdre's story vividly explores the tension between personal choice and the unyielding power of destiny. Although she defies Conchobar (Kawn-kho-bar) to follow her heart and pursue freedom, her decisions ultimately align with the prophecy, bringing sorrow to Ulster. This interplay between fate and free will echoes throughout the Ulster Cycle and underscores a cultural fascination with the limits of human agency.

At its heart, Deirdre's tale also highlights the role of women in Irish mythology. Her defiance and strength shine in a world dominated by male power. Conchobar treats her as a possession to be claimed, but she refuses to submit, even at the cost of her life. Her courage and determination to follow her own path elevate her as one of Ireland's most memorable heroines, challenging the notion of passive female figures and positioning her as a symbol of resistance and autonomy.

The bards, ancient Ireland's storytellers and cultural guardians, played a vital role in preserving Deirdre's legacy. Through their songs and poems, her story was passed down, not just as entertainment but as a reflection of Ireland's values, struggles, and beliefs. As part of the Ulster Cycle, her tale became immortal, a poignant reminder of the power of love, the inevitability of fate, and the enduring spirit of defiance. The bardic tradition ensured that Deirdre's story remained a touchstone of Irish identity, resonating across generations and connecting the past with the present.

CHAPTER 8

BATTLE OF CLONTARF

At the dawn of the 11th century, Ireland was a land of fragmented kingdoms, where rival clans vied for power and Viking influence loomed large. These Norse settlers and raiders had established strongholds across the island, integrating into Irish politics while maintaining their own ambitions. Amid this chaos, Brian Boru emerged as a leader unlike any other—a visionary who saw beyond the immediate rivalries of his time. As High King of Ireland, he sought not only to unite the Irish clans but also to free the land from the grip of Viking domination.

Brian's rise to power was no small feat. Hailing from the Kingdom of Munster, he ascended to prominence through a combination of strategic alliances, decisive battles, and an unshakable determination to bring order to a divided land. His vision of a unified Ireland resonated with many but also provoked resistance, particularly from those who had grown accustomed to wielding power in their own territories. Still, Brian pressed on, recognizing that Ireland's independence and cultural identity were at stake.

The year 1014 marked a pivotal moment in this struggle. On Good Friday, April 23, Brian led a coalition of Irish forces to confront a powerful Viking alliance bolstered by Irish factions from

Leinster. The *Battle of Clontarf* was more than a clash of armies—it was a defining moment in Ireland's history, where sovereignty and unity were fought for with immense sacrifice.

The events surrounding the battle reflect themes that resonate deeply in Irish culture: the pursuit of independence, the tension between unity and rivalry, and the enduring cost of leadership. Brian Boru's efforts to rally the clans, his ability to navigate a web of alliances and enmities, and his ultimate sacrifice underscore the complexities of Ireland's path toward sovereignty.

Brian's legacy, forged on the shores of Clontarf, continues to inspire. His determination to unify a fractured land and confront foreign powers resonates as a powerful symbol of resilience and leadership. The Battle of Clontarf stands as a testament to the sacrifices made for freedom and the enduring struggle for unity in the face of division.

In the lush green fields of Munster (Muhn-stir), a leader emerged whose dreams stretched far beyond his own borders. Brian Boru (Bree-an Boh-roo), born to the proud Dál gCais (Dawl Gosh) clan, saw his homeland plagued by division and the shadow of Viking rule. The Norse (Nor-sh), once raiders, now held power in Éire's (Ay-rah, Ireland) largest cities, like Baile Átha Cliath (Bah-lah Aw-ha Kleeh-ah, Dublin), where they ruled through strength and alliances with rival Irish clans. Brian knew this had to change.

"Ní neart go cur le chéile" (Nee nart guh kur leh keh-lah, There is no strength without unity), Brian would say to his people, reminding them that only together could they overcome the forces dividing their land. His dream was bold: a united Éire, free from Viking domination and the infighting that had weakened it for generations. But Brian was no idle dreamer—he was a man of action.

He began in his homeland, rising as the leader of Munster through a mix of determination, diplomacy, and strength in battle. Slowly, he built alliances with neighboring clans, earning their trust and loyalty by showing fairness and wisdom. Over time, his reputation grew, and he was crowned Ard Rí (Ard Ree, High King) of Éire —a title meant to unite all Irish clans under one ruler.

Not everyone embraced Brian's leadership. In Laighin (Lye-een, Leinster), the king resisted his authority and joined forces with the Norse rulers of Dublin. Together, they formed a dangerous alliance, combining Viking ruthlessness with Irish defiance. The threat was immense, and Brian knew that without unity, his vision would crumble.

At a gathering of Irish chieftains, Brian laid out his plan. Around a long table, the leaders of Éire sat, their faces marked by the weariness of years of conflict. Brian stood, gesturing to a map spread across the table. "Our land," he began, "is strong and beautiful, but it bleeds from its divisions. The Norse grow stronger with every raid, every alliance. We must stand together, or they will rule us all."

A chieftain from Connacht leaned forward, his brow furrowed with doubt. "What makes you different from the Vikings, Brian Boru? Why should we fight for you and not ourselves?"

Brian's gaze was steady. "I do not ask you to fight for me. I ask you to fight for Éire. For your children, for their future. A future where they do not live under foreign chains or fear the next raid."

The room fell silent. One by one, the chieftains nodded. Old rivalries were set aside, grudges buried for a common cause. The alliance was fragile but powerful—a united Irish force determined to reclaim their land.

Across Éire (Ay-rah, Ireland), warriors prepared for the inevitable confrontation. Men sharpened their swords, mothers said tearful goodbyes to their sons, and bards composed songs to rally spirits. The clans would fight, not just for themselves, but for the vision Brian Boru had kindled: an Éire united in purpose and strength.

Brian knew the path ahead would be steep, but in the determination of his people, he saw the spark of hope that would one day make his dream a reality.

The land of Éire (Ay-rah, Ireland) was a place of unparalleled beauty—rolling green hills, ancient forests, and rivers that glimmered in the sunlight like silver threads. But beneath its serene landscape lay a constant struggle for power. The Irish clans, proud and fiercely independent, had warred with one another for generations, each seeking to defend its own territory and honor. These rivalries, while deeply rooted in tradition, left Éire fractured, vulnerable to foreign invaders who saw opportunity in its divisions.

Among these invaders were the Norse (Nor-sh), who had arrived on longships centuries earlier. At first, they came as raiders, their sails striking fear into coastal villages. Over time, they became settlers, building strongholds in places like Baile Átha Cliath (Bah-lah Aw-ha Kleeh-ah, Dublin), where they ruled with iron fists and sharp blades. Their influence grew as they forged alliances with Irish clans who sought to use Viking strength to tip the scales of their own rivalries.

The year 1014 found Éire at a boiling point. In Baile Átha Cliath, Viking longships glided into the harbor, their black sails casting ominous shadows on the water. Warriors stepped ashore, their axes gleaming and their armor reflecting the cold sunlight. Among them was Sigurd, a chieftain from Orkney, a land to the north where the Norse still reigned supreme. He was tall and imposing, his braided hair streaked with silver, his gaze sharp and calculating.

Waiting to greet Sigurd was the King of Laighin (Lye-een, Leinster), a man who had turned to the Norse for help in his defiance of Brian Boru (Bree-an Boh-roo). Their handshake was stiff, a meeting of two men bound by ambition but divided by mistrust. "Together, we will break the High King," the King of Laighin said, his voice firm.

Sigurd nodded but said nothing. For the Norse, this alliance was a means to an end—plunder, power, and control over Éire's riches.

Meanwhile, far to the south, Brian Boru stood in the hall of his stronghold, surrounded by his closest advisors. A messenger knelt before him, breathless from a long ride. "The Norse have arrived," the man reported, his voice tense. "Their numbers grow, and they are joined by the men of Laighin."

Brian's expression did not falter. He had expected this. Turning to his commanders, he spoke with calm resolve. "The time has come. We must stand united, or we will fall divided. Gather our forces. Send word to the clans—we march for Baile Átha Cliath."

The tension in the air was palpable as the commanders moved to carry out his orders. Brian's gaze lingered on the map spread across the table before him, his fingers tracing the line of the River Liffey. This was no ordinary battle. The clash that lay ahead would determine the fate of Éire, a land that had weathered centuries of division and now faced its greatest test.

Outside, the winds carried the whispers of war, rustling the trees and stirring the hearts of warriors across the land. In the west, chieftains sharpened their swords and prepared to ride. In the east, Viking warriors feasted and laughed, their confidence growing as their ranks swelled. And in Munster (Muhn-stir), Brian Boru prepared for the battle that would define his legacy, his determination unshaken in the face of the storm that was coming.

The roads of Éire (Ay-rah, Ireland) thrummed with the sound of galloping hooves and the urgent cries of messengers. From the rugged hills of Connacht (Kon-acht) to the fertile plains of Meath, Brian Boru's summons to arms spread like wildfire. "The High King calls for unity!" they shouted in village squares and clan halls. "The Norse and their allies gather in Baile Átha Cliath (Bah-lah Aw-ha Kleeh-ah, Dublin). Stand with Brian Boru, or see Éire fall into foreign hands!"

In a small village nestled in the shadow of a mountain, a young farmer stopped his work as the messenger arrived. Villagers gathered around, their faces a mix of fear and determination. "It is time," said an elder, his voice trembling. "We fight not for Brian alone, but for Éire itself."

Across the land, warriors prepared for the coming battle. In a smoky forge, a blacksmith hammered the final touches onto a blade, the sparks flying like embers of war. A chieftain in Connacht pulled his sword from its sheath and turned to his sons. "We ride for Munster (Muhn-stir)," he said, his tone heavy with pride and sorrow. "Your mother will light a candle for us every night until we return."

Men sharpened spears, strapped on armor, and tied ribbons or charms given by their loved ones. Beneath the preparations lay the weight of what was to come. Mothers whispered prayers over their sons, fathers clapped their children on the back with trembling hands, and wives held their husbands close, knowing the road ahead was fraught with peril.

In Baile Átha Cliath, the scene was far different. The Viking stronghold buzzed with anticipation. On the docks, ships swayed gently in the harbor, their hulls laden with warriors and supplies. A captain stood on the deck of a longship, his voice booming over the gathering crowd. "Tonight, we feast," he declared, his axe glinting in the sun. "Tomorrow, we take everything!" The men roared their approval, their spirits high with promises of plunder and glory.

Within the city walls, Viking leaders gathered in a hall thick with the smell of mead and roasted meat. Sigurd of Orkney leaned over a table, his finger tracing the lines of a crude map. "The Irish will come," he said, his tone one of grim confidence. "But we have the numbers and the strength. This land will be ours by the week's end." Around him, warriors laughed and drank, their confidence swelling with each passing moment.

As the armies prepared, the winds of Éire seemed to carry the echoes of both hope and fear. On the western plains, a young warrior carved runes into his shield, the markings a prayer for protection and victory. In the forests of Munster, Brian Boru stood before his gathered forces, his voice steady and commanding. "Ní neart go cur le chéile" (Nee nart guh kur leh keh-lah, There is no strength without unity), he told them, his words igniting their spirits. "We fight not for ourselves, but for our children and their children. For Éire."

The armies of Éire were not just soldiers—they were farmers, fishermen, and blacksmiths who had taken up arms for their homeland. And though the odds seemed insurmountable, they marched with a shared purpose, their hearts united by Brian Boru's unwavering vision of freedom.

In the days that followed, warriors from every corner of Éire made their way toward the Ard Rí's (Ard Ree, High King's) banners. Old grudges were set aside, and rival clans stood shoulder to shoulder. The roads were alive with the steady beat of marching feet, the clang of swords against shields, and the songs of bards who wove courage into every verse.

In Baile Átha Cliath, the Vikings prepared their defenses, their war machines ready to unleash destruction. But even in their confidence, there was unease. They had seen Irish resilience before, and they knew this would not be a battle easily won.

As the two forces moved closer to confrontation, the air itself seemed to tighten with anticipation. The fields outside Dublin would soon bear witness to one of the greatest battles in Éire's history—a battle that would test the strength of unity against the forces of ambition and division.

The sound of marching feet echoed across the countryside as Brian Boru's forces made their way toward Baile Átha Cliath (Bah-lah Aw-ha Kleeh-ah, Dublin). Warriors from all corners of Éire (Ay-rah, Ireland) joined the march, their numbers growing with each passing day. They moved through valleys shrouded in mist and along rivers glistening under the spring sun, their banners fluttering like whispers of hope against the gaoth (gwee, wind).

In the evenings, the campfires burned bright, their light spilling across the faces of weary but determined men. Around one fire, a veteran warrior sat with a group of younger fighters. His hair was streaked with grey, and his voice carried the weight of experience. "The Vikings," he began, "are fierce, but they bleed like any other man. Stand your ground, and remember—your brothers are beside you. That's how we win. Together." The younger men nodded, their fear tempered by the wisdom of his words.

As the army pressed on, scouts returned with reports of the Viking defenses. One rode hard into the camp and dismounted quickly, his face grim. "Their numbers are great," he said, addressing Brian and his commanders. "Warriors from Orkney, the Isle of Man, and beyond. The walls of Baile Átha Cliath bristle with archers and spears."

Brian's expression remained steady, though the weight of the report was clear. "We expected no less," he said calmly. Turning to his commanders, he added, "We march at dawn. Every step forward is a step toward Éire's freedom. Let no man falter."

As they drew closer to Dublin, the camaraderie among the warriors grew. Rival clans that had once eyed each other with suspicion now shared bread and stories. A bard traveled with the army, his voice weaving tales of ancient heroes and victories, lifting the spirits of those who listened. Even as the men sharpened their swords and tightened their armor, laughter and song filled the air, a reminder of what they fought for: their families, their clans, and their homeland.

The final day of the march dawned cold and grey, the horizon shrouded in a thin veil of mist. As the army crested a hill, the sight of Baile Átha Cliath spread before them. The city's walls loomed high, bristling with Viking defenders. Longships lined the harbor, their dragon-headed prows menacing and still. The scale of the enemy forces was clear, and for a moment, a hush fell over the Irish ranks.

Brian rode among his men, his voice breaking the silence. "Look to the walls," he called out. "See what waits for us. They are many, yes, but they do not stand for Éire. They fight for plunder, for greed. We fight for something greater—for our land, for our families, for unity. And that is why we will prevail."

The words rippled through the ranks like fire, igniting the hearts of those who heard them. Even the youngest fighters stood taller, their hands gripping their weapons with renewed resolve.

Within Dublin, the Vikings and their allies were equally prepared. Warriors lined the battlements, their armor gleaming in the pale light. Inside the city, leaders like Sigurd of Orkney and the King of Laighin (Lye-een, Leinster) gathered in the great hall, finalizing their plans. "Let them come," Sigurd said with a grim smile. "We will meet them with fire and steel."

As the Irish forces set their camp within sight of the city, the tension in the air was palpable. The bards fell silent, their songs replaced by the low murmur of strategy and the scrape of swords against whetstones. The battle was near, and every man, whether hardened by years of war or new to the fight, felt the weight of what was to come.

That night, as the campfires flickered and the city walls stood dark and unyielding in the distance, Brian Boru stood alone, looking toward Baile Átha Cliath. The storm he had long prepared for was finally here, and with it, the chance to fulfill the vision that had driven him his entire life. Tomorrow, he knew, would decide not just the fate of a battle, but the future of Éire.

The dawn of Good Friday broke with a pale, cold light, the horizon tinged with the faint glow of the rising sun. A heavy mist clung to the ground, swirling around the boots of warriors as they took their positions. In the Irish camp, the air was thick with tension, the silence broken only by the clink of armor and the whispered prayers of men steeling themselves for what lay ahead. Across the field, the walls of Baile Átha Cliath (Bah-lah Aw-ha Kleeh-ah, Dublin) loomed dark and imposing, the Norse (Nor-sh) banners fluttering above them.

Brian Boru's son, Murchad (Mur-kah), moved through the Irish ranks, his presence a steadying force. "Hold your shields high," he said to a group of young warriors, his voice calm but firm. "Remember, we fight for Éire, for our families, and for those who cannot stand here with us." The men nodded, gripping their weapons tighter, their fear tempered by his courage.

On the other side of the field, the Viking forces prepared with a grim efficiency. Their captains barked orders, their voices cutting through the morning air like the ring of steel. In the front lines, berserkers paced like caged wolves, their bodies painted with symbols of war, their eyes wild with the promise of bloodshed. Sigurd of Orkney stood at the center, his axe resting against his shoulder. "Let them come," he growled, his voice low but carrying. "We will meet them with fury, and we will leave none standing."

The first horn sounded, a low and mournful note that sent a shiver through both armies. Then came the second, and with it, the Irish forces began their march forward. The ground trembled beneath their feet, the weight of thousands moving as one. The Viking ranks responded in kind, their shields locking together in a wall of iron as they advanced to meet their enemy.

The two sides clashed with a thunderous roar. Spears shattered against shields, swords met with sparks, and the cries of the wounded rose above the chaos. In the center of the fray, Murchad led the Irish charge, his blade flashing in the weak sunlight. He moved like a storm, cutting down a Viking champion with a single, brutal strike before rallying his men forward.

The Vikings countered with ferocity. A berserker broke through the Irish line, his axe cleaving through shields with terrifying strength. For a moment, panic rippled through the ranks, but a group of spearmen quickly surrounded the warrior, their weapons striking in unison. The berserker fell, his roar silenced as the Irish closed the gap he had opened.

The battle swayed back and forth, the tide of victory shifting with every charge and countercharge. In one moment, the Irish forces pushed deep into the Viking line, their unity and discipline driving the enemy back. In the next, the Vikings rallied, their shield wall holding firm as their archers rained arrows down on the advancing Irish.

Away from the chaos, Brian Boru knelt in his tent, his hands clasped in prayer. At over seventy years old, he was too advanced in age to take up arms, but his presence on the battlefield was a source of inspiration for his men. His commanders came and went, bringing reports of the battle's progress. To each, he gave quiet words of encouragement, his faith unshaken. "Ní neart go cur le chéile" (Nee nart guh kur leh keh-lah, There is no strength without unity), he murmured, his voice steady.

As the day wore on, the battlefield became a sea of bodies, the grass slick with mud and blood. The Irish forces fought with a fierce determination, their ranks bolstered by the vision of the High King and the leadership of Murchad. The Vikings, though outnumbered, held their ground with the ferocity of warriors who had spent their lives on the edge of death.

The sun climbed higher, its light piercing the mist and illuminating the battlefield in stark detail. For every man who fell, another stepped forward, driven by duty, honor, or the simple will to survive. The clash of steel and the cries of the wounded echoed across the field, a brutal symphony of war that seemed to stretch into eternity.

Through it all, the Irish held fast, their unity proving stronger than the Viking fury. But the battle was far from over, and every man on the field knew that the outcome would not be decided by strength alone but by the unyielding resolve of those who refused to fall.

As the sun began its slow descent toward the horizon, the tide of the battle shifted. The Irish forces, driven by a shared purpose and unyielding determination, began to push the Viking invaders back. Murchad (Mur-kah), at the heart of the battle, was relentless. His sword rose and fell in a deadly rhythm, carving a path through the enemy line. Around him, his warriors surged forward, inspired by his courage.

The Viking defenses began to falter. Their leaders fell one by one: Sigurd of Orkney was struck down, his towering frame collapsing into the dirt as Irish blades found their mark. The King of Laighin (Lye-een, Leinster), abandoned by his Norse allies, retreated into the chaos, his cries lost in the din of war. Panic rippled through the Viking ranks as the realization dawned—they were losing.

A great cheer erupted from the Irish forces as the enemy began to flee, their retreat a chaotic scramble toward the walls of Baile Átha Cliath (Bah-lah Aw-ha Kleeh-ah, Dublin). For a moment, victory seemed within reach. But triumph on the battlefield often comes at a heavy cost.

In the thick of the fight, Murchad fell. The details of his death would be told in many ways by those who survived, but the truth remained the same: the son of Brian Boru, the heart of the Irish army, had been struck down. When his men discovered his body, their cheers turned to anguished cries. They lifted him from the ground, carrying him on their shields as tears streaked their dirt-smeared faces.

In his tent, Brian Boru knelt in prayer, his thoughts with the men who fought for his vision of a united Éire (Ay-rah, Ireland). He did not hear the approach of the Viking raiders—a small band who, in their retreat, sought one last act of vengeance. They slipped past the defenders, their steps silent and purposeful, until they reached the High King.

The first blow came swiftly, a blade piercing the silence of the tent. Brian turned, his eyes meeting those of his attacker. Though his body failed him, his spirit remained unbroken. With his final breath, the High King murmured, "Ní neart go cur le chéile" (Nee nart guh kur leh keh-lah, There is no strength without unity).

When the Irish forces discovered what had happened, their grief was immeasurable. The battlefield, once filled with the sounds of war, fell silent as the news spread. Brian Boru, the man who had united them, was gone. His body was carried from the tent on a makeshift bier, draped in the banner of Munster (Muhn-stir).

The battlefield was a grim testament to the cost of freedom. Bodies lay strewn across the blood-soaked grass, the fallen from both sides equal in their sacrifice. The Irish, though victorious, mourned deeply. They had won the battle, but the loss of Brian and Murchad left their victory hollow.

As the sun set on that fateful Good Friday, the warriors of Éire gathered around their fallen king. One by one, they swore to honor his vision, to preserve the unity he had fought so hard to achieve. The Battle of Clontarf had ended Viking ambitions in Éire, but its cost would be felt for generations.

Brian Boru's name would echo through history, a symbol of resilience and sacrifice. Though his life was taken, his dream of a united Éire lived on in the hearts of his people, carried forward like the flame of a sacred torch. The land he had loved so fiercely stood free, its strength drawn from the unity he had inspired.

The Battle of Clontarf did more than end a single conflict—it marked a turning point in the history of Éire (Ay-rah, Ireland). Viking ambitions on the island were shattered, their military power broken. Though Norse settlers would remain in places like Baile Átha Cliath (Bah-lah Aw-ha Kleeh-ah, Dublin), they shifted from raiders to traders, integrating into Irish society over time. Clontarf had proven that a united Ireland, even if only briefly, could achieve the impossible.

The victory, however, was bittersweet. Brian Boru's death, alongside the loss of his son Murchad (Mur-kah), left a void in the hearts of his people. For many, Brian was more than a king—he was a symbol of hope, a leader whose vision of unity had inspired them to lay down their rivalries and fight for something greater. His death turned him into a martyr, a figure of ultimate sacrifice for the dream of an Éire free from foreign domination.

As the battlefield was cleared and the fallen laid to rest, bards began to craft the story of Clontarf. Around campfires and in the halls of chieftains, their songs wove together the valor of the warriors, the cunning of the leaders, and the tragedy of Brian's final moments. One such bard, his voice heavy with emotion, sang the first verses of The Song of Clontarf as warriors gathered close, their faces lit by the flickering flames. His words spoke of unity forged in battle, of blood spilled for freedom, and of a king whose dream had become their own.

In the weeks that followed, the tale of Clontarf spread across Éire. In small villages and grand fortresses alike, people mourned Brian Boru with a mixture of grief and pride. They spoke of his determination, his wisdom, and the way he had united a fractured land. Though the clans would soon return to their old rivalries, the memory of Clontarf lingered as a reminder of what could be achieved when Éire stood as one.

Far away from the battlefield, in a quiet village on the western coast, a child sat at his grandfather's feet, wide-eyed as he listened to the story of Clontarf for the first time. The old man's voice trembled as he recounted the bravery of the Irish warriors and the sacrifice of Brian Boru. "He gave his life for us," the grandfather said, "so that we might live free." The boy's gaze drifted to the horizon, where the sea met the sky, his heart swelling with wonder at the courage of those who had fought to protect their land.

The legacy of Clontarf did not end with its warriors or its songs. It became a part of Éire's soul, a story told and retold to inspire generations. It reminded the Irish people that even in their darkest moments, unity and determination could prevail. And though the man who had brought them together was gone, his vision endured, carried forward like the light of a distant star, guiding Éire toward the promise of a brighter future.

Brian Boru's name became legend, his deeds immortalized in the hearts of his people. To this day, the Battle of Clontarf stands as a testament to the strength of a united Ireland and the enduring power of a dream worth fighting for.

Sin é (Shin ay) That's it, The End

The Battle of Clontarf stands as a defining moment in Irish history, symbolizing the strength found in unity amidst division. At a time when rival clans were often at odds, Brian Boru's leadership brought together a fragmented land to fight for a shared cause. This rare moment of cohesion highlights the enduring importance of collective effort in the face of external threats. The Vikings, whose raids and settlements had long influenced Irish society, were more than invaders; they were also traders and city-builders, leaving a lasting cultural and economic legacy in places like Baile Átha Cliath (Bahlah Aw-ha Kleeh-ah, Dublin). After Clontarf, Viking power in Ireland diminished significantly, though their contributions to trade and urban development persisted.

Storytelling played a vital role in preserving the memory of Clontarf, with bards immortalizing the battle in songs and tales.

These storytellers were central to Irish culture, ensuring that the themes of sacrifice and unity remained deeply embedded in the national identity. Brian Boru's death at Clontarf elevated him to the status of a martyr, a figure whose ultimate sacrifice for Ireland's unity resonates to this day. His leadership and vision reflect the ancient Irish ideal of the rí (ree, king) as both a protector of the land and a symbol of its people's sovereignty. The story of Clontarf continues to inspire, reminding generations of the enduring struggle for freedom and the power of a united Ireland.

CHAPTER 9

WHISPER OF THE SIDHE

The Banshee's cry had haunted the Irish countryside for centuries, a sound both feared and respected. She was not just a ghost but a figure deeply rooted in Irish mythology, tied to the aos sí (ays shee), the supernatural beings who inhabited the world beyond mortal understanding. The aos sí were believed to be remnants of the Tuatha Dé Danann (Too-ah-hah Day Dan-an), the ancient godlike race who had once ruled Éire (Ay-rah, Ireland). Like them, the Banshee was a bridge between the living and the otherworldly, a presence that reminded people of the thin veil between life and death.

TALE 1: PÁDRAIG (PAW-DRIG):

The night hung heavy over the countryside, cloaked in a mist so thick it swallowed the moonlight. All was silent, save for the occasional rustle of leaves stirred by a chill breeze. Then, from somewhere deep in the hills, it came—a long, mournful wail that sent shivers rippling through the sleeping village. The cry was neither human nor animal. It was otherworldly, a sound that seemed to carry the weight of sorrow itself. It was the Bean Sí (Ban-shee, Banshee), the harbinger of death.

In a small cottage near the edge of the village, a farmer named Pádraig (Paw-drig) awoke with a start. He sat up in his bed, his breath visible in the cold night air. The cry came again, piercing and unearthly, and he felt the chill sink into his bones. Pulling his coat around him, he lit a candle and moved cautiously to the door. When he opened it, the mist seemed to curl around him, as if alive.

Far in the distance, on a rise just beyond the edge of the valley, he saw her. The figure of a woman, pale and otherworldly, her long hair streaming like silver threads in the faint moonlight. She stood as still as a statue, combing her hair with deliberate, eerie grace. Pádraig froze, his heart pounding in his chest. He knew the stories. Everyone in the village did. To see the Bean Sí was to know that death was near, tied to the ancient families of Éire (Ay-rah, Ireland). Her wail was not a curse, but a warning.

The cry rose again, more piercing this time, echoing across the valley. Pádraig slammed the door shut and leaned heavily against it, his hands trembling. "Not tonight," he whispered, as if pleading with the spirit herself. "Not my family."

But the Bean Sí did not answer. Outside, the mist thickened, and the air grew heavy with the weight of her lament. In the quiet of the village, her cry lingered, weaving through the hills and touching every soul who dared to listen. The Banshee's warning was clear: death was coming, as it always did, with the whisper of the sidhe (shee, fairies) on the wind.

He hugged his children and wife sharing his love with them. By morning his youngest son, who had been ill, was gone. Pádraig and his family wept, but Pádraig silently thanked the Bean Sí for giving him time to say goodbye to his son and the knowledge that his son was with the sidhe in the Otherworld now.

TALE 2: THE ORIGINS OF THE BANSHEE

In the village, an elder sat by the fire, recounting the tale to the gathered listeners. "The Bean Sí (Ban-shee)," he began, "is not here to harm us. She comes to mourn, to honor the dead before their passing. It is said that she is tied to the noble families—those with names beginning with Ó or Mac. Her cry is not for all, but for those whose lineages are ancient, bound to the soil of this land."

A young boy leaned forward, his eyes wide with curiosity. "But why does she cry, Daideo (Dah-djo, Grandfather)? Why doesn't she save them?"

The elder sighed, his gaze distant. "Once, she was said to be a mortal woman, like any other. But her grief in life was so great—so unbearable—that it transformed her. She became a spirit of mourning, unable to move beyond the sorrow she carried. Now, she walks among the hills and valleys, keening for those who are about to leave this world."

Outside, the mist thickened as the moon rose high above the fields. In the pale light, the silhouette of the Banshee could be seen. She sat on a low stone wall, her long, silvery hair flowing like water as she combed it with a delicate, otherworldly comb. Her movements were slow, deliberate, almost hypnotic. She neither spoke nor moved beyond her task, her pale face sorrowful as if weighed down by the grief she carried. Those who claimed to have seen her described the same haunting image—a solitary figure combing her long hair under the moonlight, endlessly weeping, her presence as eerie as it was sorrowful.

The villagers by the fire shuddered at the image. "They say," the elder continued, "that if you find her comb and take it, she will come to you, crying not in warning, but in anger. The comb is sacred to her, a symbol of her mourning."

A woman by the fire clutched a rosary in her hands, whispering a prayer. "I saw her once," she murmured. "The night my father passed. She was at the edge of the woods, her cry so soft it broke my heart. I'll never forget it."

The fire crackled as the villagers sat in uneasy silence. The Banshee was no ordinary spirit. She was a mourner, a harbinger, and a keeper of the sorrow that came with death. Her dual nature —fearsome yet tender—reflected the deep respect the Irish held for the mysteries of life and the inevitability of loss. To see her was to know that death was near, but also that it was not without honor. She mourned so that others could grieve, her cries echoing the love that tied families together, even in the face of the unknown.

TALE 3: ENCOUNTERS WITH THE BANSHEE

Stories of the Bean Sí (Ban-shee) were woven into the fabric of Irish life, told in whispers around firesides and passed down through generations. While many only heard of her through tales, others claimed to have seen or heard her themselves—an experience they would never forget. Her presence was as much a harbinger as it was a revelation, a signal that life was fragile and fleeting.

The sun hung low over the fields one autumn evening as a young farmer named Séamus (Shay-mus) worked to finish his day's labor. The golden light cast long shadows across the hills, and a chill breeze rustled through the hedgerows. He paused for a moment, wiping the sweat from his brow, when he heard it—a cry so piercing it cut through the stillness like a blade. It rose and fell, neither human nor animal, but something in between.

His chest tightened as he scanned the horizon, his eyes darting to every corner of the field. In the distance, near the edge of the woods, he thought he saw movement—a pale figure standing still among the trees. Though her form was blurred by the fading light, her long, flowing hair seemed to catch every glimmer of the sun's last rays. Séamus stumbled back, his heart racing.

He knew the stories. The Bean Sí only came for one reason. Dropping his tools, he ran home, his mind racing with thoughts of his family. That night, as his grandmother lay peacefully in her bed, she slipped away, her passing as quiet as the falling of a single leaf.

In another part of the country, the patriarch of the Ó Néill family sat alone in his study, the glow of a single candle illuminating the room. The house was quiet, the rest of his family long asleep. Outside, the wind picked up, whistling softly against the window-panes. He rose to close the shutters when he froze.

There, in the pale moonlight, she sat—her hair cascading over her shoulders, her back to him as she brushed it with an ornate comb. The sight sent a chill through him, but he could not look away. She was neither grotesque nor menacing; rather, her presence carried an overwhelming sorrow, as if the weight of her mourning filled the air.

The man staggered back from the window, clutching the edge of his desk. By the next morning, news arrived that his brother, long ill, had passed in the night. Though he mourned, he also found solace in the thought that his brother had not been alone. The Bean Sí had come to guide his spirit.

Each encounter with the Bean Sí carried with it a profound emotional weight. Her cry could vary—from a piercing wail that sent shivers down spines to a soft, heart-wrenching keening that seemed to echo the grief of those she visited. Yet, despite the fear she inspired, her presence was not malevolent. Those who heard her cry or saw her pale form often described a deep sense of inevitability, an acceptance that death was near but not to be feared.

The villagers who recounted these stories spoke with a mix of awe and reverence. "She doesn't come for all," one elder explained. "Her cry is for the families tied to the old ways, those with bloodlines stretching back to the ancient days of Éire. She mourns not just for the dead, but for those left behind."

Though the Bean Sí was a figure of fear, she was also a reminder of the bonds that tied families together. Her wail was a lament for life lost but also for the love that endures. To hear her was to face the truth of mortality, not with despair, but with a bittersweet understanding of life's fleeting beauty.

TALE 4: THE SYMBOLISM OF THE BANSHEE

The Bean Sí (Ban-shee) is more than a harbinger of death; she is a symbol of the deep, unbroken ties between the living and the departed. Her mournful cry is not merely a warning—it is a lament, an expression of grief for the lives about to be lost and the families who will be left behind. To the Irish, she embodies the enduring grá (graw, love) that binds families across generations, even in the face of loss.

In a small cottage on a misty morning, a family gathered around a still body, the eldest of their line now at rest. The room was filled with soft whispers and the occasional sound of muffled sobs. Outside, the wind carried the faint echo of a mournful cry—a sound some swore was the wail of the Bean Sí. It was not a sound of malice but one of profound sorrow, as if she too mourned the passing of someone whose life had been woven into the fabric of Éire (Ay-rah, Ireland).

The eldest daughter stepped forward to begin the caoineadh (Kwee-nah, keening), an ancient tradition passed down through the generations. Her voice, raw with emotion, rose in a haunting melody, weaving words of grief and love. The keening lament was not just for the one who had passed but for the family left behind, offering a way to release their sorrow and honor the life that had been lived.

The Bean Sí is deeply connected to this tradition, her cries echoing the keening of mortal women who sang for the dead. In ancient Ireland, professional keeners were often called upon to mourn the departed, their songs filled with both personal and communal grief. The Banshee's wail reflects this practice, a supernatural continuation of the human need to express loss and remember those who have gone before.

In the village hall, as the firelight danced on the faces of the gathered families, the stories of the Bean Sí continued to flow. "She doesn't just cry for the dying," an elder explained, his voice low and reverent. "She cries for us all—for the loss of connection, for the grá that must remain unspoken once someone is gone. But her cry also reminds us to remember, to honor, and to carry their memory forward."

Another villager added, "Death isn't the end, not here. It's part of life, part of the cycle. The Bean Sí shows us that. She's not evil. She's just a part of what it means to be alive."

This perspective reflects the uniquely Irish view of death—not as a final goodbye, but as a continuation of the journey, one that bridges the physical and spiritual worlds. The Banshee's role as a mourner speaks to the importance of acknowledging grief, of giving it voice, and of allowing it to transform into remembrance.

TALE 5: THE LEGACY OF THE BANSHEE

The Bean Sí (Ban-shee) has haunted the imagination of Ireland for centuries, her wail echoing not only through the misty hills but also through the hearts of those who keep her story alive. Though the world has changed, her legend remains, a thread woven into the fabric of Irish identity. Generations have passed down her tale, ensuring that she endures not just as a figure of fear, but as a symbol of connection to Ireland's rich and mystical past.

In a modern-day pub, a storyteller leaned against the bar, his voice carrying above the quiet murmur of patrons. "The Bean Sí," he began, his tone low and deliberate, "isn't just an old wives' tale. She's the bridge between our world and the next. You might think her cry is just the wind or the screech of an owl, but when you hear it, you'll know. You'll feel it in your bones." His audience, a mix of locals and curious visitors, leaned closer, their faces reflecting a mixture of skepticism and awe.

The storyteller continued, recounting tales of farmers who'd seen her combing her hair in the moonlight and families who had heard her cry before losing a loved one. "She's not here to scare you," he said. "She's here to remind you that death is part of life, that we all have a place in the great cycle." As he finished, a hush fell over the room, the listeners caught in the spell of his words.

In a distant village, a young child sat by the fire, their wide eyes fixed on their grandmother, who recounted the story of the Bean Sí. Her voice, soft and rhythmic, carried the weight of centuries. "She's beautiful," the grandmother said, "but her beauty is sad, like a flower that blooms only in the dark. She cries not because she hates us, but because she loves us enough to warn us when death is near."

The child clutched a blanket tightly, their imagination alive with visions of the Banshee gliding through the mist, her hair flowing and her cry piercing the night. Though they shivered at the thought, they also felt a strange comfort in the idea that she cared enough to mourn for the living.

Sin é (Shin ay) That's it, The End.

The Bean Sí continues to find her place in the modern world, appearing in literature, art, and even films. She has become a symbol of Ireland's supernatural heritage, a figure who connects the present with the mystical past. To some, she represents the loss of old ways, a reminder of the traditions that have faded with time. To others, she is a testament to the enduring power of storytelling, a character who refuses to be forgotten.

Her dual role as a warning and a comfort ensures that she remains relevant in a world that often forgets to pause and reflect on life's fragility. For those who keep her story alive, the Banshee is not just a harbinger of death, but a guardian of memory, a voice that sings of love, loss, and the unbroken ties between generations.

Whether whispered around a fire or shared in a bustling pub, the legend of the Bean Sí endures. She remains a part of the landscape of Éire (Ay-rah, Ireland), her cry woven into the ceo (kyo, mist) and her presence felt in the quiet moments before dawn. Her story reminds us all of the beauty in mourning, the strength in remembrance, and the eternal connection between the living and the dead.

CULTURAL NOTES: THE BANSHEE

The Banshee (Bean Sí, Ban-shee) is one of the most enduring figures in Irish folklore, her roots deeply intertwined with the aos sí (ays shee), the supernatural beings who inhabit the Otherworld. The aos sí are said to be remnants of the ancient Tuatha Dé Danann (Too-ah-hah Day Dan-an), a godlike race that once ruled Ireland. As part of this mystical lineage, the Banshee carries the essence of Ireland's supernatural heritage, acting as a bridge between the mortal world and the unseen realm of the spirits. Her presence is a reminder of the deep connection between the living and the departed, as well as the enduring power of familial bonds.

Central to the Banshee's legend is her cry, which echoes the ancient Irish practice of caoineadh (Kwee-nah), or keening. In traditional Irish mourning rituals, keeners—often women—would sing haunting laments for the dead, their voices rising and falling in sorrowful tones. These laments were not only a way to grieve but also a form of respect and honor for the departed. The Banshee's wail mirrors this tradition, her cries serving as both a warning and a tribute, carrying the weight of centuries of mourning. Through her keening, she reminds the Irish people of the importance of acknowledging loss and giving voice to grief.

Irish culture views death not as an end, but as a transition—a journey from one state of existence to another. The Banshee embodies this perspective, her presence signaling the inevitable but doing so with compassion and reverence. Rather than instilling terror, she acts as a guide, preparing families for the loss to come. Her role reflects the Irish belief in the cyclical nature of life and the enduring connections between generations, even beyond the veil of death.

Above all, the Banshee is a symbol of familial love and remembrance. Her cries are not born of malice but of sorrow and devotion, ensuring that those who are about to pass are honored and that their loved ones are prepared. She serves as a guardian of memory, her presence a poignant reminder that even in the face of death, the bonds of family endure. By keeping the memory of the departed alive, the Banshee reflects a core tenet of Irish culture: that to remember is to keep a part of them with us forever.

CHAPTER 10

ADVENTURES OF DIARMUID AND GRÁINNE

ADVENTURE 1: A WEDDING AND A BETRAYAL

The great hall of Tara was alight with celebration, the air thick with the scent of roasted meat and the sounds of laughter. Warriors of the Fianna gathered around long wooden tables, their goblets overflowing with ale, their voices raised in song. At the head of the hall, Fionn MacCumhaill (Fee-uhn Mac-Coo-ill), the leader of the Fianna, sat beside his bride-to-be, the beautiful and sharp-eyed Gráinne (Graw-nya).

Gráinne, dressed in a gown of deep green, her golden hair falling in waves over her shoulders, appeared every inch the perfect bride. But behind her poised smile, her heart churned with discontent. Fionn was a hero of legend, his name known across Éire (Ay-rah, Ireland), but he was no longer young. His hair was streaked with grey, and his laughter, though warm, carried the weight of years. Gráinne had not chosen this match; it had been arranged, and now, sitting beside him, her resolve hardened—she would not spend her life bound to a man she did not love.

Her gaze wandered across the hall, and there she saw him: Diarmuid Ua Duibhne (Deer-mwid Oo Duv-nah), a warrior of the Fianna. He stood apart from the others, his dark hair falling over his brow and his expression calm but watchful. Known for his ball seirce (bawl share-kah), the "love spot" that made him irresistible to women, Diarmuid was more than just handsome. His presence was magnetic, his movements graceful, his loyalty to Fionn unquestioned. Yet, as Gráinne's eyes met his, something passed between them—a spark, brief but undeniable.

Gráinne turned her gaze away, but the decision was already forming in her heart. This night would not end with her bound to Fionn. It would end with her freedom, even if it meant risking everything. The hall buzzed around her, but for Gráinne, the feast was little more than a blur. Her eyes flicked to her maid, who stood nearby, and with the faintest of gestures, she set her plan into motion.

Gráinne's maid moved swiftly and silently, weaving through the crowd with a pitcher of spiced wine. She filled goblet after goblet, offering cheerful words to the gathered warriors. The potion Gráinne had slipped into the wine earlier was subtle, designed to lull even the sharpest minds into a deep, dreamless sleep. One by one, the Fianna succumbed, their voices fading as their heads nodded against the backs of their chairs.

Fionn, seated beside Gráinne, lifted his goblet high, toasting his warriors and his bride. His face, lined with the years of battles fought and won, bore an expression of contentment. He drank deeply, unaware of the draught's hidden effects. His eyelids grew heavy, and with a final hearty laugh, he slumped forward, his arms resting on the table.

The hall grew quiet as the sleeping warriors filled it with the soft sounds of breathing. Only Diarmuid (Deer-mwid) remained awake, his untouched goblet sitting before him. Gráinne rose gracefully, her green gown rustling softly as she made her way to where he stood.

"Lady Gráinne," Diarmuid said, his voice low and cautious, "what is this? Why do the others sleep?"

Gráinne's emerald eyes met his, her expression resolute. "I cannot marry Fionn," she said simply, her voice steady. "Not when my heart belongs elsewhere."

Diarmuid took a step back, his dark brows furrowing. "Elsewhere? You cannot mean me. I am sworn to Fionn, bound by loyalty and honor. This"—he gestured to the sleeping figures around them—"is madness."

"And yet," Gráinne interrupted, her tone firm but pleading, "you know what I say is true. Diarmuid Ua Duibhne, I place a geis (gaysh, binding obligation) upon you. By the power of this binding, you must take me away from here. Protect me, or forever carry the shame of denying a woman in need."

The weight of her words—and the magical obligation they carried—fell heavily upon Diarmuid. He closed his eyes for a moment, his breath unsteady. A geis was not something to take lightly; it was an oath woven into the fabric of honor itself. To refuse would stain his name forever.

"Why me?" he asked softly.

"Because," she said, stepping closer, her voice barely above a whisper, "you have a heart that cannot deny what is right. And I see it in you—that spark of fire that Fionn has long since lost."

For a long moment, Diarmuid stood frozen, torn between his loyalty to Fionn and the undeniable truth in Gráinne's words. Finally, he nodded, his shoulders sagging with resignation. "You leave me no choice," he said. "But know this—our path will not be easy, and Fionn will not rest until he finds us."

Gráinne's lips curved into a determined smile. "I would rather face the wrath of Fionn than live a life without freedom."

With that, the two slipped into the night, leaving the sleeping feast behind. The torches flickered, the wine cooled, and the great hall of Tara stood silent, unaware of the storm that had just been unleashed.

ADVENTURE 2: THE TRIALS OF LOVE AND LOYALTY

The first rays of dawn found Diarmuid and Gráinne deep in the forest, their breath visible in the crisp morning air. The weight of their decision hung heavily between them. Diarmuid's steps were swift and sure, his eyes scanning the woods for any sign of pursuit. Gráinne followed close behind, her resolve unwavering, though her heart ached for the burden she had placed upon him.

"Fionn will not stop," Diarmuid said, breaking the silence. His tone was firm but edged with worry. "His wrath will be unrelenting. Do you understand what we face?"

Gráinne met his gaze, her chin held high. "I do. And I chose it willingly. I will not live as a prisoner to a life I did not want."

The days turned to weeks as the pair evaded Fionn's forces, their journey taking them through rugged mountains, shadowed valleys, and windswept plains. Fionn's hounds, legendary for their tracking ability, were never far behind, and the tension of the chase was constant. But the trials they faced were not only external.

Diarmuid's loyalty to Fionn, a man he had once revered, gnawed at his conscience. He found himself torn between the duty he had abandoned and the growing feelings he could not deny. Gráinne's presence—her fiery determination, her quick wit, and the way her laughter could break even the darkest moments—stirred emotions he fought to suppress.

One evening, as they camped by a riverbank, Fionn's forces set a trap. The hounds had driven the pair into a narrow gorge, where a group of warriors lay in wait. Gráinne stumbled as the hounds' baying grew louder, her breath catching as figures emerged from the shadows.

"Stay behind me," Diarmuid ordered, drawing his sword.

The battle was fierce but swift. Diarmuid moved like the wind, his blade flashing in the dim light as he disarmed and outmatched Fionn's men. His strength and precision were unmatched, and soon the warriors lay defeated or fled into the woods. Gráinne watched, her heart pounding, not with eagla (ah-glah, fear), but with awe at his skill and resolve.

Despite his victory, Diarmuid's doubts persisted. That night, as they rested in the safety of a hidden glade, he sat apart from Gráinne, his face shadowed by the firelight. "You have cursed me, Gráinne," he said softly, his voice heavy. "You've taken me from my brothers, from the only life I've ever known."

Gráinne approached, kneeling before him. Her hands reached for his, her touch warm and steady. "Diarmuid," she said, her voice gentle but firm, "you think I do not see the weight you carry? I know what I have asked of you. But I chose you because you are more than a warrior bound by duty. You are a man who follows his heart, even when it leads into darkness. That is why I love you."

Her words settled over him like the first light of dawn. Though his doubts did not vanish, her reassurance kindled something within him—a flicker of belief that their bond was worth the trials they endured.

Gráinne, too, proved herself a force to be reckoned with. On a cold, misty morning, the pair sought refuge in the territory of a local chieftain. Fionn's forces had cut off their path, and without aid, escape seemed impossible.

Diarmuid prepared to plead their case, but Gráinne stepped forward, her voice commanding. "My lord," she began, addressing the chieftain, "we are not mere fugitives. I am Gráinne, daughter of Cormac Mac Airt, a descendant of kings. Aid us, and you align yourself with the blood of Éire itself."

The chieftain, struck by her confidence and eloquence, agreed to grant them shelter. That night, as they rested under the chieftain's protection, Diarmuid looked at Gráinne with new admiration. She was more than a companion—she was a partner, her strength matching his own in every way.

Their journey was one of constant trial, but with each challenge, their bond deepened. Though Fionn's pursuit loomed like a shadow, Diarmuid and Gráinne found moments of light amid the darkness —a stolen laugh, a quiet embrace, a shared dream of a future free from fear. Their love, forged in the crucible of adversity, became a beacon that guided them through the trials yet to come.

ADVENTURE 3: THE RELENTLESS PURSUIT

The sound of Fionn's hounds, their baying sharp and relentless, echoed through the hills. The animals were legendary, with noses said to be guided by the Otherworld itself. Fionn had spared no effort in his pursuit of Diarmuid and Gráinne, driven by a fury that was equal parts betrayal and wounded pride. His warriors, hardened and loyal, followed close behind, their swords gleaming in the dim light of the moon.

In the heart of a dense forest, Diarmuid and Gráinne paused to catch their breath. Diarmuid crouched low, his ears straining to catch the sounds of their pursuers. "They're close," he said, his voice barely above a whisper. Gráinne leaned against a tree, her chest rising and falling with exertion, but her eyes were steady. "What do we do?" she asked.

Diarmuid's mind raced. He was as skilled in strategy as he was in combat, and his thoughts turned to the tricks and illusions he had learned from his time with the Fianna. He grabbed a fallen branch, smearing it with the scent of their trail, and tied it to the tail of a passing stag. With a swift slap, the animal bolted into the woods, carrying the scent away from their true path.

Moments later, the hounds burst into the clearing, their noses to the ground. They followed the scent of the branch, their howls fading into the distance. Diarmuid pulled Gráinne to her feet. "Come," he said, "we don't have much time."

Their flight took them through landscapes that seemed to belong to another world. One night, they found themselves on a vast plain, the grass shimmering silver under the starlight. The air was still, and the horizon stretched endlessly in every direction. But as they walked, strange shapes began to emerge—ghostly figures that flickered and danced at the edges of their vision.

"It's an illusion," Diarmuid said, his hand tightening around

Gráinne's. "Fionn's druids have enchanted this place to lead us astray." The figures grew bolder, their forms shifting into familiar shapes: Gráinne's father, her sisters, her childhood home. For Diarmuid, the forms were more haunting—Fionn's face, stern and unforgiving, and the brothers of the Fianna, their eyes filled with disappointment.

Gráinne stopped, her voice cutting through the silence. "These are shadows, nothing more. We won't let them deceive us." With her words, Diarmuid's resolve solidified, and they pressed forward, ignoring the phantoms that tried to block their path. At last, they reached the edge of the plain, the enchantment breaking like a veil falling away.

Meanwhile, Fionn stood atop a rocky outcrop, the moonlight casting his face into sharp relief. He held a small bowl of water in his hands, the surface rippling as his eyes searched its depths. Through the art of divination, he glimpsed the trail of the fugitives, the water revealing fleeting images of forests and plains, caves and rivers. Yet for all his power, the visions were incomplete, the couple's bond shielding them from his sight.

For the first time since the chase began, doubt crept into Fionn's mind. He thought of his own youth, of the days when his heart burned with passion and his spirit defied all restraint. Could he blame Diarmuid for following his heart? Could he blame Gráinne for seeking freedom? The thoughts unsettled him, and he set the bowl down, the ripples fading into stillness.

In the days that followed, the chase continued, but so did the resilience of Diarmuid and Gráinne. They found refuge in hidden glades, their love and trust deepening with each trial. Diarmuid's cunning and Gráinne's determination proved a formidable match for Fionn's relentless pursuit.

Though the hounds' baying and the warriors' shouts were never far, the couple pressed on, their bond unshaken. Each step forward was an act of defiance, their love a beacon that guided them through the enchanted landscapes and the shadows of doubt. The chase was far from over, but Diarmuid and Gráinne knew that as long as they stood together, they could face whatever lay ahead.

ADVENTURE 4: THE SANCTUARY OF THE WILD

The valley was like a world apart, cradled by mountains that seemed to shield it from the chaos of pursuit. A stream cut through the lush greenery, its gentle murmur the only sound apart from the songs of birds. Here, Diarmuid and Gráinne found a fleeting respite, their journey's hardships momentarily forgotten in the embrace of the wild.

Diarmuid (Deer-mwid), ever vigilant, ensured their survival. He hunted in the dense forests, his movements as silent as the wind, while Gráinne gathered herbs and berries along the stream's edge. Their days were simple yet fulfilling, a stark contrast to the tension of their flight. The valley became their sanctuary, a place where love could flourish despite the shadow of Fionn's vengeance looming beyond the mountains.

One evening, Diarmuid returned from the forest, a rare flower in his hand. Its petals shimmered faintly in the fading sunlight, a vibrant blue unlike anything Gráinne had seen before. "It reminded me of you," he said, kneeling before her. His voice, usually steady and guarded, softened as he placed the flower in her hands.

Gráinne's eyes glistened as she looked at the gift. "Even here, in this fleeting peace, you find ways to make me feel as if the world is ours," she said. Her fingers traced the delicate petals, and she met his gaze with a mixture of love and sorrow. "I know what you've given up for me, Diarmuid. I know what it's cost you."

Diarmuid took her hand in his, his rough palms a testament to the life they had built together. "I gave up what I had to," he said simply. "Because what we have is worth more than anything I left behind."

But their peace was not without its shadows. One morning, as mist clung to the valley like a veil, a figure appeared at the edge of the forest. A druid, cloaked in grey, stepped into their sanctuary. Diarmuid rose immediately, his hand on the hilt of his sword, but the druid raised a hand in peace.

"I come not as a foe, but as a messenger," the druid said, his voice low and grave. "The valley has offered you peace, but it cannot shield you from what lies ahead."

Gráinne stepped forward, her chin lifted. "What do you mean? Speak plainly."

The druid's gaze rested on her, his eyes filled with both sorrow and respect. "Your love is strong, and it has carried you through great trials. But grá (graw, love) alone cannot change the will of fate. The bond you share has angered forces beyond even Fionn MacCumhaill. A time will come when this sanctuary will fall, and your journey will end."

The words hung in the air like a storm cloud. Diarmuid's jaw tightened, but he said nothing. Gráinne, ever defiant, placed her hand on Diarmuid's arm. "If this is to be our fate," she said, "then we will face it together."

The druid nodded, his expression unreadable. "May your grá give you the strength to endure what is to come." With that, he turned and disappeared into the mist, leaving the couple alone once more.

The prophecy lingered over them in the days that followed, but Diarmuid and Gráinne refused to let it steal their joy. They embraced each moment as if it were their last, their grá burning brighter against the inevitability of the future. The valley, though temporary, became a testament to what they had fought for—a fragile haven carved out of a world intent on tearing them apart.

Yet, deep down, they both knew the truth. The sanctuary of the wild could not last, and their bond would soon face its greatest test.

As they watched the sun set over the mountains, their hands entwined, they silently vowed to hold on to their grá, no matter what lay ahead.

ADVENTURE 5: THE INEVITABLE CONFRONTATION

The peace of the valley was shattered at dawn. The sound of Fionn's hounds, their baying sharper and more relentless than ever, echoed through the mountains. Birds scattered from the treetops, and the stillness that had cradled Diarmuid and Gráinne was replaced by the harsh reality of pursuit. The sanctuary they had cherished was no longer safe.

Diarmuid stood at the edge of the clearing, his spear in hand, his expression grim. Gráinne, beside him, gripped his arm. "We cannot run forever," she said, her voice steady despite the fear in her eyes. "It was always going to come to this."

He nodded, his jaw set. "Stay behind me," he said, his tone leaving no room for argument. "I will face him."

Fionn and his warriors emerged through the trees, the hounds at their heels. The leader of the Fianna cut an imposing figure, his silver hair gleaming in the morning light, his expression a mask of fury. Behind him, the warriors fanned out, their weapons ready but their movements cautious. They knew Diarmuid's reputation and his skill; even outnumbered, he was a force to be reckoned with.

Diarmuid stepped forward, placing himself firmly between Fionn and Gráinne. His spear glinted as he held it steady, his stance one of defiance. "This ends here, Fionn," he said, his voice calm but resolute. "I will not let you harm her."

Fionn's face twisted with anger. "You speak of harm, Diarmuid, when it is you who have betrayed me? You, who swore loyalty to me, who ate at my table and called me a friend!" His voice cracked with emotion, the pain of betrayal evident beneath his rage. "Why? Tell me why you would do this."

Diarmuid hesitated, his spear lowering slightly. "It was never my intention to betray you," he said. "I was bound by a geis (gaysh), a bond I could not break. I did what honor demanded, though it broke my heart to do so."

Before Fionn could reply, Gráinne stepped forward, her eyes blazing. "Do not lay all the blame at his feet," she said, her voice sharp and commanding. "It was I who chose this path. I could not marry a man I did not love, and I would not be a prisoner to a life I did not want. Diarmuid has done nothing but honor the vows placed upon him. If you must punish someone, let it be me."

Her words cut through the tension, forcing Fionn to pause. His gaze shifted to Gráinne, and for a moment, his anger wavered. He saw not a rebellious girl, but a woman of strength and conviction, someone who had made her choice and stood by it. His pride and his pain warred within him, but the sight of her determination stirred something deeper—something he had long since buried.

Fionn turned back to Diarmuid, his expression softening, though his voice remained firm. "You have betrayed me, but I see now that it was not for selfish gain. You have fought for her, protected her, and faced death for her. Perhaps you are more loyal than I gave you credit for."

Diarmuid's grip on his spear tightened. "Do what you must, Fionn," he said, his voice steady. "But leave her out of it."

Fionn's shoulders sagged, the fire of his anger dimming. "No harm will come to her," he said at last. "But I cannot forgive this. Your choices have consequences, Diarmuid, and those consequences are yours to bear."

The confrontation ended not with blood, but with heartbreak.

Fionn's men withdrew, their leader silent as he turned his back on the pair. Diarmuid and Gráinne stood together, their hands entwined as they watched the Fianna disappear into the forest. The price of their grá had been high, and though they remained together, the shadow of their choices loomed large.

As the sun rose higher, the couple shared a bittersweet embrace. "Whatever comes," Diarmuid said softly, "we face it together."

Gráinne nodded, her voice steady despite the tears in her eyes. "Together," she whispered.

But in the depths of their hearts, both knew the truth: the peace they had fought for was fleeting, and their grá (graw, love), though strong, could not shield them from the fate that awaited. The inevitable confrontation had passed, but the story of Diarmuid and Gráinne was far from over. In the years that followed, they wandered Ireland as fugitives, their love, though true, was fated to end in sorrow.

Their end came not in a clash of swords, but in the shadow of a prophecy. On the slopes of Ben Bulben, Diarmuid faced the enchanted boar, a beast of magic and might foretold to bring his end. Though his spear struck true, the creature's tusks found their mark, leaving him gravely wounded.

As life ebbed from him, Diarmuid called for Fionn, who possessed the power to heal through water. But Fionn hesitated, the bitterness of betrayal holding him back. By the time his heart relented and he brought the water to Diarmuid's lips, it was too late. Diarmuid's story remained forever unfinished, leaving behind the weight of a love and loyalty that neither fate nor forgiveness could mend. It is said that when word reached Gráinne of his death, her grief was immeasurable—a love forged in defiance and sealed in sorrow, now left to endure in solitude.

Sin é (Shin ay) That's it, The End.

CULTURAL NOTES: ROMANCE AND LOYALTY IN IRISH MYTHOLOGY

In Irish mythology, the concept of a geis (gaysh, magical obligation) is a recurring theme that shapes the lives of heroes and heroines. A geis binds individuals to a course of action, often challenging their sense of duty and morality. This supernatural force reflects a deeply rooted belief in destiny and the inescapable consequences of one's choices. For Diarmuid, the geis Gráinne placed upon him was not just a demand—it was a sacred bond, forcing him to choose between his loyalty to Fionn MacCumhaill and his obligation to protect Gráinne. The geis becomes the catalyst for their journey, driving the narrative forward and illustrating the tension between duty and desire.

Irish folklore often explores the complexity of relationships, where love and loyalty are rarely simple. Diarmuid and Gráinne's story is a prime example of this dynamic, as their passion defies societal expectations and personal allegiances. Diarmuid's unwavering sense of honor clashes with his growing feelings for Gráinne, creating an emotional and moral dilemma that lies at the heart of the tale. Similarly, Fionn's role as both betrayed leader and jilted lover reveals the human struggle between forgiveness and vengeance. These layered relationships reflect the Irish cultural fascination with the fragility and strength of human connections, where love and loyalty often coexist in conflict.

The story of Diarmuid and Gráinne also embodies the Irish cultural view of love as a force of both great strength and profound sacrifice. Their love drives them to endure relentless trials, from the physical hardships of their flight to the emotional burden of knowing the pain they've caused others. Yet, despite these challenges, their bond remains steadfast, serving as a testament to the resilience of love. At the same time, their story is tinged with tragedy, as the sacrifices they make ultimately lead to a bittersweet conclusion. This duality of love as both empowering and devastating is a hallmark of Irish mythology, where the greatest passions are often accompanied by the deepest sorrows.

Diarmuid and Gráinne's tale continues to resonate because it speaks to universal themes of choice, consequence, and the enduring power of love. Through the lens of Irish myth, their story reminds us that love, while fleeting and fragile, has the power to shape destinies and leave an indelible mark on those who dare to embrace it.

CHAPTER 11

THE QUEEN'S AMBITION

In the heart of Connacht, Queen Medb (Mayv) stood tall in the grand hall of her fortress at Cruachan (Croo-kawn), her presence as commanding as her ambition. Her voice, sharp yet captivating, rang out as she addressed her court, the flickering light of the hearth dancing in her keen eyes. Medb was no ordinary ruler; she was cunning, fearless, and determined to secure her place as the most powerful sovereign in Éire (Ay-rah, Ireland).

"We have wealth," she declared, her voice firm as she surveyed the gathered chieftains and warriors, "lands that stretch farther than the eye can see. Yet, among all our riches, there is one thing that eludes us—a bull to rival my husband's. Without this, our power is incomplete."

The bull she coveted was no ordinary beast. Donn Cúailnge (Dun Koo-ul-nyuh), the Brown Bull of Cooley, was a creature of legend, its strength and beauty unmatched across the land. Owned by Dáire (Daw-rah), a chieftain of Ulster, it symbolized prosperity and dominance, the very qualities Medb sought to embody. "We will take it," she said, her tone leaving no room for doubt. "For Connacht, for our legacy, and for me."

As her words spread, warriors and allies from across Ireland answered her call, eager for the wealth and glory she promised in return for their loyalty. Medb's charm and determination united an army that seemed unstoppable. Yet, in the shadows of her court, a druid stepped forward, his face lined with the weight of visions yet to be spoken.

"My queen," he said, his voice heavy with foreboding, "this raid will not bring only victory. Blood will flow across the land, and a hero will rise—one whose name will echo through the ages."

Medb's lips curved into a smile, sharp as the edge of a blade. "Let him rise," she replied. "He will fall, as will all who stand in my way."

While Medb's forces gathered, far to the north in Ulster, the seeds of resistance were sown. The men of Ulster lay stricken by a curse, their strength sapped at the worst possible moment. Only one stood untouched—Cú Chulainn (Coo Hull-un, Hound of Culann) a warrior still in his youth but already a figure of legend. Known for his unmatched skill in combat and his unyielding loyalty to his homeland, he alone rose to face the coming storm.

The stage was set: a queen's unrelenting ambition, a young hero's courage, and a battle that would shape the history of Éire. The raid for the Brown Bull of Cooley was no mere act of greed—it was the spark of a conflict that would test the limits of loyalty, power, and destiny.

The plains of Connacht teemed with activity as Medb's army began to assemble. Warriors from every corner of Éire answered her call, lured by promises of wealth and glory. The clang of forging weapons and the low murmur of battle chants filled the air, a symphony of preparation that reflected the queen's unrelenting ambition. Chieftains swore oaths of loyalty, their banners fluttering in the crisp morning breeze, each representing clans eager to carve their names into legend alongside hers.

Medb (Mayv) moved through the camp, her gaze sharp and calculating. She paused to watch a line of warriors practicing with spears, their movements precise yet powerful. "You fight for more than a bull," she told them, her voice clear and commanding. "You fight for Connacht's honor, for its place as the greatest kingdom in Éire." Her confidence was infectious, and her warriors cheered, their resolve hardening under her fiery leadership.

In her tent that evening, Medb sat with her closest advisors, poring over maps and plans. Each route, each strategy, was scrutinized and perfected. Medb's focus never wavered; she knew the strength of her forces and believed her victory inevitable. But the druid's prophecy lingered in her mind, a shadow she refused to acknowledge. The hero who would rise to oppose her might be formidable, but Medb was convinced that her cunning and her army's might would crush him.

Far to the north in Ulster, the lands were eerily quiet. The warriors of the province, struck down by a mysterious curse, lay helpless in their beds, their strength sapped as if by an unseen hand. Only one figure moved through the stillness: Cú Chulainn (Coo Hull-un), the boy-hero who had already proven himself in battles far beyond his years.

By the banks of a river that wound through Ulster's green hills, Cú Chulainn knelt, sharpening his spear. His movements were steady and deliberate, his expression calm but intense. The reflection in the water showed not a boy, but a warrior determined to defend his land, no matter the odds.

The voices of his foster father, Fergus (Fur-gus), and his mentor, Scáthach (Scah-hah), echoed in his memory, urging him to honor the warrior's code and protect Ulster at all costs. The curse that had incapacitated his comrades left him as Ulster's only hope, a burden he carried with quiet pride. "If Medb comes," he whispered to himself, "she will find more than she bargained for."

The contrast between Medb and Cú Chulainn could not have been greater. Where Medb relied on her charisma and calculated ambition to rally her forces, Cú Chulainn drew strength from his unwavering loyalty and raw, youthful courage. She marched with an army at her back; he stood alone, his resolve unshaken.

As the sun set over Connacht, Medb's forces began their march toward Cooley, their torches lighting up the horizon like a sea of fire. Meanwhile, in Ulster, Cú Chulainn rose from the riverside, his weapons gleaming in the fading light. He looked toward the south, where the first whispers of war began to stir, and vowed to stand firm against whatever came his way.

The storm was gathering, and both sides knew that the coming conflict would not be easily won. For Medb, it was a quest for power. For Cú Chulainn, it was a fight for home, honor, and the land he loved. The battle for the Brown Bull of Cooley was about to begin.

Cú Chulainn stood at the ford, the cold water lapping at his ankles as he gazed across at Medb's approaching forces. The first rays of dawn lit the sky, casting long shadows over the land. Alone, he faced the might of Connacht's army—a sea of warriors armed with blades, shields, and the confidence of superior numbers. Yet there was no fear in his heart, only the quiet resolve of a warrior defending his homeland.

He raised his spear, its tip glinting in the early light. "If you seek to pass," he called out, his voice echoing across the water, "you must face me first. Send your champions, one by one, and I will meet them here. Or turn back and spare yourselves the shame of defeat."

Medb's forces hesitated, murmurs spreading through the ranks. Many had heard the tales of Cú Chulainn's prowess, whispered like warnings in the dark. He was no ordinary boy, they said, but a warrior touched by the gods, his strength unmatched, his skill unparalleled. Still, pride and duty demanded they answer his challenge.

One by one, Medb's champions stepped forward, each confident in their ability to end the young warrior's defiance. The first charged into the ford, his blade flashing as he swung at Cú Chulainn. But the boy-hero was quicker, his movements a blur as he parried and struck, his spear finding its mark with deadly precision. The champion fell, the river running red around him.

Another came, and another. Each met the same fate, their strength and numbers no match for Cú Chulainn's speed, cunning, and unyielding determination. As the sun climbed higher, the ford became a testament to his heroism, its waters bearing the marks of his stand.

But Cú Chulainn's strength was not purely mortal. As the battle wore on and his foes grew more numerous, a transformation began to overtake him. The ríastrad (ree-uh-strahd), the warp-spasm, coursed through his body, twisting and contorting him into a form both terrifying and awe-inspiring. His muscles bulged, his hair stood on end, and his face darkened with an otherworldly fury. His body seemed to glow with an inner fire, his movements becoming even faster and more brutal.

To Medb's forces, he appeared less like a man and more like a creature of legend—a being whose wrath was fueled by the land he protected. Even seasoned warriors hesitated, their confidence faltering as they faced the monstrous figure in the ford.

From her vantage point, Medb watched the scene unfold with growing frustration. Each champion she sent was defeated, and her army, once so sure of its victory, began to falter. She called her advisors to her side, her voice sharp and commanding. "This boy cannot hold us forever," she said, though her tone betrayed a hint of doubt. "What must we do to overcome him?"

Her advisors spoke in low tones, their faces grave. "He fights not only with skill but with the strength of the aos sí (ays shee)," one said. "His bond to this land makes him unstoppable. But even the greatest warriors have their limits. We must wear him down—force him to fight until he is too weak to stand."

Medb's eyes narrowed as she considered the advice. She turned her gaze back to the ford, where Cú Chulainn still stood, his spear raised, his body trembling with the energy of the ríastrad. She knew this battle would not be won through brute force alone. To claim victory, she would need to outmaneuver not just the warrior, but the legend.

As the day waned, Cú Chulainn remained unyielding, his defiance a beacon of hope for Ulster. Medb's forces, though formidable, found themselves at a standstill, their momentum halted by a single warrior's courage and skill. But the fight was far from over, and both sides knew that the battle for the Brown Bull of Cooley had only just begun.

Medb paced within her war tent, her mind racing. The ford had become a choke point, one boy holding her entire army at bay. The defeat of her champions had stung her pride, but it was the growing whispers of fear among her warriors that stung more. Still, Medb was not a queen to be deterred by brute force alone. Her mind turned to subtler strategies—trickery, persuasion, and alliances with forces beyond the mortal realm.

"This is not a battle of swords alone," she told her advisors. "If Cú Chulainn relies on cunning and strength, then we shall match him with guile and numbers."

That night, under the cover of darkness, Medb sent spies into the hills surrounding the ford, their mission to find a way around Cú Chulainn's defenses. The spies moved silently, their steps careful as they crept through the underbrush. But Cú Chulainn, guided by the keen instincts of the warrior and the subtle whispers of the aos sí (ays shee), anticipated their approach.

Using the terrain to his advantage, he set traps along the spies' paths—hidden pits, tripwires, and ambush points that left them disoriented and vulnerable. By dawn, they returned to Medb empty-handed, some injured and others too shaken to speak. Medb's frustration grew, but she refused to give up.

"If the land protects him, we will use the land to break him," she said, her eyes narrowing. "Fetch the druids."

Meanwhile, the toll of the conflict weighed heavily on Cú Chulainn. Though his victories were many, the relentless fighting began to sap his strength. By the ford, he sat sharpening his spear, his hands trembling slightly from exhaustion. It was then that a figure emerged from the mist—a druid cloaked in grey, his staff tapping softly against the earth.

"You fight well, boy," the druid said, his voice low and resonant. "But the path ahead is long, and Medb's cunning is not yet spent."

Cú Chulainn looked up, his expression guarded but respectful. "What must I do?" he asked simply.

The druid extended his hand, offering Cú Chulainn a bundle of herbs and muttering a chant under his breath. "These will strengthen your spirit and sharpen your mind. Remember, not all battles are won with the blade. The aos sí watch over you, but your wits and resolve will guide you through the trials ahead."

The druid's words lingered as he disappeared into the mist, leaving Cú Chulainn to ponder the balance between strength and strategy.

Medb's next move was as bold as it was desperate. She sought out alliances with supernatural forces, druids and witches who owed their loyalty to Connacht. With their aid, she attempted to turn the land itself against Cú Chulainn. The river's currents were enchanted to swell against him, the trees whispered false trails, and illusions of warriors loomed where none stood.

Yet Cú Chulainn, drawing on his inner strength and the wisdom of the aos sí, overcame each obstacle. He used the enchanted river's strength to his advantage, creating whirlpools that trapped Medb's advancing forces. He cut through the illusions with precision, trusting his instincts over his eyes. His resilience became a legend in itself, his name whispered in awe even among Medb's own ranks.

Despite the mounting losses and the growing fear among her warriors, Medb refused to abandon her quest. She called her commanders together, her voice sharp and unyielding. "We have come too far to turn back now," she declared. "Let him stand against us. Let him fight until he breaks. No man, no matter how strong, can hold against the tide forever."

Medb's obsession with victory drove her forces onward, each scheme more desperate than the last. Yet with every failure, her frustration deepened, and her army's morale wavered. The battle for the ford was no longer just a test of strength and strategy—it was a war of wills, with Cú Chulainn standing unbroken against Medb's relentless ambition.

Both sides knew that the final clash was nearing, and the outcome would not only determine the fate of the Brown Bull but would cement the legacy of those who fought for it.

The sun rose over the borders of Ulster, casting its golden light on a land poised for battle. Medb's forces stretched across the horizon, a sea of warriors armed and ready for the final push. The air was thick with tension, the weight of the campaign bearing down on both sides. Medb stood at the forefront, her gaze fixed on the fields ahead, where the last obstacle to her ambition awaited: Cú Chulainn (Coo Hull-un). The Brown Bull of Cooley remained elusive, its capture tantalizingly close yet frustratingly out of reach.

But the warriors of Ulster, once incapacitated by the mysterious curse, were beginning to stir. Their strength returned slowly, like the tide rising after a storm. Word spread among Medb's ranks that the men of Ulster were awakening, their legendary ferocity ready to answer the call of battle. Yet Medb, ever defiant, pushed her army forward. "Before they rise, we will break their champion," she declared. "Cú Chulainn cannot hold forever."

At the ford, Cú Chulainn prepared himself for what he knew would be his greatest test. His body bore the marks of countless battles—cuts, bruises, and the deep ache of exhaustion—but his resolve remained unshaken. The young hero stood alone, his spear gleaming in the morning light, as the might of Connacht bore down upon him.

From Medb's army, her mightiest champion emerged: Ferdiad (Fair-dee-ah), a warrior of equal renown and, once, a dear friend to Cú Chulainn. Bound by honor and Medb's promises, Ferdiad approached the ford with a heavy heart, knowing the duel ahead would test not only their skill but their bond.

The duel began with a clash of spears, the sound reverberating across the battlefield. Both warriors fought with precision and power, their movements a blur as they exchanged blow after blow. Ferdiad's strength was formidable, his strikes relentless, but Cú

Chulainn matched him with speed and cunning, his body twisting and contorting with the supernatural energy of his ríastrad (ree-uh-strahd).

The fight raged on for hours, neither side gaining the upper hand. The warriors of Medb's army and the awakening Ulstermen watched in awe as the two legends pushed each other to their limits. Blood stained the ford, the river flowing red as the battle reached its peak. Finally, with a burst of strength born of desperation and love for his homeland, Cú Chulainn delivered the decisive blow, striking Ferdiad down. As his friend fell, Cú Chulainn knelt beside him, his grief mingling with his triumph.

"Forgive me," he whispered, his voice choked with sorrow. "I fought for Ulster, as you fought for Connacht. May your name be remembered with honor."

Medb's forces, demoralized by the loss of their greatest champion, began to falter. News of the Ulster warriors' recovery spread through the ranks, sowing fear among the men. Seeing her ambition slipping away, Medb called for a retreat, her dream of claiming the Brown Bull slipping from her grasp. Yet even as she ordered her forces to withdraw, she could not help but admire the young warrior who had thwarted her.

From the hilltop, Medb turned to watch Cú Chulainn, his figure silhouetted against the rising sun. "He is no mere boy," she said to her advisors, her voice tinged with both frustration and respect. "He is a force of nature, a legend in his own time."

As the battlefield emptied, Cú Chulainn stood alone once more, the weight of the conflict pressing heavily upon him. The ford, once a symbol of defiance, now bore the scars of his struggle—fallen warriors, shattered weapons, and the blood of friends and foes alike. His body ached, and his spirit was weary, but his homeland was safe. Ulster stood unbroken, thanks to his sacrifice.

Gazing across the battlefield, Cú Chulainn reflected on all he had lost: the bond with Ferdiad, the innocence of youth, and the ease of a life unburdened by duty. Yet he also saw what he had protected—the land he loved, the people who would sing of his deeds for generations to come.

Sin é

The raid for the Brown Bull of Cooley was over, its ambitions crushed. But for Cú Chulainn, the story was far from finished. He had secured his place as Ulster's greatest hero, though the cost of such greatness was etched deeply into his soul. As the wind carried the distant sound of Medb's retreating army, Cú Chulainn tightened his grip on his spear and turned back toward his homeland, ready to face whatever trials lay ahead.

The story of the Táin Bó Cúailnge (Tawn Boh Koo-ul-nyuh), or The Cattle Raid of Cooley, transcended the battlefield where it was forged. It became more than a tale of warriors and kings—it grew into one of the greatest epics in Irish literature, passed down through generations by the bards who wove its events into song and story. Around the fires of chieftains' halls, the deeds of Queen Medb and Cú Chulainn were recounted with reverence, their names becoming touchstones of Ireland's heroic age.

At the heart of the Táin lies a tapestry of themes that resonate deeply with the cultural values of ancient Ireland. Loyalty, honor, and sacrifice are woven into every twist and turn of the tale. Cú Chulainn's unwavering dedication to Ulster, even when faced with insurmountable odds, exemplifies the warrior's code: to protect one's homeland, no matter the cost. His defense of the ford and his tragic duel with Ferdiad are more than moments of heroism—they are symbols of the sacrifices demanded by duty and love for one's people.

Medb's ambition, though cast as a foil to Cú Chulainn's loyalty, is equally compelling. Her cunning, determination, and ability to command an army of disparate forces highlight her as a figure of immense power. She embodies a different kind of heroism—one rooted in the pursuit of sovereignty and legacy, even at great personal and political risk. Together, Medb and Cú Chulainn represent the duality of human nature: ambition and loyalty, strength and vulnerability, triumph and tragedy.

The Táin also preserves the deeper cultural elements of ancient Ireland, where cattle symbolized wealth, status, and survival. Medb's desire to possess Donn Cúailnge (Dun Koo-ul-nyuh), the prized Brown Bull, underscores the societal importance of prosperity and power. Yet the epic shows that the cost of such ambition can be immense, leading to loss and bloodshed that far outweigh material gain.

In the hands of the bards, the Táin became a living story, evolving with each telling. One such bard, seated in the hall of a chieftain, recited the tale with vivid detail, his voice rising and falling with the rhythm of battle and sorrow. Warriors listened, their faces illuminated by firelight, their hearts stirred by Cú Chulainn's bravery and Medb's unyielding drive. A young warrior, barely out of boyhood, clenched his fists as the story unfolded, inspired to emulate the courage and loyalty of Ulster's great hero.

The legacy of the Táin endures not only as a cornerstone of Irish mythology but as a reflection of the human spirit. It captures the eternal struggle between personal ambition and communal responsibility, between the pursuit of greatness and the sacrifices it demands. Queen Medb and Cú Chulainn remain timeless figures, their stories echoing across the ages as reminders of the complexity of heroism and the enduring power of storytelling.

Through the Táin, the voices of ancient Ireland continue to speak, reminding us that even in the face of overwhelming odds, the ideals of courage, loyalty, and honor shine as brightly today as they did in the time of heroes.

The Táin Bó Cúailnge (Tawn Boh Koo-ul-nyuh), often called "The Cattle Raid of Cooley," stands as the centerpiece of the Ulster Cycle, one of the four great cycles of Irish mythology. This epic embodies the richness of Ireland's storytelling tradition, weaving together themes of heroism, ambition, and the deep ties between people and the land. Passed down through oral tradition before being committed to writing, the Táin captures the essence of Ireland's heroic age, serving as both entertainment and a cultural touchstone that reflects the values of its time.

Cattle held profound significance in ancient Irish society, serving as symbols of wealth, power, and survival. Medb's desire to possess Donn Cúailnge (Dun Koo-ul-nyuh), the Brown Bull of Cooley, was not merely an act of greed but a demonstration of her ambition to assert Connacht's dominance. In the Táin, cattle represent more than material wealth—they are tied to identity, legacy, and the strength of a kingdom. Medb's obsession with the bull mirrors the fierce competition among rulers of the time, where power was measured not just in land or armies, but in the prosperity symbolized by livestock.

Cú Chulainn stands as one of the most iconic figures in Irish mythology, embodying the complexities of the tragic hero. His supernatural strength, marked by his ríastrad (ree-uh-strahd), or warp-spasm, sets him apart as a warrior and demigod blessed by the Otherworld. Yet, his story is also one of human vulnerability—his youth, his loyalty, and the weight of the expectations placed upon him. Cú Chulainn's defense of Ulster at the ford demonstrates both his bravery and the loneliness of his burden. His duel with Ferdiad, a friend turned enemy, underscores the pain of heroism, where victory often comes at great personal cost.

The Táin resonates beyond its mythological roots, exploring universal themes of leadership, resilience, and the cost of ambition. Medb and Cú Chulainn, though adversaries, share a deep connection to these themes. Medb's drive for power and Cú Chulainn's unwavering loyalty both lead to triumphs and tragedies, reflecting the duality of human nature. Their stories remind us that greatness often demands sacrifice, and that the line between hero and villain is often blurred by perspective and context.

What makes the Táin enduring is its ability to speak to audiences across time. The tale of Medb's ambition and Cú Chulainn's heroism has inspired countless retellings, each generation finding new meaning in its themes. As part of Ireland's epic literary tradition, the Táin not only preserves the history and mythology of its people but continues to ignite the imagination, offering lessons on leadership, perseverance, and the eternal struggles between duty, love, and ambition.

CHAPTER 12

FAIRY QUEEN ÁINE

In the rolling hills of Knockainey (Knock-aw-nee), or Cnoc Áine in Irish, where the mists of dawn kiss the emerald grass, whispers of an otherworldly presence linger in the air. This is the home of Áine (Awn-ya), the radiant Fairy Queen of Munster, whose beauty rivals the golden glow of the summer sun. Her name is spoken with reverence and caution, for Áine is not merely a figure of myth but a force that binds the land, its people, and the unseen realms together.

Áine is both guardian and enigma. By day, her presence is felt in the warmth of the fields and the bloom of wildflowers, but by night, she is said to walk among mortals, her footsteps light as dew and her laughter echoing in the breeze. In her dual nature lies her power: she can bless a harvest with abundance or curse the land with blight, depending on the hearts of those who seek her favor.

Fairy Queen Áine

One fateful evening, as the moon rose high over Knockainey, a humble farmer tending his late crop paused. From the corner of his eye, he caught a glimpse of a figure cloaked in silvery light, dancing among the shadows. He stood transfixed as the melody of her laughter filled the air, mingling with the rustle of the leaves. It was Áine (Awn-ya), they say, weaving her magic beneath the stars.

The farmer, wise enough to know the tales of the Fairy Queen, dropped to one knee, averting his gaze to show respect. His crops, which had struggled through the season, thrived in the weeks that followed, their bountiful yield a silent thanks from Áine.

But not all who crossed Áine's path were so fortunate. Her generosity was matched by her retribution against those who disrespected her or the land she cherished. A lord, arrogant and greedy, once tried to claim Knockainey as his own, dismissing the warnings of the villagers. They say his wealth turned to dust, and his lands grew barren under Áine's curse.

Her presence became a tale of duality—love and vengeance, beauty and power, mortal and divine. Áine's legend endures not only as a story of magic and mystery but as a reminder to respect the balance of the world and the unseen forces that shape it. For those who walk the hills of Knockainey, her spirit is said to linger, a radiant guide and a formidable protector of the land she holds dear.

Áine's bond with the mortal world was as complex as the shifting seasons. To those who respected the land and its unseen forces, she was a guardian and benefactor, her blessings subtle yet profound. Farmers spoke of fields blooming unexpectedly after harsh winters, of streams running clear even in the driest months, and of illnesses vanishing with the dawn. Yet, for those who crossed her—through arrogance or greed—the consequences were swift and unforgiving, her retribution a reminder of the delicate balance between the mortal and the supernatural.

One such tale told of a poor family living on the outskirts of Knockainey. Struggling through a lean harvest, they shared the last of their bread and milk with a cloaked stranger who knocked on their door one stormy night. The next morning, their barren fields shimmered with golden stalks of wheat, and their cows, once frail, produced milk rich and plentiful. Though the stranger was never seen again, the family whispered in awe of Áine's hand in their fortune. They left offerings at the foot of Knockainey Hill each year thereafter—wildflowers, honey, and bread—tokens of gratitude to the Fairy Queen who had watched over them.

Yet, Áine's favor was not given lightly. In her role as a protector, she demanded respect for the land she cherished. A tale of a nobleman serves as a cautionary lesson. This lord, haughty and dismissive of local customs, ordered his men to plow the sacred fields at the base of Knockainey Hill, claiming them for his estate. Despite warnings from the villagers, he scoffed at the notion of a Fairy Queen and her power.

The night after the first furrow was cut, a fierce storm swept through the land, uprooting the lord's fields and shattering his estate. By morning, his wealth had vanished, his gold turned to brittle leaves, and his horses reduced to wandering shadows. The villagers, shaken but unsurprised, spoke of Áine's wrath and the folly of defying the unseen forces of the aos sí (ays shee).

But Áine was not only a figure of reverence and fear; she was also capable of love, a rare connection between the human and fairy worlds. One moonlit evening, by a shimmering lake nestled deep in the hills, a mortal man encountered Áine. He was a musician, his harp slung across his back, drawn to the lake by a melody he could not resist. As he approached the water's edge, he saw her, radiant in the silver light, her golden hair cascading like rivers of sunlight.

The man played a tune, soft and enchanting, as Áine listened with a smile that seemed to hold the secrets of the world. In that moment, their connection felt timeless, the boundary between mortal and fairy blurring. Though Áine's presence hinted at love, it also carried an unspoken warning—the human heart, no matter how earnest, must tread carefully in the realm of the supernatural.

The union of Áine (Awn-ya), the radiant Fairy Queen, and her mortal love was as fragile as it was beautiful. Their bond defied the boundaries between worlds, drawing the awe and envy of both mortals and fairies. For Áine's kin among the aos sí (ays shee), her love for a mortal was a betrayal of their otherworldly nature, a weakening of the ancient veil that kept their realms apart. Among humans, whispers of the Fairy Queen's favor spread uneasily, blending wonder with fear.

In the early days of their love, Áine bestowed her mortal partner with an enchanted cloak, woven with threads of moonlight and imbued with protective magic. "Wear this always," she said, her golden hair catching the morning sun. "It will shield you from harm, but only if your heart remains true to me. Betray my trust, and its magic will turn against you."

The cloak's brilliance shielded the man as he traveled through forests and fields, his steps unnoticed by those who might harm him. Yet, as the cloak's magic grew admired, so too did it spark jealousy. Among the aos sí, a rival fairy, long envious of Áine's prominence, saw the union as an opportunity to sow discord. This rival spread whispers among Áine's kin, claiming that the mortal's loyalty was fragile and that his presence endangered their realm.

Suspicion brewed, but the greatest threat came from the mortal world. Humans, uneasy with what they could not understand, began to distance themselves from the man who had won Áine's love. "He's bewitched," some said. Others spoke of the Fairy Queen's wrath and wondered if their own lives might be in peril should her favor shift. The man, torn between his love for Áine and his connection to his community, felt the weight of the divide grow heavier with each passing day.

Amid these challenges, Áine's powers became both a source of protection and a reminder of the barriers between them. When storms threatened their valley, she called the winds to shield their home. When shadows stirred in the forest, she summoned light to drive them away. Yet, each act of magic seemed to widen the gap between Áine's otherworldly nature and the mortal life her partner once knew.

One night, as they sat by the shimmering lake where they had first met, Áine rested her head on her mortal love's shoulder. "I have given you my heart," she said softly, her voice carrying the weight of both joy and sorrow. "But our love exists between two worlds, neither of which will accept us as we are."

Her mortal love took her hand, the warmth of her touch grounding him even amid his doubts. "Then we will make our own world," he said. Yet, in his eyes, Áine saw the shadow of uncertainty. Love bound them, but the pressures of their divided lives threatened to unravel all they had built together.

The rival fairy, seizing this moment of vulnerability, struck with deception. Disguised as a traveler, the rival sought out the mortal man and planted seeds of doubt. "Why cling to a love that can never last?" the fairy asked. "Her magic may protect you now, but what of the cost? What of your people, who speak your name with fear?"

The mortal's heart wavered, the words stirring the uncertainties he had tried to suppress. Áine, sensing his turmoil, confronted the rival fairy, her radiance blazing with fury. "You would harm him to spite me?" she demanded. "Be gone, before I bind you to the winds!" The rival fled, but the damage was done. The trust between Áine and her love had been shaken.

Despite the trials, moments of happiness still bound them. On a clear summer evening, Áine led her love to a hidden grove, where flowers bloomed in colors no mortal had seen, and the air hummed with soft, unearthly melodies. "For now," she whispered, "let us leave the world behind. Let this place be ours."

They danced beneath the stars, their laughter rising into the night like music. But as dawn approached, they both felt the fragility of their joy. Love, no matter how strong, could not erase the divide between the mortal and the magical. They held each other tightly, knowing their bond was as fleeting as the mist that kissed the hills of Knockainey.

The bond between Áine and her mortal love, forged in defiance of two worlds, was as delicate as the morning dew. Their love had weathered the trials of jealousy and suspicion, but even the strongest bonds can break when trust is shaken. It was not malice that led to the mortal's betrayal, but the weight of fear, doubt, and the impossibility of living between two realms.

One evening, while speaking with a trusted friend from his

village, the mortal let slip the secret of Áine's true nature. "She is no ordinary woman," he admitted, his voice low but tinged with pride. "She is Áine, the Fairy Queen of Knockainey." He meant no harm, but his words, once spoken, could not be unsaid. The friend, unable to resist the allure of such a revelation, spread the tale across the village and beyond.

The villagers, who had long harbored a mix of awe and unease about the mortal's relationship, reacted with fear. Some whispered that Áine's presence brought blessings; others claimed her magic endangered them all. A few, driven by greed, plotted to capture her or coerce her into using her powers for their gain. The mortal man, realizing too late the consequences of his words, tried to shield Áine from the brewing storm, but the damage had already been done.

Áine, sensing the change in the air, confronted her love by the shimmering lake where they had first met. Her golden hair caught the fading light, her eyes filled with both sorrow and anger. "You spoke of me," she said, her voice soft yet laced with hurt. "You revealed what was meant to remain hidden."

The mortal fell to his knees. "I did not mean to betray you," he pleaded. "I was foolish, but my heart remains true. Please, forgive me."

Áine's gaze softened, but her heartbreak was clear. "It is not only my heart you have endangered," she replied. "The veil between our worlds is fragile, and your words have torn it. The trust between us was all that kept it whole."

Her sorrow turned to fury as the first villagers arrived, bearing torches and shouting demands. Áine raised her hand, and the torches extinguished with a hiss, leaving only the moonlight to illuminate the scene. The flowers around the lake, once vibrant and alive with her magic, began to wilt, their colors fading to grey.

"I gave you my love and my trust," Áine said, her voice trembling with emotion. "But now, I must leave. I will not be bound by fear or greed, and I cannot remain where trust is broken."

Her mortal love reached for her, but she stepped back, her

radiant form beginning to fade. The wind stirred, carrying her voice like a lament across the hills. "You will live with what you have done, and I will return to the Otherworld, where the bonds of trust are sacred and unbroken."

As Áine disappeared, the world around the lake seemed to dim. The villagers, overcome with a mix of fear and regret, retreated, leaving the mortal man alone with his sorrow. The vibrant hills of Knockainey, once alive with Áine's magic, grew quiet and subdued. The man wandered the hills for days, calling her name and pleading for her return, but the Fairy Queen was gone.

In the years that followed, the mortal man's tale became a cautionary legend. He lived with the weight of his regret, his life marked by the absence of the one he had loved and lost. On quiet nights, he would sit by the lake, listening to the wind and hoping to catch even a whisper of Áine's laughter.

Áine's departure served as a stark reminder of the delicate balance between the human and fairy worlds. Her love had bridged the gap for a time, but trust was the cornerstone of that union. Without it, the bridge could not stand. The story of Áine and her mortal love endures not just as a tale of heartbreak but as a lesson: the bonds between worlds are fragile, and the consequences of breaking them are profound. In the hills of Knockainey, where her magic lingers faintly, her name is still spoken with reverence—a symbol of love, loss, and the enduring power of trust.

Though Áine withdrew from mortal life, her spirit was never truly gone. In the rolling hills of Knockainey (Knock-aw-nee), her presence lingered, woven into the very fabric of the land. The wind that rustled the wildflowers, the golden glow of the summer sun, and the shimmering light of the moon on the lakes all whispered of Áine, the radiant Fairy Queen of Munster.

Generations of villagers carried her story, passing it from parent to child. They spoke of her beauty and power, her blessings and her wrath, and the love that bridged worlds. Áine's tale became more than a memory—it was a lesson. To respect the land was to honor her, and to approach the unseen forces with humility and reverence was to live in harmony with the world. On midsummer nights, when the air seemed alive with magic, offerings of flowers, honey, and milk were left at the base of Knockainey Hill, small gestures of gratitude to the Queen who once walked among them.

One such night, a child followed their grandmother to the edge of the hill, carrying a garland of daisies. "Why do we leave flowers here?" the child asked, their voice curious and soft. The grandmother smiled, kneeling to place the garland at the foot of the hill.

"This is for Áine," she said, her voice tinged with reverence. "She watches over us still, though we may not see her. Her blessings bring life to the fields and beauty to the hills. But we must also remember her sorrow and the price of forgetting the balance she taught us."

The child gazed at the hills, their imagination ignited by the thought of Áine, her golden hair flowing as she danced beneath the stars. The story became a part of them, as it had for so many before, ensuring that Áine's legacy endured.

Sin é

The beauty of Munster's hills remained a testament to Áine's enduring magic. On clear nights, the land seemed to shimmer beneath the moonlight, as if her spirit breathed life into every blade of grass and every ripple on the lakes. Farmers spoke of unexpected blessings—a bountiful harvest after a difficult spring, a cow's sudden recovery from illness—and attributed them to Áine's unseen hand.

But Áine's tale was also a reminder of caution. Her story taught that love and trust, when broken, had far-reaching consequences, and that the mortal and fairy realms, though interconnected, required balance and respect. The aos sí (ays shee), of whom Áine was one of the most radiant, were guardians of this balance, their legends deeply rooted in Ireland's cultural consciousness.

Through her story, Áine became more than a figure of myth; she became a symbol of the interconnectedness of love, nature, and the unseen forces that shape the world. Her radiance continues to inspire those who hear her tale, a reminder that even in sorrow, beauty endures, and that in the quiet places of the world, magic lingers. For those who walk the hills of Munster, Áine is still there, her spirit a quiet guardian, her name carried on the wind.

Áine (Awn-ya) holds a central place in Irish fairy lore as one of the most revered and powerful fairy queens. She is emblematic of the aos sí, the supernatural beings of Irish mythology who inhabit the Otherworld. As a figure of beauty and grace, Áine embodies both the allure and the danger that comes with the realm of the fairies. Her role as a guardian of nature, protector of the land, and keeper of its magical secrets reflects the deep connection between the aos sí and the natural world in Irish belief.

In Irish mythology, fairies are often seen as beings of dual nature —capable of both kindness and wrath, offering blessings or curses depending on how they are treated. Áine, like many fairy figures, is a guardian of the land, and her actions—both benevolent and vengeful—are directly tied to the respect given to the land and the beings who inhabit it. Her home, the hills of Knockainey, symbolizes the sacredness of the earth, a place where the veil between the mortal world and the Otherworld is thin. Just as the fairies could bestow good fortune upon those who respected nature, they could also withdraw their magic, causing misfortune to those who acted out of greed or disrespect.

Ireland's deep respect for fairies is closely tied to its connection of these beings with natural landscapes, especially hills, lakes, and sacred sites. These sites were believed to be the homes of the aos sí, places where the veil between worlds was thin and the magic of the fairies could be felt. The hills of Munster, where Áine is said to dwell, are not just geographical locations but are considered sacred spaces. Locals would offer gifts to the fairies—such as flowers, milk, and bread—as a gesture of respect, ensuring their favor and protection. This connection to the land reflects Ireland's deeply rooted belief that nature is imbued with supernatural power, and that the fairies serve as its guardians.

Fairy tales in Irish mythology often carry a strong moral message about respect and caution. These stories emphasize the importance of honoring agreements made with fairies and understanding the delicate balance between the seen and unseen worlds. Áine's tale is no exception—her love for a mortal man, while beautiful and transcendent, ultimately serves as a reminder of the potential dangers of crossing the boundary between human and fairy realms. When that trust is broken, as in the case of the mortal's betrayal, the consequences are swift and severe. This dynamic underscores the theme of balance in Irish folklore: harmony with the fairy world brings prosperity and blessings, but disrespect or betrayal can result in misfortune or punishment.

Áine's story, like many fairy tales in Irish tradition, blends universal themes of love, betrayal, and the power of nature. Her love for a mortal man illustrates the transient nature of such unions, highlighting the challenges that come when humans seek to merge their world with that of the supernatural. The power of nature in the tale is not just literal but symbolic, representing the forces beyond human understanding and control. Áine's magic, like the natural world itself, is beautiful, but it is also unpredictable and can turn destructive when misused or disrespected.

Áine's legacy in Irish folklore speaks to universal human emotions—love that transcends boundaries, the pain of betrayal, and the deep connection to nature. At the same time, her story preserves the unique cultural heritage of Ireland, where the supernatural is intertwined with the natural world and where respect for both realms is essential. In Áine's tale, we see not only the power of fairies but also the enduring belief in the unseen forces that shape the world and the lives of those who walk upon it.

CHAPTER 13

VOYAGE OF BRAN

Bran (Brawn), a noble hero of Irish mythology, was known for his connection to the sea and his adventurous spirit. He was a man who spent much of his life at the edge of the world, where land met the endless ocean. As the son of a great chieftain, Bran had grown up surrounded by the teachings of warriors, bards, and druids. Yet despite the strength of his lineage, it was the sea that called to him, with its promises of adventure, discovery, and the unknown.

His life had been peaceful—until the fateful day when the sound of an eerie, melodic voice carried across the waves. Sitting at the shore, Bran felt a strange stirring in his heart. The voice seemed to speak directly to him, soft and haunting, promising knowledge of ancient lands, mystical powers, and secrets hidden in the depths of the ocean. "Bran, son of the waves," the voice whispered. "Come, and I shall show you a realm beyond your wildest dreams, a world untouched by time."

The call from the Otherworld, as it came to be known, was not the voice of a mortal. It was something greater, more ancient—a voice that could not be ignored. Bran (Brawn) had heard legends of the Otherworld, a place where gods and fairies dwelled, a realm where time bent to the will of those who ruled it. The mortal world, with its wars, struggles, and familiar faces, seemed so distant in comparison. The call promised not only adventure but a journey that could reshape his destiny.

Bran's heart quickened as he considered the offer. It was a journey into the unknown, one that would take him far from the shores of Ireland. But something deep inside him told him that this was the path he was meant to take. This was the adventure that would define him.

Despite the quiet comfort of his life, Bran could not shake the feeling that his destiny lay beyond the known world. With a heart full of courage and a sense of wonder, Bran began to make preparations. He gathered a crew of brave companions, warriors who trusted his judgment and shared his thirst for adventure. Together, they would set sail on a voyage that would lead them to lands untouched by human feet, to a world where the supernatural and the divine were within reach.

As the ship prepared to depart, the wind seemed to beckon them, calling them to the horizon. The sea, once a vast and untamed wilderness, now felt like a gateway, a path that would lead them into the mysteries of the Otherworld.

For Bran, this was not just an adventure—it was a test of spirit, an invitation to step beyond the ordinary and enter a world where anything was possible. The themes of adventure, uncertainty, and wonder, which defined Bran's character, were reflected in the very act of setting out on this journey. The sea was no longer just a body of uisce (ish-keh, water); it was a realm of possibility, where legends were born, and where Bran would face challenges beyond his comprehension.

As Bran and his companions sailed into the unknown, they left behind the familiar shores of Ireland. With each wave they crossed, the boundary between the human world and the mystical realms grew thinner, and the promise of the Otherworld began to take shape on the horizon.

Their journey was just beginning, but already they could sense that what lay ahead would change them forever.

As the ship sailed further from the familiar shores of Ireland, the world seemed to shift. The sea, once boundless and wild, now felt strangely still, as if it were holding its breath. The air grew heavier, charged with a quiet energy. The horizon stretched on endlessly, but in the distance, faint lights began to flicker—glistening islands that shimmered with an otherworldly glow. Bran and his companions could feel it: they were no longer on a journey through the mortal world, but crossing the threshold into the realm of the supernatural.

The crew, initially excited by the unknown, grew uneasy as the winds began to change, and the sea's once rhythmic flow turned into a steady, eerie current. The landscape around them seemed to warp and shift, as if reality itself were bending in response to their presence. Bran stood at the bow, watching the uisce (ish-keh, water) stretch into a strange, dream-like mist, and felt the first stirrings of both awe and apprehension.

As they ventured further, the voice that had called to him once more resonated within his mind. It was clearer now, as if the distance between them had shortened. "Bran, son of the waves, you have come far. But remember: the path you walk is not for the faint of heart. To cross the boundary is to leave behind the world you know forever."

The crew, now more alert and weary, began to question the wisdom of the journey. "What if the tales are true?" one of the sailors asked, his voice tight with anxiety. "What if we never return?" Others nodded in agreement, casting uneasy glances toward Bran.

Bran, however, remained resolute. This was his calling, his fate. The voyage was not just a physical journey, but one of the soul. He turned to his men with a calm smile, though he too felt the weight of the unknown pressing in on him.

"Do not fear," Bran said, his voice firm and steady. "What lies ahead is the realm of the gods and the fairies, a place where magic lives and time bends. We go not just to explore, but to learn. The answers we seek will define our world, as well as the next."

With Bran's words, the crew found renewed courage, though the tension remained. The further they sailed, the more they felt the pull of the mysterious realm. The sea, in its endless expanse, was both a barrier and a bridge—one that separated the mortal world from the unknown, but one that Bran was determined to cross.

As they approached the first island, a strange stillness enveloped the ship. The sea had grown calm, the mist parting to reveal an island bathed in an ethereal light. The land seemed impossibly green, and towering trees stretched high into a sky that shimmered with unnatural colors. It was a place unlike any Bran had ever seen, and yet it felt familiar, as if it were a dreamscape come to life.

The island beckoned them, drawing them closer with its otherworldly charm. As Bran stepped onto the shore, the ground beneath him seemed to hum with magic. His companions, unsure of what to expect, followed him hesitantly, sensing that this was a place where nothing could be taken for granted.

On the island, Bran and his men encountered strange creatures —beings that defied explanation, yet seemed to understand them as if they had always been part of the land. Some appeared as humans, though their eyes gleamed with the light of stars. Others were animals with the wisdom of ancient beings, their voices soft but laden with meaning.

A figure approached Bran—an old woman with long silver hair, her skin glowing faintly in the twilight. She welcomed him in a voice that was both comforting and commanding.

"You have crossed the veil, Bran," she said. "Here, time does not measure as it does in your world. What you seek is closer than you think, but it comes with a price. The journey of the soul is not without sacrifice."

Bran listened intently, feeling the weight of her words. He had come seeking knowledge, but the price, it seemed, was not just of this world, but of his very soul.

As Bran and his companions explored the island, they were struck by its beauty, but also its strangeness. Time flowed differently here—what seemed like hours in the mortal world stretched into days, and yet the sun never quite set, casting the land in a perpetual golden twilight. It was a realm where rules did not apply, where the laws of nature could be bent or broken. The inhabitants, though kind and welcoming, spoke in riddles and parables, as though they were aware of the delicate balance between worlds.

Bran began to understand that this was not just a journey through physical space but a journey into the unknown corners of existence. The island was a reflection of his soul's quest—one that challenged him not only to explore the supernatural but to confront the mysteries within himself. Each step, each encounter with the strange creatures, revealed more about the nature of the Otherworld, but also about the human desire for meaning and transcendence.

And yet, as Bran ventured deeper into the island, the pull of the mortal world remained strong. He could not forget the life he had left behind, nor the people who depended on him. This was a place of wonder and terror, where every step forward seemed to push him further from the life he knew.

As the ship waited on the shores of the island, Bran knew his journey was far from over. The call of the Otherworld was growing louder, but the lessons of the mortal realm would always remain within him. The journey of the soul, it seemed, was one that could never truly be completed. It was a path that would continue to unfold, leading Bran to answers, but also more questions—until the end of time itself.

Bran's journey carried him from one magical island to the next, each a realm in itself, where the rules of the mortal world seemed to blur and bend. These islands were not merely physical places, but spiritual landscapes that represented different aspects of the Otherworld—each embodying a unique blend of beauty, mystery, and peril. Through his encounters with these islands, Bran's understanding of life, death, and the divine grew deeper, and he began to see that the Otherworld was as much a place of lessons as it was of enchantment.

The first island they arrived at was one of breathtaking beauty —a land that seemed to exist outside of time. Here, the air was thick with the scent of flowers in bloom, the skies perpetually a soft hue of blue, and the waters crystal clear. As Bran and his companions stepped ashore, they noticed something odd: there were no signs of aging, no tired faces, no decay of any kind. Everyone they encountered appeared as young as the day they were born. The people lived in perfect harmony, their laughter echoing in the air, their homes simple yet magnificent, built with materials that seemed to hum with magic.

"This is the Island of Eternal Youth," one of the islanders explained, smiling with ageless eyes. "Time here does not pass as it does in your world. We live free from sickness and death, in perfect peace."

The island was a paradise, but it was also a place of reflection. Bran saw that although the inhabitants were blissful and immortal, they lacked the wisdom that comes with the trials of life and death. Their lives were timeless, but their experiences were shallow, and the island seemed eerily static. No one ever left, and no one ever arrived.

As Bran walked through this timeless world, he realized that immortality without challenge was a gift that came at a cost—the richness of life could not exist without the shadow of death, the passing of time, and the lessons learned in its flow. He found himself wondering whether the absence of death here made life meaningless, despite the island's apparent beauty.

From the Island of Eternal Youth, Bran sailed onward, driven by the voice that had guided him, towards a place darker and more mysterious. As he journeyed across the water, the air began to grow thick and the waves began to stir uneasily. Soon, a strange and otherworldly sea creature surfaced alongside the ship—a vast, serpentine form, its scales shimmering in iridescent colors that reflected both light and darkness.

The creature's voice, deep and resonant, spoke to Bran without moving its lips. "You seek knowledge, Bran of the mortal realm," it said, its eyes glowing like distant stars. "But knowledge comes with a price. There are things you will see that cannot be unseen. There are truths you will learn that may drive you to madness or despair."

Bran, both awed and frightened by the creature, asked, "What is the price of this journey?"

The creature's eyes narrowed as it replied, "Do not be too eager to return to your world, for when you leave the Otherworld, you may not recognize what awaits you. The time you seek to find will slip away, and you will find the past and future confused. Beware, Bran, of the tide that draws you home."

The creature's cryptic words hung in the air long after it had disappeared beneath the waves, leaving Bran with a foreboding sense of uncertainty. It was a reminder that the path to wisdom was fraught with peril. While the Otherworld offered knowledge and wonder, it also held mysteries that could overwhelm even the bravest soul.

The next island they reached was unlike any they had encountered so far. Here, the laws of time seemed utterly warped. The sky above was a swirling mass of colors that shifted and changed, while the land itself appeared to distort, growing and shrinking in moments. Bran and his crew found themselves trapped in a cycle where moments bled into one another. One instant, they were standing in a lush forest, and the next, they found themselves in a barren wasteland. The landscapes morphed, not gradually, but with disorienting speed.

On this island, time seemed fluid—one moment they were in the present, and the next, Bran saw visions of his past and future unfolding before him. He saw his younger self, setting sail from Ireland, filled with hope and courage. Then, he saw glimpses of his future: a world he did not recognize, where everything had changed, and he was no longer the man he had been. His heart ached as he watched these fleeting moments, unsure whether they were prophecies or illusions conjured by the island's magical nature.

"Time here bends," a voice said behind him, and Bran turned to see an elderly woman, her face lined with age but her eyes as sharp as a hawk's. "Here, you will witness your own life, but not as you know it. Time flows backward, forward, and sideways. But it is all an illusion."

Bran asked, "What am I meant to learn here?"

The woman's gaze softened. "You are meant to understand that time, in the grand scheme of things, is a mere ripple in eternity. The past and future are not fixed, but fluid. What you do today echoes in ways you cannot imagine. Choose wisely, for the ripple you create today may change the world forever."

As Bran absorbed her words, the visions of his life continued to unfold, revealing both triumphs and failures. He saw the faces of those he had loved, those he had lost, and those yet to come. The fluidity of time made him realize how interconnected his journey was with the lives of others. Nothing existed in isolation, and each moment shaped the next.

The islands Bran visited each held their own unique mystery and challenge, forcing him to confront different aspects of the Otherworld and the spiritual forces that guided it. Each island brought a new understanding of the world beyond, from the eternal peace of the Island of Eternal Youth to the warning of the cryptic sea creature, and the distorted time of the final island. These encounters deepened Bran's understanding of life, death, and the divine, revealing the fluid nature of time and the intertwined relationship between the mortal and the supernatural.

With each step, Bran moved closer to the core of the Otherworld and to the profound truths that awaited him. He began to understand that the journey was not just an exploration of the world beyond, but also a path of inner discovery, where the true meaning of existence could only be glimpsed in the most mysterious and mystical corners of the universe.

As Bran's voyage through the Otherworld continued, the adventure evolved into something far more profound than he had initially anticipated. The islands, with their enchantments and mysteries, were not just physical destinations—they were realms of transformation and self-discovery. Each moment spent in the supernatural landscape deepened his understanding of the connection between life, death, and the divine. Bran began to realize that this journey was not merely a test of courage or skill, but one of the soul, designed to reveal hidden truths about the nature of existence itself.

The first spiritual revelation came when Bran experienced a mystical vision. One evening, as the ship floated in still waters beneath a sky filled with strange constellations, Bran drifted into a deep, dreamlike trance. In the vision, he found himself standing on a vast plain, surrounded by ancient trees that seemed to pulse with life. The air shimmered with an ethereal glow, and the earth beneath his feet hummed with an ancient rhythm.

In the distance, a great river flowed, its waters reflecting the light of a thousand stars. As Bran gazed into the river, he saw images of life—past, present, and future—swirling in its depths. He saw the faces of those he had loved, the lands he had known, and the souls of those who had passed before him. The river was not just a body of uisce (ish-keh, water), but a symbol of the interconnectedness of all things, weaving together life, death, and the forces that governed the universe.

The voice of the river spoke to him, its tone soft but clear. "All things are connected, Bran. Life and death are two sides of the same coin, ever flowing in harmony. The land, the sea, the sky— they are all part of one great cycle. You are not separate from this cycle. You are both the journey and the traveler."

This vision, though fleeting, left Bran with a deep sense of peace and understanding. He realized that his journey was not just about seeking knowledge but about understanding the eternal flow of life. The boundaries between the mortal world and the Otherworld seemed to disappear, as he began to grasp the idea that death was not an end, but part of a never-ending cycle—a journey that transcended the limitations of time and space.

Bran's newfound understanding was further deepened by a dream-like encounter with a divine figure who appeared to him one night as he rested on a rocky shore. The figure was tall and radiantly beautiful, with eyes that seemed to hold the wisdom of the ages. The divine figure spoke in a voice that resonated with the power of the cosmos.

"Bran, son of the waves," the figure said, "you seek knowledge beyond your world, but you must understand that the journey of the soul does not follow the paths you know. Life and death are not separate; they are parts of the same cycle. You cannot have one without the other. The soul must pass through death, not as an end, but as a necessary passage."

The figure went on to explain that the soul's journey after death was cyclical, with each life a continuation of a greater cosmic journey. Every soul was part of the grand dance of creation, destruction, and rebirth. The figure spoke of the divine forces that guided this cycle—the Tuatha Dé Danann (Too-ah-hah Day Dan-an), the ancient gods and goddesses who watched over the worlds, ensuring the continuity of life and the balance between the mortal realm and the Otherworld.

As Bran absorbed the divine figure's teachings, he began to see the journey for what it truly was—a path of spiritual growth. It was not merely a physical journey to distant lands but an internal quest to understand the essence of the soul's connection to the divine. Bran now understood that every choice, every action, was part of a larger, cosmic flow, and that each soul played a role in the great cycle of life and death.

Bran was not alone in his transformation. His companions, each grappling with their own fears and desires, found their own spiritual revelations as they journeyed through the Otherworld. One companion, a seasoned warrior named Ciarán (Kee-rawn), found himself reflecting on his past battles and the lives he had taken in the name of honor. On the island of eternal youth, where no one aged and time stood still, Ciarán saw his reflection in the waters, and for the first time, he faced the guilt and grief of his past actions. He realized that true peace would not come through victory or valor but through forgiveness and self-acceptance.

Another companion, a young bard named Eoghan, experienced a similar transformation on a magical island where he heard the voices of the ancestors singing songs of old. The melodies were filled with sorrow and joy, tales of love and loss, victories and defeats. Eoghan felt the deep connection between his own life and the ancient stories of Ireland, realizing that his role as a bard was not just to entertain, but to preserve the stories of the past and to help others understand their place in the grand tapestry of life.

Bran, too, was forever changed by the journey. As he continued his exploration of the Otherworld, he grew in wisdom, learning that the boundaries between the mortal realm and the supernatural were not as rigid as they seemed. The world, in all its forms—both seen and unseen—was interconnected. Life was not a straight path but a winding journey filled with twists, turns, and lessons that could only be understood when one looked beyond the surface.

For Bran, the spiritual journey was not about finding answers in the traditional sense. It was about embracing the mystery, understanding that the quest for truth was as important as the truth itself. In the Otherworld, he discovered that the soul's journey was infinite, and that no matter where one traveled, the cycle of life, death, and rebirth would continue, forever intertwined with the natural and spiritual forces of the universe.

Bran's voyage was far from over, but each step had brought him closer to understanding the true nature of existence. As he sailed further into the Otherworld, Bran carried with him the knowledge that the journey of the soul was a continuous one, ever-evolving, ever-growing. And as he looked out at the horizon, he realized that the search for meaning, the pursuit of spiritual growth, was the greatest adventure of all.

As Bran's journey through the Otherworld neared its end, he found himself at a crossroads. The voice that had first called him to the sea now spoke again, echoing through his mind with the same urgency that had guided him from the start. The divine figure he had encountered spoke once more, its tone both gentle and firm.

"Bran, son of the waves, you have witnessed much, and your journey has brought you closer to the heart of the universe. But now the choice is yours: return to the world you left behind, or remain here in the eternal realm of the gods. The Otherworld offers you immortality, a life untouched by time, but with it comes a cost—the loss of everything you once knew."

Bran stood at the threshold between the two worlds, the horizon stretched before him, a gateway between the mortal realm and the eternity of the Otherworld. He could feel the pull of both. The promise of eternal life, filled with wisdom and peace, tempted him. Yet, the weight of his past—the people he had loved, the land he had sworn to protect—reminded him of his duty. Could he truly abandon everything for the allure of immortality?

Reluctantly, Bran made his decision. He chose to return to Ireland, to the world he had left behind. But as the ship sailed back across the waters, he knew that the world awaiting him was no longer the same one he had left. The winds felt different now, heavier with the weight of knowledge, and the sea seemed vast and lonely. The Otherworld had offered him wisdom beyond measure, but it had also changed him in ways he could not yet fully understand.

When Bran and his companions finally returned to Ireland, the land seemed unchanged, yet profoundly different. The hills they had once known now felt distant, the faces of those they had left behind seemed older and more distant, as if time itself had moved on without them. The passing of years in the Otherworld had taken its toll on the mortal realm, and Bran realized that the world he had left behind had aged, as had those he once knew. The people, the places, and the customs—all seemed out of place now. Time, which had stood still in the Otherworld, had marched on here without pause.

The companions who had sailed with Bran felt the same alienation. They, too, found that the world had moved on. The homes they had once known were now ruins, their families no longer where they had left them. The bonds of kinship that had once tethered them to the mortal world had frayed, and they were left with nothing but the knowledge and the memories of a journey that had changed them forever. The people of Ireland, seeing their strange appearance and hearing their otherworldly stories, could not comprehend the vastness of their experience. In a way, Bran and his companions had become outcasts, no longer fully part of the world they had once known.

As Bran walked across the familiar, yet now foreign, land of Ireland, he couldn't help but reflect on the price of his return. His soul had been forever touched by the divine, but his mortal life, with all its human joys and sorrows, seemed fleeting in comparison. The knowledge he had gained in the Otherworld, while profound, was now a burden. It was a reminder of the delicate balance between the mortal and the supernatural realms, and how the pursuit of wisdom could, at times, distance one from the very life they once cherished.

On a quiet evening, Bran sat alone on a hill overlooking the sea, the place where his journey had begun. The sun was setting, casting a golden hue across the water, and the gentle waves lapped against the shore. In that moment, Bran felt the weight of both worlds pressing down on him. The peace he had found in the Otherworld seemed far away, but the struggles of the mortal world—its fleeting nature, its beauty, and its pain—were now part of him, too.

As Bran reflected on his choices, he felt a strange sense of peace. He had learned much, but he understood now that there were no easy answers. The journey of the soul, like the tides of the sea, was endless. Some knowledge, once attained, could never be forgotten, and some paths, once taken, could never be retraced. Bran's final moment of peace was not one of clarity, but of acceptance. He had glimpsed eternity, and in doing so, had come to understand the preciousness of the fleeting moments that made up a mortal life.

Though the world had changed in his absence, and his place within it had shifted, Bran knew that the journey was far from over. There was wisdom in every step, and every choice, no matter how difficult, was part of the greater cycle. The sea, which had called him in the beginning, would continue to call, just as the Otherworld would always be there, waiting for those who were brave enough to seek its truths.

Sin é

The Voyage of Bran (Immram Brain) stands as one of the most significant tales in Irish mythology, not only because of its epic adventure, but also because of the deep spiritual themes it explores. Bran's journey to the Otherworld became a cornerstone in the development of Irish mythological thought, representing the Irish people's adventurous spirit, their innate connection to the supernatural, and their ceaseless quest for meaning beyond the mortal world.

As a central figure in Irish mythology, Bran's voyage captured the imagination of the Irish people and was passed down through the generations. His adventure across the sea, from one mystical island to another, symbolizes the ancient desire to understand the mysteries of existence, the afterlife, and the divine. The Otherworld in Bran's tale is not merely a place of supernatural beauty and peril—it is a spiritual realm that challenges the boundaries between life and death, between the mortal and immortal, reflecting the Irish belief in the interconnectedness of all things. Bran's journey, filled with mystical beings, trials, and profound revelations, mirrors the Irish perception of the human soul's quest for wisdom, peace, and ultimately, understanding.

The Voyage of Bran also helped to establish the immram genre —Irish tales of voyaging heroes who journey to the Otherworld.

These stories became a rich part of Irish oral tradition, with each subsequent immram building upon the themes Bran's story introduced: the tension between the mortal and the supernatural, the price of knowledge, and the transformative power of the Otherworld. Bran's tale influenced generations of storytellers, who used the immram genre to express not only the physical voyage of the hero but the deeper, spiritual voyage that humans undertake in their search for meaning.

The immram stories often highlight themes of death, transformation, and the cyclical nature of existence—concepts deeply embedded in Irish culture. In Bran's journey, we see the blurring of lines between life and death, where immortality and mortality are not separate but intertwined. The Otherworld becomes a place where the soul is tested, where spiritual wisdom is gained, and where the boundary between the human experience and divine knowledge is continually challenged. This reflects Ireland's belief in the afterlife—not as a final end, but as part of the eternal journey of the soul.

Bran's journey also symbolized the importance of spiritual exploration. While physical travel could reveal new lands, it was the journey of the soul, the quest for wisdom and understanding, that was most significant. The Immram Brain became more than just an adventure; it became a spiritual model for those who sought deeper truths about their own lives. The voyage through the Otherworld was not just a literal sea journey, but a metaphor for the inner journeys that all humans must take to understand their own nature, their connection to the divine, and their place in the cosmos.

In Ireland, The Voyage of Bran became a beloved tale. It was told by bards in the courts of kings, passed from generation to generation, its spiritual lessons remaining relevant across the ages. Each retelling kept Bran's memory alive, immortalizing his voyage and its lessons for those who came after him. Through these stories, the Irish people were reminded of their connection to the land, the sea, and the supernatural forces that shaped their world.

One evening, a young child sitting at a fire in a remote village listens in awe as an elder recounts the tale of Bran. The child's eyes widen, captivated not just by the adventure but by the mystery that lies beyond the visible world. For the child, Bran's journey is not just a story from the past, but a door opening to new possibilities—the beginning of their own spiritual journey. The child, inspired by the heroism and wisdom of Bran, dreams of a future where they too might embark on a voyage, not across the seas, but deep into their own soul.

Even in modern Ireland, the appeal of immram tales continues to endure. They remain an integral part of Ireland's rich literary and cultural heritage, capturing the timeless human fascination with the mysteries of the soul, the afterlife, and the divine. Today, immram stories are still told, their themes of adventure, self-discovery, and spiritual growth resonating with people across the world. In a world that is constantly changing, the quest for meaning, for knowledge, and for a connection to something greater than ourselves, remains as powerful as ever.

CULTURAL NOTES: IMMRAM AND IRISH MYTHOLOGICAL VOYAGES

The genre of immram (voyage tales) occupies a central place in Irish mythology, offering a rich blend of adventure, spirituality, and the supernatural. In these stories, heroes embark on epic sea voyages to distant and mysterious realms, often crossing boundaries that separate the mortal world from the divine or otherworldly realms. Immram tales were more than mere adventures; they were spiritual quests designed to explore the limits of human understanding, the mysteries of the afterlife, and the complex relationships between the mortal and supernatural worlds.

In these stories, the sea is both a literal and symbolic barrier, separating the known world from realms of unimaginable wonder and peril. The voyages often take the heroes to islands that are inhabited by gods, fairies, or mystical beings, each place representing a different facet of existence and spirituality. The idea of crossing the sea, venturing beyond the visible world, embodies the Irish belief in a reality that stretches beyond what is immediately perceivable. The hero's journey is not just a physical passage but a spiritual one, meant to test their resolve, expand their understanding, and challenge their perceptions of life and death.

The Otherworld plays a pivotal role in immram tales, serving as both the destination and the backdrop for the hero's spiritual journey. In Irish mythology, the Otherworld is a place of profound beauty, where time operates differently, and where the boundaries between life and death are often fluid. It is described as a realm of immortality, eternal youth, and unending happiness, but it is also fraught with uncertainty. The Otherworld is often depicted as a paradise where the souls of the worthy find peace, yet it can also be a place of danger, trickery, and deception. It is where the gods dwell, where heroes encounter divine forces, and where profound lessons about existence are learned.

The Otherworld in immram tales is not simply a utopia—it is a realm of dualities. It represents both the beauty and the fragility of life, offering insights into the human condition, yet also revealing the price of immortality and the pursuit of forbidden knowledge. The heroes who venture into the Otherworld do not return unchanged. Whether they learn the truth about the afterlife, discover hidden wisdom, or are forced to confront their own inner darkness, these journeys symbolize the complex and often perilous path to spiritual understanding.

One of the key themes of immram tales is the idea of the hero's journey as a reflection of the soul's voyage. As the hero sails across the sea, they not only travel through physical space but also through their own consciousness, experiencing profound transformations. This spiritual journey is one of self-discovery, where the hero learns about the nature of existence, the balance between life and death, and their place in the grand scheme of the universe.

In The Voyage of Bran, this theme is central to the narrative. Bran's journey to the Otherworld is not just an adventure in a literal sense, but a voyage of the soul. Along the way, Bran learns that immortality, wisdom, and power come with great responsibility. He is forced to confront the tension between the mortal world and the allure of the divine, facing the consequences of seeking knowledge that may not be meant for humans. The journey represents the quest for enlightenment, but it also reveals the dangers of that pursuit. Bran's experience in the Otherworld teaches him that true wisdom is not just about what one learns, but about the choices one makes in seeking that knowledge.

In immram tales, the hero's spiritual exploration often carries significant consequences, reflecting the Irish belief in the importance of balance between the seen and unseen worlds. Bran's return to Ireland after his voyage is marked by a deep sense of loss. Though he has gained profound wisdom, his return to the mortal world leaves him disconnected from the life he once knew. This reflects a recurring theme in Irish mythology: that the pursuit of spiritual knowledge often comes at a great cost. The hero may learn sacred truths, but those truths can be alienating, leaving them forever changed and, in some cases, isolated from the world they once understood.

The Voyage of Bran offers a vivid illustration of this theme. Bran's decision to return to the mortal world, after learning so much from the Otherworld, brings with it a sense of irreversibility. While the knowledge he has gained elevates his understanding of existence, it also separates him from his former life. The sacrifice Bran makes is symbolic of the greater Irish cultural belief that certain journeys—particularly those involving the divine or supernatural—are not without their costs. The pursuit of wisdom, no matter how pure or noble, requires a price, and in the case of Bran, that price is the loss of his connection to the mortal world.

The immram tales, including The Voyage of Bran, are timeless reflections on the themes of human curiosity, the search for deeper meaning, and the tension between the mortal and the supernatural.

They underscore the importance of spiritual exploration in Irish culture, portraying the heroes' journeys as both physical and metaphysical quests. These stories invite audiences to contemplate the mysteries of life and death, the pursuit of knowledge, and the boundaries between human limitations and divine potential. Ultimately, the immram genre speaks to a universal human desire: the desire to understand the unseen forces that shape our existence and the world beyond.

CHAPTER 14

TALE OF SÉTANTA'S TRAINING

Sétanta (Shay-tan-tah), later known as Cú Chulainn (Coo Hull-un), was a young warrior from the kingdom of Ulster, already renowned for his strength, courage, and quick reflexes. Yet, despite his natural abilities, he felt incomplete. His prowess in combat was undeniable, but without formal training, he understood that he could not achieve the greatness he desired. Sétanta longed to be not just another skilled fighter, but a true hero —someone whose name would echo through the annals of Irish history.

In the tales passed down through the generations, Sétanta had heard stories of Scáthach (Skah-hakh), the legendary warrior woman who lived in a far-off land. She was renowned not only for her immense strength but for her ability to turn young warriors into legends. Her fortress, set in the mystical lands of Skye, was a place where the most promising fighters went to train under her watchful eye. It was said that no one who trained under Scáthach left the same; they emerged as skilled warriors, not just physically but with the wisdom and discipline to lead.

Sétanta felt the pull of adventure, and more importantly, the call to challenge himself in ways that would elevate him beyond what he had already achieved. Despite the dangers of the journey, the uncertainty of what awaited him in Scáthach's land, and the fear of what he might encounter, Sétanta knew that he had to go. This was the next step in his quest to become a true hero.

Leaving the comforts of home behind, Sétanta set off alone. He knew this journey would change him, but what he did not yet understand was just how much it would transform him—not just into a warrior, but into a man. The trials that awaited him would test not just his strength, but his spirit. The land of Scáthach would challenge him in ways he could never have imagined, shaping him into one of the greatest heroes in Irish mythology.

And so began Sétanta's journey—not just a journey across the land, but a journey into himself, one that would lead him to confront his limits, his passions, and the true meaning of heroism.

Scáthach (Skah-hakh), the legendary warrior woman, lived in a remote, mystical land where the very air seemed thick with magic. Her fortress, Dún Scáith (Fortress of Shadows), perched on a craggy hill in the wilds of Skye, was surrounded by high, jagged mountains that seemed to stretch into the heavens. The land itself was steeped in ancient power, with mist-cloaked forests, rushing rivers, and vast, untamed plains. To reach her fortress, Sétanta had to cross treacherous terrain, but his heart surged with anticipation. The stories of Scáthach had inspired him since childhood, and now he had come to test himself in the very place where warriors were made.

The fortress itself was a reflection of Scáthach's power—its towering stone walls fortified by ancient magic. It was said that no one could enter without Scáthach's permission, and that the very land responded to her will. Inside, the training grounds were as wild and unforgiving as the land surrounding them, with weapons strewn across the earth, as though waiting for those who dared to take them up and prove their worth. This was a place where legends were forged, where young warriors like Sétanta could come to seek the training that would shape them into heroes—or break them altogether.

Sétanta approached the gates with awe and respect, feeling the weight of the moment. He was a strong young man, already skilled in combat, but here, in Scáthach's domain, he was nothing but a novice. His excitement was tempered with a deep awareness that to prove himself worthy of the warrior queen's teachings, he would need more than just raw strength. He would need discipline, focus, and a spirit ready to face the challenges of true battle.

Scáthach, unlike the other warrior leaders Sétanta had known, was a woman. In a world where men dominated the martial arts, Scáthach's reputation stood out—not just for her prowess in battle, but for her ability to train warriors. Her lineage was that of the great warrior women of ancient times, and her reputation stretched far beyond the borders of Ireland. It was said that she had defeated armies single-handedly, and that no one who trained under her left the same—either they were broken by the harshness of her methods, or they emerged as some of the finest warriors Ireland had ever known.

Her backstory was steeped in both triumph and tragedy. She was the daughter of a powerful king, but she had chosen the warrior's path, casting aside the comforts of royal life in favor of battle and discipline. She had trained under the greatest warriors of her time, eventually surpassing them all and earning the title of mná na réalta (muh-nah nah rayl-ta), "woman of the stars"—a name given to her by those who saw her as a living legend.

What made Scáthach particularly unique in the world of Irish warriors was her ability to lead not just through strength, but through wisdom and insight. As a woman in a male-dominated world, she had to fight twice as hard to prove herself, but her reputation was beyond question. Her warriors revered her, not just for her prowess in combat but for the guidance she provided. It was said that when Scáthach spoke, even the bravest warriors listened.

Sétanta's first sight of her was as awe-inspiring as the stories had promised. Scáthach stood tall, her posture straight and unyielding, her armor gleaming in the sunlight. Her eyes were sharp, like a hawk's, scanning the land around her, but when she turned to meet

Sétanta's gaze, there was a deep intelligence in her expression, a silent understanding that spoke volumes. There was no need for words; the moment Sétanta stepped into her presence, he knew that his journey had truly begun.

She did not speak immediately, but instead, she studied him, her eyes narrowing as she sized him up. "You have traveled far," she said at last, her voice steady and commanding. "But the journey ahead is not one of distance, but of spirit. Your strength is apparent, but strength alone will not make you a true warrior. Tell me, Sétanta, what brings you here?"

Sétanta, his heart pounding in his chest, took a deep breath and spoke without hesitation. "I seek to be the greatest warrior of Ireland. I wish to learn from you, to become as great as those who have walked before me."

Scáthach studied him for a long moment before nodding. "Very well," she said, her voice calm and measured. "But know this: training here is not for the weak of heart. Many have come seeking my guidance, but few have survived. You must prove yourself worthy, for I do not hand power lightly."

With that, Scáthach gave Sétanta his first challenge. "You will face me in combat. Show me your skill, your strength, your will to endure. And know this: I will not hold back."

Sétanta's heart raced with anticipation. Here was the test he had sought, the chance to prove himself. Scáthach raised her sword and took her position, her eyes never leaving his. It was clear that she was not only testing his combat skills but also his ability to learn and adapt. This was not just a battle of strength—it was a battle of the mind, where every move mattered, and every decision could be the difference between success and failure.

The clash of their swords echoed through the fortress, and Sétanta realized in that moment that the true journey had just begun.

The path to becoming a legendary warrior under Scáthach's tutelage was not an easy one for Sétanta. From the moment he stepped onto the training grounds, he was thrust into a world of rigorous discipline, physical hardship, and mental trials. Scáthach, a strict and demanding teacher, believed that a true warrior's strength lay not just in the body, but in the mind and spirit as well. Sétanta quickly realized that this was a far cry from the straightforward combat he had known before. The lessons were as much about endurance and perseverance as they were about skill.

Each day, Sétanta's body ached from the intense physical demands placed upon him. He practiced long hours with weapons —first learning the spear, then the sword, perfecting his aim, precision, and timing. He sparred with Scáthach's other students, sometimes one-on-one, sometimes in group battles, each encounter pushing him to his limits. Often, he found himself lying on the cold earth, breathless, with bruises and cuts from his training. But Scáthach never let him give up. "A warrior does not falter in the face of hardship," she would say, her voice sharp as a blade. "He rises again, stronger than before."

Though his body began to grow stronger, the true challenge lay in overcoming his mind. Sétanta was used to fighting with passion, with the fire of his youthful spirit, but Scáthach taught him that true mastery of combat required calm and control. He had to learn to manage his rage, to channel his emotions, and use them in a way that served him, rather than letting them rule him. Each day, Sétanta struggled with his temper, resisting the urge to fight recklessly. Scáthach's teachings on restraint were not easy to follow, but over time, Sétanta began to see the wisdom in her words.

In addition to physical training, Scáthach introduced Sétanta to the mystical aspects of the warrior's path. She taught him about the geis (gaysh, magical obligations) that bound a warrior's destiny. These geis were powerful forces, not merely rules to be followed, but ancient laws that connected the mortal world with the divine. They spoke of the warrior's duty to protect his people, uphold justice, and maintain honor at all costs. Scáthach explained that a warrior's fate was often shaped by these geis, and a breach of them could lead to destruction. Sétanta learned that his destiny was not entirely his own; it was shaped by the spirits and forces that

guided his path, and his choices would have far-reaching consequences.

Through it all, Sétanta learned the core values that would define
him as a hero: honor, loyalty, and the balance between rage and
restraint. Scáthach didn't just teach him how to fight; she taught
him how to embody the warrior's way, how to live with integrity,
and how to lead with wisdom. The bond between teacher and pupil
deepened with each passing day, and Sétanta began to understand
the true nature of heroism. He wasn't just learning to be a great
warrior; he was learning what it meant to be a man of honor and to
take on the responsibilities that came with his power.

Sétanta's first real test came when he was sent to face a rival
warrior, one of Scáthach's most skilled students, in a battle of skill.
Sétanta had been training for months, but the reality of the combat
was still intimidating. The duel took place in the training arena,
where the sky hung heavy with clouds, and the air buzzed with
tension. The two warriors faced each other, their eyes locked in a
fierce gaze, knowing that this would be a defining moment for
Sétanta.

The battle was long and brutal, with each combatant pushing
the other to their limits. Sétanta, though younger and less experienced, had learned well from Scáthach's teachings. He didn't fight
with the same wild intensity that had marked his earlier battles.
Instead, he moved with purpose, controlling his emotions, and
using every lesson he had learned about strategy, timing, and
patience. His opponent, strong and skilled, was confident, but
Sétanta's cool-headed determination proved stronger.

In the end, Sétanta emerged victorious, his rival lying defeated
on the ground. It was not just his strength or speed that had won
the fight—it was his discipline, his focus, and his understanding of
the warrior's path. Scáthach watched from the sidelines, her expression one of quiet approval. She had not only seen Sétanta's growth
in skill but also in spirit. In that moment, Sétanta understood the
true meaning of being a warrior.

The victory was a turning point for Sétanta. No longer just a boy with raw talent, he had become a skilled and disciplined fighter, one who had learned to blend his physical prowess with the wisdom of a true warrior. Yet, even with this first victory, Sétanta knew that his training was far from over. Scáthach had given him the tools, but the road ahead would still be full of challenges. It was not enough to simply win battles; he had to continue learning, growing, and refining the path that lay before him.

As Sétanta stood, looking at his fallen opponent, Scáthach approached him and placed a magial spear in his hand. "You have taken the first step, and I gift you this deadly spear, Gáe Bulg, that only you can wield," she said. "But the warrior's journey is never finished. You must always seek to grow, to learn, and to serve. You are on the path, Cú Chulainn, but it is a path that will test you again and again. Only the bravest and wisest ever truly become legends."

Sétanta nodded, his heart swelling with pride and purpose. The road ahead would be long, but with Scáthach's teachings in his heart, he knew that he was on the path to greatness.

Through his training under Scáthach, Sétanta's transformation was not just physical but spiritual, as he learned the values and principles that would guide him throughout his life. The hardships, the lessons in restraint, and the battles fought with both mind and body would shape him into the legendary Cú Chulainn, the greatest of all Irish warriors.

As Sétanta's training under Scáthach continued, he began to evolve in ways that extended beyond his physical strength. The raw talent he had arrived with was now tempered with wisdom and discipline, and his time in Scáthach's land had molded him into something far greater. Sétanta was no longer merely a gifted warrior; he had become the embodiment of the warrior class, a man who understood the true meaning of strength—not just in his muscles, but in his character. His pride was not in his victories but in his ability to maintain his honor, his self-restraint, and his commitment to the warrior's code.

The transformation was slow but undeniable. Sétanta's ability to control his emotions and to make decisions with a clear mind marked his growing maturity. No longer did he fight with reckless abandon, but with a sense of purpose and wisdom. He had learned the value of both rage and restraint, understanding when to unleash his fury and when to remain calm, and this balance gave him a strength few warriors possessed. His time with Scáthach had shaped him into the type of man who was not only a warrior by training but a true hero in spirit.

It was during a final trial that Sétanta's transformation into the legendary Cú Chulainn became complete. Scáthach, ever the wise and perceptive mentor, had seen the changes in him over time, but she knew that a true hero was forged not just by success in battle, but by confronting one's deepest fears. For Sétanta, this trial would not just be physical; it would be a test of his heart and mind.

Sétanta was taken to a sacred place on the edge of Scáthach's land, a place where the veil between the mortal world and the Otherworld was thinnest. There, Scáthach challenged him with a vision of his own death, an image that would haunt any warrior who saw it. Sétanta was forced to face the moment of his downfall, knowing that every warrior had to face death one day. It was a test of courage, not just to fight, but to confront the inevitability of mortality.

For hours, Sétanta remained in the presence of this haunting vision, unable to move, paralyzed by the weight of what he saw. But eventually, his will—honed through years of training under Scáthach—triumphed over the fear. He stood tall, facing the vision and accepting his fate with the same courage he would face any battle. By embracing his fear, Sétanta proved that he had become a true warrior, unflinching in the face of death.

This trial marked the final stage in his transformation. The young man who had arrived at Scáthach's fortress—confident yet untested—was now a warrior of unparalleled skill, wisdom, and fortitude. In a solemn and heartfelt moment, Scáthach raised her hand in recognition of Sétanta's accomplishments and spoke the words that would bind his fate forever.

"You have proven yourself worthy, Cú Chulainn," she said, her voice steady but full of pride. "You are Cú Chulainn, the Hound of Culann. You are a warrior, a hero, and a champion of Ireland. May your name echo in the songs of our people forever."

As Scáthach's words echoed in the wind, Sétanta's heart swelled with pride and purpose. The young Hound of Ulster who had left Ulster seeking fame and fortune had now become a hero in his own right. But his transformation was far from over—he had yet to face the true tests that awaited him in Ulster, including battles that would define his legacy and trials that would prove his place among the greatest warriors Ireland had ever known.

Scáthach's teachings were not just about fighting—they were about living with honor, understanding the responsibility that came with great power, and embracing the larger cosmic forces that shaped a warrior's fate. Her final lesson to Cú Chulainn was one that would serve him well in the years to come: A true warrior must understand that his strength is not for himself alone, but for the protection of his people, his land, and the values that define him. Scáthach had shaped Cú Chulainn into more than just a great warrior—she had forged a legend.

As Cú Chulainn prepared to leave Scáthach's land and return to Ulster, he knew that the world would never be the same. His training was complete, but the true test of his heroism awaited him. The lessons he had learned under Scáthach's watchful eye would carry him through countless battles, but it was the warrior's heart that would guide him in the most important fight of all: the fight for his people, for his honor, and for the future of Ulster.

His journey was just beginning, but Cú Chulainn knew that with the strength of Scáthach's teachings behind him, he was ready for whatever challenges lay ahead.

Sin é

In Irish warrior culture, mentorship was a cornerstone of both personal development and the preservation of tradition. Warriors were not simply trained to fight; they were shaped by the values, honor, and principles instilled in them by their mentors. This passing of knowledge from one generation to the next was a deeply ingrained aspect of warrior life, ensuring that the legacy of great leaders like Scáthach (Skah-hakh) would endure.

Scáthach herself embodied the intersection of the mortal and the mystical. As a warrior woman, she had surpassed the boundaries of what was traditionally expected of women in Irish society, leading her own school of warriors and imparting not just battle skills, but spiritual wisdom. Her training grounds, shrouded in the mystical power of the aos sí (ays shee), bridged the gap between the human realm and the supernatural. Scáthach's students learned that their strength and honor were not solely products of physical combat but were tied to the land and the unseen forces that governed their world. The aos sí, the fairies or otherworldly beings, played an essential role in shaping the training of these warriors, offering guidance and protection to those deemed worthy. These spirits were thought to walk among the warriors, helping to shape their fates and ensuring that the bonds between the human world and the divine were kept intact.

As Cú Chulainn (Coo Hull-un) grew under Scáthach's guidance, he began to understand the deeper aspects of warrior life. It was not enough to simply possess strength or skill; a warrior had to embody values such as honor, courage, and loyalty. These values were reinforced through the relationships formed between mentors and their students. Scáthach's teachings went beyond the mechanics of battle with Gáe Bulg; she instilled in Sétanta a sense of responsibility to protect his people, to serve the greater good, and to uphold the traditions of his ancestors.

Scáthach's role as a teacher also marked a critical moment in Cú Chulainn transformation from a headstrong youth into a disciplined, wise warrior. It was through Scáthach's tough love and steadfast mentorship that Cú Chulainn learned to balance his natural abilities with wisdom and restraint. His training was not only a means to gain power but also a process of learning how to wield that power responsibly. Every lesson, every challenge he faced, was designed to bring him closer to his destiny as a hero of Ireland, but also as a keeper of the warrior's code.

Once Cú Chulainn's training was complete, he returned to Ulster, a man transformed. No longer the brash, brave boy who had sought out Scáthach, Cú Chulainn's name would be etched in Irish history forever. Yet his journey was not over. Like his mentors before him, Cú Chulainn understood that his legacy was not built solely on his victories or feats of strength. He knew that his true role was to pass down the knowledge he had gained, just as Scáthach had passed it down to him.

Cú Chulainn's legacy would go on to influence future generations of warriors. He would teach the young of Ulster not just how to fight, but how to live by the warrior's code—how to balance strength with wisdom and leadership, how to be fierce not only in battle but in spirit, and how to protect the land and people they loved. In this way, the cycle of mentorship and the passing of knowledge would continue, ensuring that the ideals of the warrior class lived on long after Cú Chulainn's own time had passed.

As Cú Chulainn mentored the next generation of heroes, he became not just a warrior, but a living symbol of the values that had shaped him. He embodied the lessons of Scáthach—the importance of honor, loyalty, and balance—and carried those teachings forward into the hearts of those who followed him. In doing so, he ensured that the warrior code would endure, passed down through the ages, shaping the future of Ulster and all of Ireland.

This passage of wisdom from teacher to student, from one generation to the next, is a central theme in Irish mythology. It reflects the deep respect for knowledge, tradition, and the responsibility that comes with being a warrior. Through Scáthach's mentorship, Cú Chulainn's legacy would shaping the future of Ireland's warriors for centuries to come.

Cú Chulainn (Coo Hull-un), the ultimate warrior in Irish mythology, became the embodiment of the ideals and virtues that defined the warrior class in ancient Ireland. His legacy, shaped profoundly by his rigorous training under Scáthach (Skah-hakh), transcended the physical battles he fought. Through Scáthach's mentorship, Cú Chulainn gained more than just martial prowess; he acquired the wisdom, discipline, and honor that would establish him as the quintessential hero-warrior.

The qualities that Cú Chulainn represented—strength, loyalty, courage, leadership, and sacrifice—were held in the highest regard in Irish society. His training was designed not just to make him a formidable fighter, but to shape him into a leader who could carry the weight of responsibility for his people. Cú Chulainn was not merely a product of his strength but of his moral and ethical decisions, grounded in the lessons of Scáthach, who taught him the balance between rage and restraint. While he possessed immense power, it was his sense of honor and his unshakeable loyalty to Ulster that defined him as a true hero.

Throughout the Ulster Cycle, Cú Chulainn's training and his adherence to the warrior's code remain central themes. His story exemplifies the ideal of the hero-warrior: a figure who stands not only as a champion in battle but as a symbol of the virtues that hold society together. His training story reflects the Irish belief that a warrior's strength is intertwined with their sense of duty, that physical might must be tempered by wisdom and a deep understanding of one's place in the world.

Cú Chulainn's role as the archetypal warrior went beyond mere combat. His moral decisions and the trials he faced—many of which were steeped in the supernatural—demonstrated the complexities of the warrior's life. His actions embodied the Irish understanding of heroism: a hero was not just one who fought for glory, but one who fought for something greater than themselves, whether it was their community, their leaders, or the gods they served. In this way, Cú Chulainn's training was not just a path to individual greatness but a means of ensuring the continued strength and honor of Ulster and its people.

Cú Chulainn's relationship to his community and the gods is also a reflection of the broader societal structure in ancient Ireland.

Warriors like Cú Chulainn were bound by more than just physical training—they were tied to their clans and to the divine forces that governed the land. Their loyalty was not only to their leaders but to the land itself, and in Cú Chulainn's case, this deep connection to his homeland has made him one of the most beloved and revered figures in Irish folklore. His commitment to Ulster and his unyielding defense of his people highlighted the warrior's role as a protector, both of the people and the values that defined Irish society.

This sense of duty was reinforced by the spiritual aspects of his training. Scáthach, a teacher of both mortal and mystical combat, imbued Cú Chulainn with a deep understanding of his role in a world where the boundaries between the supernatural and the mortal were often blurred. The training in the land of Skye, which was as steeped in magic as it was in martial tradition, ensured that Cú Chulainn did not just see himself as a man of muscle and might but as a warrior chosen by fate, one who was part of a larger cosmic order.

Cú Chulainn's final moments of training marked a pivotal moment in his evolution. He had surpassed the expectations of his teacher, Scáthach, who, upon witnessing his transformation, recognized that he had become more than a student—he had become the living embodiment of the warrior ideals she had taught him. As Cú Chulainn took his place among the greatest warriors of Ireland, he was not just remembered for his victories but for the way he lived his life, the choices he made, and the values he upheld.

His story, immortalized in the Ulster Cycle, continues to serve as a model of the warrior spirit: someone who stands for the greater good, who fights with both strength and wisdom, and who sacrifices personal desires for the defense of those they love. The impact of Scáthach's teachings lived on through Cú Chulainn, ensuring that future generations of warriors would carry forward the lessons of honor, loyalty, and the delicate balance between rage and restraint.

Cú Chulainn's legacy extended far beyond the battlefield. He became a mentor to others, just as Scáthach had mentored him, passing on the teachings that defined him as both a warrior and a leader. His story continued to inspire not only warriors but also the poets, bards, and historians who preserved his legend for generations to come. Through his actions, Cú Chulainn became a symbol of what it meant to be a true hero—someone who understood that power was not an end in itself, but a means of serving something far greater.

Ultimately, Cú Chulainn's role in Irish warrior culture and his place in Irish mythology highlight the dual nature of the hero: the physical warrior who fights for honor and the spiritual figure who embodies the virtues that define the Irish people. His story remains a testament to the values of ancient Ireland, and his legacy continues to shape the ideals of courage, duty, and wisdom in Irish culture today.

CHAPTER 15

WRATH OF MACHA

Macha (Mah-ka) was a figure both revered and feared in ancient Irish mythology. Known for her otherworldly beauty and incredible strength, she was a woman of great power, yet her story was marked by injustice and heartbreak. Born of the mystical aos sí (ays shee), the fairy folk of Ireland, Macha was destined for greatness, but her life would be forever shaped by the brutal treatment she received from the men of Ulster.

Macha's story began in the fertile lands of Ulster, where she married Crunnchu (Kroonn-khoo), a man of Ulster who had long admired her beauty and strength. Despite their marriage, Macha's relationship with the men of Ulster was tense. They were proud and boastful, believing themselves to be the greatest warriors in all of Ireland, yet they lacked the humility to recognize the strength of the woman they had married into their land. As a result, Macha was often looked upon with suspicion, her strength envied by men who could not reconcile their pride with her power.

Ulster, a land of warriors and heroes, was marked by its incredible strength and martial prowess, but beneath its prideful exterior lay deep flaws—flaws that would eventually lead to Macha's curse upon the province. The men of Ulster, consumed by their sense of superiority, failed to recognize that their land was not invincible and that its future was tied to the respect and balance of all its forces, including those of the supernatural.

It was in this environment of pride and misplaced arrogance that Macha's troubles began. Her strength was both a blessing and a curse in a world where women were expected to remain silent and passive. The men of Ulster, intoxicated by their own pride, mocked Macha and subjected her to a humiliation that would forever change her fate. It was a moment of disrespect—one that they would come to regret—that set the stage for the catastrophic curse that Macha would unleash upon them.

Macha, though beautiful and strong, was not without vulnerability. She felt the weight of the injustice done to her, and it was this mistreatment that ignited the fire of vengeance in her heart. Macha's decision to curse Ulster was not taken lightly; it was the culmination of years of mistreatment and scorn. The humiliation she suffered at the hands of the men of Ulster became the catalyst for a tragedy that would haunt the province for generations to come.

This story is one of vengeance, justice, and the consequences of failing to honor strength, particularly the strength of a woman. Macha's curse was not simply an act of retribution—it was a reminder of the balance that must be maintained between the mortal and supernatural worlds. When that balance is broken, as it was by the men of Ulster, the consequences are both severe and far-reaching.

Macha's wrath, unleashed upon the land, would serve as a stark reminder of the power that resides in the unseen forces of Ireland. Her strength was not just physical—it was the strength of a woman who had been wronged, a strength born from the ancient magic of the aos sí and the deep-rooted connection she had to the land. Her curse was not just an act of vengeance; it was a lesson. The men of Ulster would learn, too late, that their pride had not only dishonored her but had also called down the wrath of powers far beyond their understanding.

As Macha's story unfolds, it will become clear that her curse on Ulster is as much a reflection of the world she inhabited as it is a cautionary tale for the future. In this land of warriors, strength is revered, but respect—especially the respect of those who wield power—is what holds that strength together. Without it, as Macha would show, even the mightiest of kingdoms can fall victim to forces that cannot be seen, only felt.

The insult that Macha endured was one of great humiliation and one that would be etched into the annals of Irish myth. The men of Ulster, drunk on their pride and filled with the arrogance that often accompanies strength, made a wager that would cost them dearly. It was said that the men, gathering one day in their pride, boasted of their unmatched skill and swiftness on horseback. In their boastfulness, they challenged Macha to a race, not understanding the depth of her strength or the true nature of the being they were insulting.

Macha, having long been recognized for her beauty, intelligence, and power, was no stranger to the admiration of others, but the men of Ulster treated her as little more than a prize, a subject for their amusement. They sneered at the idea that a woman, no matter how strong, could possibly outmatch their horses. Driven by their own egos, they pressed her into a race against their fastest steeds.

At first, Macha hesitated, for she knew the stakes were high. But she could not bear the weight of the insult. Her pride as a goddess and aos sí (ays shee) was intertwined with her sense of justice and respect. The moment the challenge was made, the decision to race was no longer hers—it was a matter of her dignity, of being seen not as a mere object but as a force to be reckoned with.

With a steely resolve, Macha accepted the challenge, not only to show the men of Ulster her strength but to remind them that no being, mortal or immortal, should be mocked or belittled. The race commenced, and to the astonishment of the men, Macha easily outran their finest horses, leaving them behind in the dust.

However, in their prideful disrespect, the men, especially the chief among them, Crunnchu, who was Macha's husband, scoffed at her victory. Their cruelty only grew with their embarrassment. They demanded that she race again, this time not on horseback, but in a footrace against the fastest men in the land.

Macha, enraged and humiliated beyond words, found herself facing an insult that no woman should have to endure. The pride of the men of Ulster had crossed a line, and her heart burned with fury. But it was not enough to simply race and win again. She knew that the men of Ulster had crossed a threshold that could not be undone with mere words or deeds.

As Macha stood victorious, the men's mockery continued, turning her victory into a spectacle of shame. In that moment, something within her snapped. With a voice that echoed with the power of the aos sí, Macha invoked a curse so potent that it would forever change the fate of Ulster.

She called upon the ancient gods and the fairies, whose power flowed through her veins, and swore vengeance on the men who had humiliated her. Macha's words rang with finality: "From this day forth, whenever the men of Ulster are most in need of their strength—on the eve of battle—they will find their bodies weak, their minds clouded, and their courage gone. For the price of their disrespect, they will never know the power of their full might in battle again."

With these words, she placed the curse upon them, invoking the power of the supernatural to bind the men of Ulster to her wrath. The curse would not simply make them physically weak; it would render them unable to act in the face of their greatest need. In a time when war and honor were everything, their inability to fight at the crucial moment would cost them dearly.

Not long after Macha's curse was cast, the men of Ulster faced their first trial under its weight. When an army of invaders from a neighboring kingdom threatened the province, the warriors of Ulster should have been able to rally to their defense. Yet, when the time came to fight, the men found themselves stricken by an inexplicable weakness, their bodies betraying them at the worst possible moment. The warriors, once known for their fearsome strength and indomitable courage, could barely lift their weapons, let alone stand against the invaders.

The battle was disastrous. The warriors of Ulster, weakened by Macha's curse, could not defend their land. Ulster's fields were overrun, its cities plundered, and its people left vulnerable. Macha's curse had stripped them of the one thing they held most dear—their ability to protect their homeland.

The curse was not just a physical one. It was a blow to Ulster's pride, to the very heart of its warrior culture. The warriors, who had once been invincible in their battle prowess, now faced the ultimate humiliation. This was the price of their arrogance, the cost of disrespecting the strength of a woman who was far more than they ever imagined.

As Macha's curse took root, the people of Ulster were left to face the consequences of their actions. The warriors, though once mighty, were now bound by a supernatural force that made them impotent in the face of their greatest trials. The men of Ulster would never again be able to fight with the strength they once had during the most critical moments. Macha's vengeance had reshaped the future of their kingdom and marked it with the stain of their dishonor.

Her curse, while devastating, also served as a harsh reminder: the strength of the land, and the people who inhabited it, were inextricably linked to the respect given to all beings—mortal or divine. No one, man or woman, could be treated as lesser, for the power of the supernatural was always watching, waiting for the moment when the balance would tip.

Macha's wrath became not just a personal act of revenge but a cultural lesson that would reverberate through the generations:

respect is the foundation of all strength, and when that respect is violated, even the strongest will fall.

The men of Ulster never anticipated the fury they had provoked. Macha's curse was not born of mere anger—it was a direct response to the wrongs she had suffered, and in Irish mythology, justice and revenge often walked hand in hand. The two were intertwined like the roots of the earth, inseparable in their power and purpose. Justice was not merely a passive concept; it demanded action, and for Macha, that action was swift and severe.

As the men of Ulster stood in the wake of their arrogance, unable to defend their homes and lands, they learned a harsh lesson. Macha's vengeance was not just for herself; it was an embodiment of a cosmic balance that could not be ignored. In Irish lore, the supernatural was deeply tied to the earth, and the earth itself demanded respect. For the men of Ulster to treat Macha with such disrespect, to challenge her in a race and mock her strength, was to tip that balance. It was a sin against the natural order, and Macha, as a powerful figure of the aos sí (ays shee) and a protector of the land, had the power to restore that order—no matter the cost.

Sin é

In many ways, Macha's story represents the complexity of justice in Irish mythology. Her actions, though driven by a personal wound, were also a reflection of the deeper principles that governed Irish society. The values of honor, respect, and balance were sacred, and any disruption to that balance demanded retribution. Macha's curse wasn't just a personal vendetta; it was an act of cosmic justice. She wasn't merely avenging an insult to her pride, but responding to an imbalance that threatened the very fabric of the world.

Yet, her actions also blurred the line between justice and revenge. In the Irish tradition, revenge often held the same weight as justice—it was seen as a necessary tool to right wrongs and restore balance. But Macha's vengeance was harsh, punishing an entire province for the pride and arrogance of a few men. The question of whether it was just or excessive is one that echoes through Irish mythology, where the gods, heroes, and warriors alike often grapple with the consequences of their actions.

Macha's strength, however, was more than just an instrument of retribution—it was the essence of her being. She was not just a powerful figure in the mythological world, but a representation of the raw, untamable power of nature itself. In the world of Irish mythology, women like Macha were not just passive figures—they were forces to be reckoned with, embodying both creation and destruction, beauty and terror.

Her strength transcended that of ordinary women. It was a strength that was rooted in the earth and the supernatural, something beyond the mortal realm. As a member of the aos sí, she was not bound by the same rules as men, nor was she beholden to the expectations placed upon women in her time. In a world dominated by male warriors, Macha stood as a figure who could command the forces of nature and bend them to her will. Her curse, and the power she wielded, was a direct manifestation of this strength.

Macha's power was not just physical—it was spiritual, tied to the land and the cycles of life and death. In many ways, she was both a protector and a punisher, reflecting the duality that exists in all powerful figures. Her actions were a reminder that women in Irish mythology held sway over more than just the domestic realm; they were intertwined with the earth, nature, and the divine. The curse she laid upon Ulster was a reminder that to disrespect a woman's power, especially one as connected to the land and the supernatural as Macha, was to invite ruin.

In Irish mythology, women like Macha embody strength and autonomy that transcended societal expectations. While men were expected to be the warriors, the protectors, and the rulers, women were often the keepers of the land's magic, the wielders of divine power, and the arbiters of fate. Macha's story underscores the importance of respecting women's strength and autonomy, especially in a society that often overlooked them. Her curse was a powerful reminder that even the greatest warriors must pay heed to the women who walk among them, for their power is not to be underestimated.

Revenge in Irish mythology was often viewed as a necessary and just response to disrespect and dishonor. The concept of honor was central to the warrior ethos, and when that honor was violated, retribution was seen as a rightful means of restoring balance. Macha's curse was an act of revenge, yes, but it was also a statement of her unshakable sense of justice. She had been wronged, and in the eyes of the supernatural forces that governed her world, she was justified in her actions.

The men of Ulster had failed to recognize the sacredness of their connection to the earth and the divine. They had mocked her strength, disregarded her power, and treated her as if she were a mere woman to be put in her place. In Irish society, where the balance between man, nature, and the divine was so crucial, their actions were a direct affront to the gods. Macha's curse was, in many ways, the manifestation of that affront. Her vengeance wasn't just for herself—it was for the land, for the divine, and for the honor of women everywhere.

In a culture that valued honor above all else, Macha's curse served as a harsh but necessary reminder of the consequences of dishonor. Her decision to curse the men of Ulster was not an act of unchecked rage; it was a calculated response, a correction of the imbalance they had created. And while her revenge might have seemed excessive, it was precisely the kind of action that Irish mythology often deemed necessary to restore balance and order. It was a reminder that in a world filled with gods, heroes, and powerful women like Macha, no insult could go unpunished.

Ultimately, Macha's story highlighted the complex relationship between justice, revenge, and respect in Irish mythology. It shows how vengeance can be both a righteous act and a dangerous one, how the strength of women can change the course of history, and how the supernatural forces of the aos sí can shape the world in ways that cannot be ignored.

The air in Ulster was heavy, as if the weight of Macha's words lingered, carried by the winds to every corner of the province. Farmers whispered of crops that seemed slower to grow, warriors glanced at their weapons with unease, and the elders warned of an imbalance that could not be undone. Macha's curse was not just an act of vengeance—it was a ripple in the fabric of the world, a force both feared and respected.

Curses in Ireland were never taken lightly. They were not mere words spoken in anger but deeply tied to the supernatural, carrying the power of the aos sí and the ancient gods. Every curse was a bridge between the mortal and mystical realms, a reminder of how thin the veil between them truly was. When Macha invoked her curse, she did more than punish the men of Ulster; she tapped into the primal forces that governed the world, binding her words to the natural laws of life, death, and honor.

In the days following Macha's curse, the people of Ulster could feel the shift in their land. The warriors, once so proud and strong, now felt a shadow upon them. Their strength remained intact during peace, but the mere whisper of battle brought a sickness to their limbs, a trembling to their hands. It was as if the curse had rooted itself not just in their bodies but in the very soil beneath their feet. The curse became not just a punishment but a lesson— one that would be told and retold as both warning and explanation.

Macha's curse was not the first, and it wouldn't be the last, to ripple through Irish lore. The bards often sang of such events, where curses shaped the destinies of kingdoms and heroes alike. "A curse is the hand of the unseen," the old storytellers would say. "It is the weight of justice that mortal hands cannot carry."

In a quiet village near Emain Macha (Eh-mawn Mah-ka), a farmer sat by his hearth, telling his children tales of curses long past. He spoke of the druid Cathbad (Kah-thahd), whose words could bend the will of nature, and of the Fomorians, who cursed the land with blight after their defeat by the Tuatha Dé Danann (Too-ah-hah Day Dah-nahn). "Curses," the farmer said, "are not mere words. They are promises, woven into the world itself."

Macha's curse was different. It was not cast by a druid or a god but by a woman who had suffered. This made it more potent, the farmer explained, for it carried not just the weight of the supernatural but the raw power of a wounded heart. "When you disrespect the forces of this world," he warned, "you risk drawing the wrath of something greater than yourself."

The people of Ireland understood curses not just as punishments but as reminders of the balance that had to be maintained. A curse was a disruption, but it was also a correction, a way to restore harmony when it had been broken. Macha's curse, as harsh as it was, became a symbol of this principle. It was more than revenge—it was a declaration that arrogance and disrespect could not go unchecked.

The supernatural was woven into every aspect of Irish life, and curses served as one of the most direct connections to that unseen world. When the warriors of Ulster fell to their knees in moments of need, their weakness was more than physical. It was a reflection of their collective failure to honor the balance between strength and respect. Macha's curse reminded them that their power, no matter how great, was still subject to the laws of the divine and the natural world.

Years later, a bard sang of Macha in the court of a neighboring king. He described her beauty, her strength, and her tragic tale. "She was wronged," he sang, his voice rising with emotion, "and she answered not with tears but with a curse so great that the earth itself shuddered beneath her words."

The king, leaning forward, asked the bard, "And what became of her?"

"She returned to the hills," the bard replied, "to the land of her kin among the aos sí. But her words remained, bound to the men of Ulster as tightly as their swords to their scabbards. Even now, when they march to battle, her curse marches with them."

The king nodded, his face grave. "A powerful tale," he murmured. "A powerful lesson."

The winds that swept across the hills of Ulster carried whispers of Macha's name long after her departure. Her curse, uttered in fury and pain, didn't fade with time. It grew. It seeped into the soil, into the very marrow of the warriors who called Ulster their home. The men of the province, once so proud and invincible, found themselves forever marked, forever scarred, by the words of the wronged goddess.

When the warriors of Ulster gathered for battle in the years that followed, a strange unease would settle over them. They could feel the curse lingering, a silent specter that waited to strike. At times, the curse lay dormant, allowing them to fight with the ferocity that they had once been known for. But in moments of greatest need, when the battle cries rose and their land demanded their strength, Macha's curse would awaken.

It was said that on those days, the strongest of men would fall to their knees, their arms trembling as if weighed down by invisible chains. Their vision blurred, and their hearts raced with an inexplicable fear. Those who tried to stand found their legs betraying them, their breath stolen by an unseen force. The warriors of Ulster would clutch at their weapons, desperate to defend their homeland, only to find their bodies rendered useless. The shame of it was worse than any wound.

Macha's name became a warning passed down through generations. In the courts of kings, the bards sang her tale with reverence and caution. "Macha of the hills," they would say, "whose wrath can fell even the mightiest warriors." Her story became legend, a testament to the strength of a woman wronged and the power of the supernatural to shape the fate of men.

The curse became part of Ulster's identity, an inescapable mark on its warriors. They were known across Ireland not just for their bravery but for the shadow that hung over them. Other provinces spoke of Macha with fear and respect. Her name was etched into the history of Ulster, as much a part of its legacy as its victories and heroes.

Even in the greatest tales of the Ulster Cycle, Macha's curse loomed large. It shaped the destiny of Cú Chulainn (Coo Hull-un), Ulster's greatest hero. When the armies of Queen Medb (Mayv) marched on Ulster during the events of the Táin Bó Cúailnge (Tawn Boh Koo-ul-nyuh, The Cattle Raid of Cooley), the warriors of the province were stricken by the curse, leaving Cú Chulainn to stand alone against an entire army.

In those moments, the curse was not just a burden—it was a crucible. It tested the resolve of the warriors and the strength of their will. For Cú Chulainn, it became both a challenge and a calling, forcing him to rise above the weaknesses of his kin and embody the ideals of a true hero. Yet even he could not escape the shadow of Macha's curse, as the weight of her words shaped his life and the destiny of Ulster itself.

Among the common folk, Macha's story became a symbol of respect for the supernatural and the strength of women. In the villages, women whispered her name with both pride and sorrow, seeing in her a reflection of their own struggles for respect and recognition in a world dominated by men. Her curse was a lesson, a reminder that power came in many forms, and that to disregard it —especially the power of a woman—was to court disaster.

In quiet moments, the people of Ulster left offerings on the hills believed to be her home. They placed flowers and whispered prayers, asking for her forgiveness or seeking her blessing. Though she had cursed their warriors, they knew that Macha's strength was something to be revered, not feared. Her connection to the land, to the aos sí, and to justice made her more than a figure of vengeance —she was a force of nature, a guardian of balance who had acted in the only way she could.

As centuries passed, Macha's story endured. The bards wove her tale into the fabric of Irish mythology, ensuring that her name would never be forgotten. Her curse, though devastating, became a part of Ulster's identity, a reminder of both its strength and its flaws. Macha's legacy was one of justice, of standing against disrespect and dishonor, and of the consequences of failing to recognize the power of those who walk among us, unseen but ever-present.

Her wrath, born of pain, became a lesson for all of Ireland—a lesson of respect, balance, and the enduring strength of a woman whose words could shape the destiny of her province. To this day, the hills of Ulster seem to whisper her name, and her story remains a testament to the power of justice and the price of arrogance.

CHAPTER 16

DEATH OF CÚ CHULAINN

The dawn broke cold and gray over Ulster, the sky heavy with clouds that seemed to mirror the unease of the land. Cú Chulainn (Coo Hull-un), the Hound of Ulster, stood at the threshold of his home, the chill air biting at his skin. He had known this day would come—the day when his strength would be tested for the last time, and the weight of his destiny would press down upon him like a blade.

Years of battle had left their mark on him. His once-youthful face was lined with the scars of war, his eyes shadowed with memories too painful to name. Yet, even with the passage of time, he remained a figure of unmatched power and grace, a warrior whose name struck fear into the hearts of his enemies and pride in the hearts of his people. The Hound of Culann had never turned from a fight, and he would not start now.

The omens had been clear. For nights, Cú Chulainn had been haunted by dreams of shadowy figures and flickering lights, their voices calling him to the Otherworld. A raven had perched on his windowsill at twilight, its dark eyes unblinking as it stared into his soul. The druids had warned him—this was no ordinary battle. "Your fate is upon you," they had said, their voices trembling with the weight of their vision. "The threads of your life are woven tightly now. What remains will be written in blood and remembered in song."

Still, Cú Chulainn felt no fear. His heart, though burdened by years of loss and sacrifice, beat steadily with the rhythm of duty. He was a warrior of Ulster, bound not by choice but by destiny. The land had claimed him long ago, and he had given himself to it without question. The people of Ulster needed him, and that was all that mattered.

The call came with the rising sun—a messenger, breathless and pale, bringing news of Connacht's advancing armies. Their forces were vast, united by a shared hatred for Ulster and a desire to see its great champion fall. Cú Chulainn listened in silence, his expression unreadable. When the messenger finished, he simply nodded and turned to prepare. His weapons, worn yet still deadly, lay ready, and as he lifted his spear, its weight felt heavier than ever before.

As he stepped outside, the wind stirred around him, carrying the faint scent of the sea and the whispers of the past. He paused for a moment, his gaze fixed on the horizon where the enemy would come. He thought of all he had fought for—his home, his people, the honor of his name. And though he knew what awaited him, he felt no regret. If this was to be his last stand, he would face it with the courage and ferocity that had defined his life.

The hero of Ulster tightened his grip on his spear and walked into the cold light of morning, the weight of fate heavy on his shoulders but his spirit unbroken. This was his moment, the culmination of a life lived for the land and its people. And whether he lived or died, his name would echo across the hills of Ireland for all time.

The winds carried whispers of war across Ulster, their cold touch bringing dread to the hearts of its people. On the borders, scouts returned with grim news: Connacht's forces were gathering once more. Queen Medb (Mayv), relentless and cunning, had united the enemies of Ulster under her banner, promising wealth and vengeance to those who would march against the province. The warriors of Ulster, once fierce and proud, now spoke in hushed tones, their spirits dampened by the shadow of Macha's curse.

In his hall, Cú Chulainn sat alone, his spear laid across his lap. The weight of it seemed heavier now, its edge dulled by years of battle. He had carried this weapon into countless fights, each one a test of his strength and will. Yet this time, the burden felt different. This was not just another skirmish. This was the storm that had been building for years, the culmination of all the bloodshed and sacrifice. And though Cú Chulainn's body bore the scars of his past, it was the wounds unseen—the loss of comrades, the loneliness of a hero—that ached the most.

Cú Chulainn's mind wandered to the days of his youth, when he was known simply as Sétanta, the boy with dreams of glory and the fire of untested strength. He had stood alone at the fords, his enemies falling before him like wheat to a scythe. Back then, he had believed in the purity of battle, the honor of defending his land. But time had revealed the cost of such ideals. Each victory had come at a price, each life taken leaving its mark on his soul.

The door creaked open, and a young messenger entered, his face pale with fear. "My lord," he stammered, "the armies of Connacht gather near the borders. Their numbers are vast."

Cú Chulainn rose slowly, his movements deliberate. He looked at the boy, his eyes filled with the weight of countless battles. "How long do we have?" he asked.

"Not long," the boy replied. "They will be upon us by sunrise."

Outside, the land seemed to echo the hero's turmoil. The skies darkened, the wind howled through the trees, and the rivers ran heavy as if mourning what was to come. Cú Chulainn stepped out into the cold, his breath visible in the chill air. He gazed at the horizon, where the enemy would soon arrive, and felt the familiar pull of his geis (gaysh). He had always known that his destiny was bound to Ulster, that his strength was not his own but a gift to his people.

And yet, he felt the weariness in his bones, the years of fighting and loss pressing down on him. He thought of Emer (Em-er), his beloved wife, and the quiet life they might have had if fate had been kinder. But such thoughts were fleeting. He was not a man born for peace. He was a warrior, and warriors did not turn away from their duty, no matter the cost.

As the sun dipped below the hills, casting the land in shadows, Cú Chulainn prepared for the battle to come. He sharpened his weapons with practiced precision, each stroke a reminder of the life he had chosen. The world around him seemed to hold its breath, the calm before the storm.

He knew this would be his greatest fight. And though the odds were against him, he welcomed the challenge. For Ulster, for his people, and for the honor that defined him, Cú Chulainn would stand alone once more. And this time, he would give everything he had, even if it meant giving his life.

The armies of Connacht had learned much from their previous defeats at the hands of Cú Chulainn. They knew they could not match his strength in single combat, nor could they hope to outlast his relentless determination. To defeat the Hound of Ulster, they needed cunning. Queen Medb (Mayv), shrewd and calculating, called upon her advisors, druids, and spies to devise a plan that would exploit the one weakness no warrior could escape: their honor.

"The Hound fights not for himself but for his land and his people," Medb said, her voice sharp as steel. "We will turn his loyalty into his downfall."

Word spread quickly of a supposed threat to Ulster's people. A small village, nestled near the border, was said to be under siege by Connacht's forces. The villagers, it was whispered, had sent desperate pleas for help, their fate resting in the hands of the province's defenders. When this news reached Cú Chulainn, he wasted no time. Despite warnings from his companions that it could be a ruse, he prepared to ride out alone.

"This is my duty," he said firmly, his jaw set with determination. "If there is even a chance that my people are in danger, I must act."

As he approached the supposed battlefield, an unnatural stillness greeted him. The air was heavy, the trees eerily silent. It was only when he reached the clearing that the trap sprang into motion. The "villagers" he had come to save melted away, revealing a host of Connacht's warriors, their weapons gleaming in the fading light. Behind them stood the druids, their chants weaving an invisible web of geasa (gas-uh, magical obligations plural) around Cú Chulainn, binding him to fight on their terms.

He recognized the trickery immediately, his sharp mind piecing together the betrayal even as the warriors closed in around him. For a moment, rage flared in his chest—not at his enemies, but at the manipulation of his honor. Yet, as quickly as the anger came, it faded. Cú Chulainn had always known the risks of his path. The geis placed upon him was unbreakable, and his duty to his people was absolute.

Steeling himself, he gripped his spear tightly and stepped forward. "If this is the way you choose to face me," he called out, his voice carrying across the field, "then let us end it here. I will not run, and I will not cower. Come, and face the Hound of Ulster!"

The battle began with a ferocity that shook the earth. Connacht's warriors attacked in waves, their numbers overwhelming, but Cú Chulainn met them with unmatched skill and ferocity. His spear danced like a living thing, striking with precision and power. For every warrior that fell before him, another took their place, but he fought on, his resolve unbroken.

The druids' magic, however, began to take its toll. The geasa weighed on him like chains, sapping his strength and clouding his mind. His movements slowed, his strikes grew less sharp, and the wounds he sustained bled more heavily than they should have. Yet still, he fought, driven by an unshakable sense of duty.

At last, as the sun dipped below the horizon, casting the battlefield in shadow, Cú Chulainn stood alone amidst the bodies of his foes. His breathing was labored, his vision blurred, but he remained defiant. He knew this battle had been his enemies' trap, and though he had fought valiantly, the cost had been great.

In that moment of quiet, as his enemies regrouped and prepared to strike again, Cú Chulainn felt a strange sense of peace. He had faced betrayal and fought not for himself but for the land and people he loved. His honor remained intact, untainted by the treachery that surrounded him.

As the next wave of warriors charged, Cú Chulainn raised his spear one final time, ready to face them all, knowing that no matter the outcome, he would remain true to his path.

The battlefield lay bathed in the blood-red light of dusk, its silence broken by the clash of steel and the cries of the wounded. Cú Chulainn stood alone, his spear in hand, surrounded by the bodies of those who had fallen to his wrath. His enemies encircled him, wary of the legend who had defied their might time and time again. But this time, they could feel the shift in the air—the Hound of Ulster was weary, his strength waning under the weight of battle and betrayal.

The warriors of Ulster, crippled by the curse of Macha, lay scattered across the province, unable to rise and defend their land. Cú Chulainn, bound by his duty and unyielding honor, was left to stand against Connacht's army alone. Yet even in the face of overwhelming odds, he refused to falter. His spear was steady, his gaze unwavering.

The first wave came with the howl of war horns, and Cú Chulainn met them like a storm. His movements were a blur of precision and power, every strike a calculated dance of death. He fought with the ferocity of a cornered wolf, his enemies falling one after another. The ground beneath him turned slick with blood, but he pressed on, his body moving as if guided by the gods themselves.

And then, the change began.

Cú Chulainn's ríastrad (ree-uh-strahd), the warp-spasm that transformed him into a force of otherworldly terror, overtook him.

His muscles twisted and swelled, his face contorting into a mask of primal rage. His eyes burned like embers, and his hair stood on end, a fiery halo that crowned his head. He became a creature of chaos and destruction, no longer bound by mortal limits.

His enemies hesitated, their courage faltering as they faced the wrath of a warrior who seemed more god than man. With a roar that echoed across the battlefield, Cú Chulainn surged forward. His spear carved through armor and flesh like a blade through water. His war cries drowned out the shouts of his foes, the sound of his fury shaking even the most seasoned warriors.

But even the warp-spasm could not last forever. The supernatural energy that fueled his rage began to fade, leaving him drained and vulnerable. His enemies, sensing an opportunity, closed in with renewed determination. Cú Chulainn fought on, his spear heavy in his hands, his body crying out in pain. Yet he did not yield. His love for Ulster, his unwavering loyalty, and his refusal to abandon his people drove him forward.

The battle had raged for hours, the clash of swords and the cries of the fallen echoing across the blood-soaked plains. Cú Chulainn, though battered and weary, still stood defiant, his spear gripped tightly in his hand. He had faced countless waves of enemies, each more determined than the last, but his resolve had never wavered. Yet his enemies, knowing they could not defeat him through sheer strength, turned to deceit.

A shadowy figure emerged from the ranks of Connacht's army—a druid, cloaked in gray, chanting under his breath. He carried with him a gae bolga (gay bowl-guh), a barbed spear said to be imbued with dark magic, a weapon meant for a single purpose: to bring down the Hound of Ulster. Hidden among the enemy ranks, the druid raised his voice, weaving spells into the wind that carried toward Cú Chulainn. They were not spells of strength but whispers of doubt, illusions meant to distract and disorient.

For the first time, Cú Chulainn faltered. His vision blurred, and the ground beneath his feet seemed to shift. He saw shapes in the distance—faces of those he had loved and lost, Emer (Em-er), his beloved wife, among them. A voice, soft and haunting, called his name. "Sétanta," it whispered, using the name of his youth. For a brief moment, he turned his head, and in that instant, the enemy struck.

The barbed spear found its mark, piercing his side with a sickening thud. Pain, sharp and searing, radiated through his body as the weapon lodged deep within him. Cú Chulainn staggered but did not fall. He gritted his teeth, blood dripping from his lips as he turned to face his attackers. Even wounded, even bleeding, he fought back with the fury of a storm, cutting down those who dared approach him.

But the wound was mortal, and he knew it. His strength ebbed with every passing moment, his vision dimming. Yet the Hound of Ulster would not die on his knees. Summoning the last of his strength, he dragged himself to a standing stone that jutted from the earth nearby. With shaking hands, he unfastened his belt and tied himself to the stone, his legs barely holding him upright.

There he stood, defiant to the end. His enemies circled warily, their weapons drawn, but none dared approach. To them, he was no longer just a man but a force of nature, a legend that refused to fade. The sun dipped below the horizon, casting the battlefield in shadow. The men of Connacht whispered among themselves, glancing at one another with unease.

It was only when a raven descended, landing on Cú Chulainn's shoulder, that they dared to move closer. The bird's black eyes gleamed, a silent signal that the Hound of Ulster had breathed his last. Even in death, he stood tall, his body tied to the stone, his head bowed but unbroken.

As the warriors of Connacht approached, they felt not triumph but a deep and lingering respect. They had defeated a man, but they had faced a legend. One by one, they lowered their weapons, their voices hushed in reverence. The Hound of Ulster, the greatest champion Ireland had ever known, had fallen—but his spirit would never die.

The field grew silent as the warriors departed, leaving the lone figure standing against the backdrop of the darkening sky. Cú Chulainn's sacrifice had saved Ulster, but at a cost that echoed far beyond the battlefield. His death marked the end of an era, but his name would live on, carried in the songs of bards and the hearts of those who revered him.

The news of Cú Chulainn's death spread quickly through Ulster, carried by messengers with heavy hearts and weary steps. The Hound of Ulster was gone. In the halls of Emain Macha (Eh-mawn Mah-kha), the seat of Ulster's power, a deep and profound grief took hold. The warriors who had fought beside him wept openly, their pride and stoicism breaking under the weight of their loss. Women keened in sorrow, their mournful cries echoing across the hills, while druids lit sacred fires to honor his passing.

The people of Ulster felt more than just the loss of their champion; they felt the end of an era. Cú Chulainn had been more than a warrior—he had been a symbol of their strength, their defiance, and their unyielding spirit. Without him, the province seemed smaller, its future uncertain. Yet, even in their grief, the people began to weave stories of his life, ensuring that his deeds would not be forgotten.

Bards took up their harps, composing songs that celebrated his courage and mourned his sacrifice. Around hearths and in great halls, they recounted the tales of Cú Chulainn's youth, his legendary battles, and his unwavering loyalty to Ulster. They spoke of the warp-spasm that made him invincible, the single-handed defense of the province, and the tragic nobility of his final stand. In their verses, he became larger than life, a figure whose bravery could inspire generations to come.

The land itself seemed to remember him. The standing stone where he had tied himself remained a solemn monument, a place of pilgrimage for those who sought to honor his memory. Travelers whispered of ravens that lingered there, as if watching over the spirit of the fallen hero. The rivers and hills of Ulster, once soaked with his blood, became imbued with his presence, a silent testament to his love for the land he had given everything to protect.

As time passed, Cú Chulainn's legacy grew, his name becoming synonymous with the ideals of the warrior. His life and death embodied loyalty, courage, and the willingness to sacrifice for a greater cause. For the people of Ireland, he was not just a hero but a symbol of their enduring spirit. His story, rooted in the Ulster Cycle, became one of the cornerstones of Irish mythology, a tale of triumph and tragedy that resonated across centuries.

Parents told their children of the Hound of Ulster, his name spoken with reverence and pride. Warriors invoked his memory before going into battle, seeking to channel even a fraction of his strength. Even in times of peace, his story served as a reminder of what it meant to stand for one's homeland, one's people, and one's honor.

In the end, Cú Chulainn was more than a man, more than a legend. He was Ireland itself—fierce, resilient, and unyielding in the face of adversity. His death, though tragic, ensured that his spirit would live on, carried in the hearts of those who called Éire their home. And so, the Hound of Ulster, tied to his standing stone in defiance of death, stood eternal in the memories and stories of a people who would never forget.

Sin é

Cú Chulainn (Coo Hull-un) embodies the Irish ideals of loyalty and sacrifice, values deeply ingrained in the culture of ancient Éire (Ay-rah). His unwavering dedication to Ulster and its people drives him to face overwhelming challenges, even when he knows the outcome will lead to his death. This sense of loyalty extends beyond his land to the broader concept of clann (klawn), or kinship, which was central to Irish society. Cú Chulainn's story reflects the belief that personal sacrifice is not only noble but necessary to protect one's community and uphold honor, no matter the cost. His choices resonated with the cultural emphasis on selflessness as a heroic virtue, a legacy that endures in Irish storytelling.

The role of fate (cinniúint, kin-yoo-int) in Cú Chulainn's life underscores a key theme in Irish mythology: the tension between human agency and predestined outcomes. From birth, his path is shaped by prophecy, and his heroic deeds are shadowed by the inevitability of his demise. His adherence to the geis, or the taboo, that seals his fate reflects the deep respect for these sacred laws in Irish culture, even when they conflict with survival. This tragic inevitability mirrors the belief that fate cannot be escaped, a recurring motif in Irish lore that lends a poignant, bittersweet quality to the stories of its heroes.

Cú Chulainn's death marks the emotional and narrative climax of the Ulster Cycle. It encapsulates its central themes of heroism, loyalty, and loss. His fall represents the end of an era, as the greatest champion of Ulster was vanquished, it left the kingdom vulnerable. Yet, his story endures as a testament to the resilience of the human spirit and the enduring value of courage in the face of insurmountable odds. Through his sacrifice, Cú Chulainn becomes more than a hero; he becomes a symbol of the virtues that define Irish cultural identity, ensuring his legacy lives on in the hearts and stories of Éire.

CHAPTER 17

THE SECRET KING

In the land of Éire, where the rolling hills of green met the endless blue of the sky, there ruled a king unlike any other. Labhraidh Loingseach (Lahv-reeh Ling-shock), whose name meant "Labra the Voyager," was celebrated across his kingdom for his wisdom and fairness. Under his rule, the people of his court flourished, and tales of his just decisions spread far and wide. Yet, beneath the golden crown that adorned his noble head, the king held a secret so strange, so carefully hidden, that even his closest advisors dared not speak of it.

Beneath the ornate crown, which never left his head, King Labhraidh hid a pair of donkey's ears.

The truth of his condition was known only to the king and to the barbers who trimmed his hair—once. Every year, a new barber was summoned to the palace to perform this task, and every year, that barber mysteriously disappeared. Whispers crept through the kingdom like ivy climbing a crumbling wall. The people speculated about the fate of these unlucky barbers, but none dared to voice their fears too loudly, for Labhraidh was not a king to be crossed.

The court, too, was uneasy. Ministers and advisors noticed the king's peculiar habits, the way he adjusted his crown with an almost obsessive regularity, or how his gaze would linger just a moment too long when someone mentioned his appearance. Yet no one dared question him. After all, he was Labhraidh Loingseach, the wise and just. What harm could there be in his quirks?

But the king's secret weighed heavily on him. Though he ruled with a steady hand, the knowledge of his deformity gnawed at the edges of his mind. He feared ridicule, the loss of respect, and, most of all, the betrayal of his people's trust. So, year after year, he clung to his secret, trusting no one with the truth.

Yet secrets, as all stories will tell, have a way of escaping. And Labhraidh's secret was no different.

In the court, tension grew. Rumors began to spread among the servants and villagers: "Why does the king need a new barber every year?" "What happens to those who trim his hair?" The questions hung in the air, unanswered but insistent, a quiet rebellion against the silence that the king had imposed.

On a quiet morning, as Labhraidh sat in his chamber and gazed into a polished mirror, the weight of his secret felt heavier than ever. The crown that hid his ears now seemed like a shackle, and the whispers from his people felt like distant waves crashing against the fortress of his mind. He knew, deep down, that the truth would not stay buried forever. The winds of Éire carried whispers, and soon enough, they would roar.

Thus began the tale of Labhraidh Loingseach and the truth he could no longer hide—a story of humor, humility, and the unexpected freedom that comes with embracing oneself.

Each year, when the blossoms of spring painted the hills of Éire (Ay-rah) in vibrant colors, King Labhraidh Loingseach (Lahv-reeh Ling-shock) performed a solemn and secretive ritual. A messenger would ride out into the villages surrounding the court, seeking a barber—just one—for the most prestigious task of the year: trimming the king's hair. The promise of gold and favor was irresistible, but the villagers spoke of the task in hushed tones, for they knew the price of accepting the king's summons. No barber who had entered the palace had ever returned.

The chosen barber would be brought before the king, their tools gleaming in the light of the grand hall. They would kneel as Labhraidh's steely gaze fixed upon them, and the terms of their service were made clear: they were to swear an oath of secrecy, binding them to silence about what they would see beneath the king's crown. But what good was an oath to those who vanished before they could even think of breaking it?

In the village of Glenvar, a young barber named Donal received the summons. His family had fallen on hard times, and the gold promised for his service could lift them from their struggles. Yet, as the messenger handed him the king's decree, Donal's stomach churned with dread. He had heard the whispers. He had seen the solemn expressions of the townsfolk whenever the subject of the king's barbers arose.

Still, he had no choice. His mother needed medicine, his siblings needed food, and the weight of their survival rested on his shoulders. With trembling hands, Donal packed his tools and made the journey to the palace, his heart heavy with fear but resolute in his decision.

The court was more magnificent than Donal had imagined. Marble floors gleamed under his feet, and tapestries of rich emerald and gold adorned the walls. But the opulence did little to ease his nerves. As he was led into the king's private chamber, he felt the air grow heavy, and the murmurs of servants fell silent.

King Labhraidh sat upon an intricately carved throne, his crown gleaming as it caught the morning light. He was an imposing figure, his piercing eyes betraying no emotion. "You are Donal," he said, his voice steady and commanding. "Do you understand the oath you are about to swear?"

Donal nodded, his throat dry. The king's guards stood at attention, their hands resting on the hilts of their swords, a silent reminder of the stakes. With a wavering voice, Donal recited the oath, promising on his life that he would reveal nothing of what he saw that day.

As Donal set to work, the tension in the room was palpable. With each snip of his scissors, he felt as though he were peeling back layers of a mystery too great to comprehend. And then, as the crown was lifted from the king's head, Donal saw them: a pair of donkey's ears, pointed and unmistakable.

Shock coursed through his body, but he kept his expression neutral, his hands steady. The king watched him carefully, his eyes sharp, searching for any hint of ridicule or disdain. Donal finished the haircut in silence, his mind racing with questions he dared not ask.

When the task was complete, the king leaned forward, his voice low and deliberate. "You will leave this chamber with your life," Labhraidh said. "But only if your silence remains eternal. Should you speak of what you have seen, you will pay the price."

Donal nodded fervently, bowing as he gathered his tools. Relief washed over him as the guards escorted him from the chamber, but the weight of the king's secret was a heavy burden on his soul. For the first time, he understood the curse that hung over those who dared to wield a barber's scissors in the service of the King with Donkey's Ears.

The gold Donal received for his service glimmered brightly in the humble cottage he called home, but it did little to ease the shadows that hung over him. The secret of the king's donkey ears weighed heavily on his mind, a burden that seemed to grow heavier with each passing day. At first, he tried to focus on his work, trimming the hair of villagers and merchants, but his hands would tremble, and his eyes would dart around the room as if searching for eavesdroppers.

Donal became withdrawn. His cheerful banter with customers faded into awkward silences, and his laughter, once frequent and hearty, disappeared entirely. People began to notice. "What's wrong with Donal?" they whispered among themselves. "He looks as if he's seen a ghost." They asked him outright, but Donal only shook his head and forced a tight-lipped smile. To speak, to even hint at what he had seen beneath the king's crown, would mean his life.

At night, Donal found no peace. He would wake from restless sleep, drenched in sweat, the king's stern warning echoing in his mind: "Your silence must remain eternal." Even when he was alone, he felt as though unseen eyes were watching him, judging him. The secret became a living thing, gnawing at his thoughts and robbing him of rest. Every time a friend or neighbor asked him why he seemed so troubled, he had to fight the urge to blurt out the truth, just to be free of it.

The villagers noticed his pale complexion and the way he avoided their gazes. Even Donal's family began to worry. His mother pressed him for answers one evening as they sat by the fire. "Donal, my son, what is it that weighs on you so heavily? You've returned from the palace with gold, yet you seem poorer in spirit than before you left."

"I'm fine, Mother," Donal said, his voice hollow. But the truth pressed against his lips, threatening to escape. He excused himself and stumbled out into the cool night air, clutching his chest as though he could physically hold the secret inside him.

Unbeknownst to Donal, King Labhraidh had been observing him from afar. Word of the young barber's troubled demeanor had reached the court, and the king, who was no stranger to the weight of secrets, began to feel the first pangs of guilt. Labhraidh summoned Donal to the palace once more. When Donal entered the chamber, his face was drawn, his shoulders slumped. He looked more like a condemned man than one who had been rewarded by the king.

"You are struggling," Labhraidh said, his tone surprisingly gentle. "The secret I have placed upon you is a heavy one, and I see that it has taken its toll."

Donal's eyes widened. He bowed his head. "My king, I would never betray your trust. But... I feel as though the weight of it will break me."

For a long moment, Labhraidh was silent. Then, with a sigh, he rose from his throne and placed a hand on Donal's shoulder. "I have made many mistakes," he said. "Perhaps the greatest is believing that the fear of death could ensure silence. I see now that fear can crush a man's spirit, and I would not have you suffer any longer."

Labhraidh took a deep breath. "You may keep your life, Donal. But you must promise me this: find a way to lighten your burden without revealing my secret to others."

Donal looked up, his eyes brimming with relief and gratitude. He nodded, his voice steady for the first time in weeks. "I swear it, my king."

As Donal left the palace, a flicker of hope ignited in his heart. The secret was still his to bear, but he no longer feared for his life. And though the burden remained heavy, he resolved to find a way to carry it without breaking. For the first time since that fateful haircut, he dared to believe that peace might yet be within his reach.

The days passed, and though King Labhraidh's pardon had spared Donal's life, the barber still felt the unbearable weight of the secret gnawing at his soul. No amount of gold could lift the burden, and he feared that one day, the truth would spill out despite his efforts to hold it in. He avoided people entirely, taking his meals alone and declining even his closest friends' invitations to gather. The isolation only deepened his torment.

One evening, as the sun dipped low and bathed the fields in golden light, Donal made his way to a nearby grove, desperate for solitude and answers. It was there he encountered an old druid, his robes tattered but his eyes sharp with wisdom. The druid regarded Donal with a curious expression, as if he could see the turmoil raging within the young man.

"You carry a great weight," the druid said, his voice calm and knowing. "It clings to you like a shadow. Tell me, what troubles your heart?"

Donal hesitated, his hands trembling. "I cannot say it aloud," he replied. "To speak the truth would be my doom."

The druid's gaze softened. "Then do not speak it to men. Speak it to the earth. Dig a hole in the ground, whisper your secret into it, and bury it there. The earth is a patient keeper of truths, and it will not betray you."

That night, under the pale light of the moon, Donal took a spade and made his way to a quiet field far from the village. He dug a small hole, his heart pounding as he knelt before it. The cool night air wrapped around him, and for a moment, he hesitated. But the thought of relief pushed him forward.

He leaned close to the hole and whispered, as softly as the rustling of leaves, "The king has donkey's ears."

The words spilled out, and with them came a wave of release. Donal felt as though a weight had been lifted from his chest. He quickly covered the hole with soil, patting it down with trembling hands. For the first time in weeks, he felt calm. The secret was no longer his alone—it had been given to the earth, and he believed it was safe there.

But the earth is a strange keeper of secrets, and its ways are not always silent. From the spot where Donal buried his confession, a cluster of reeds began to grow, tall and green, swaying gently in the breeze. Weeks passed, and as the wind played through the reeds, they began to sing a haunting melody. To the ears of passersby, it was not just a song but a message: "The king has donkey's ears."

At first, the villagers thought it was a trick of the wind. But as the reeds continued to sing the same words, their curiosity grew. Crowds gathered near the field, whispering and murmuring. The message spread from one person to another until it reached the court itself.

"The reeds speak of the king," the villagers said. "They know his secret."

When word of the singing reeds reached King Labhraidh, his fury was swift. He summoned his guards and demanded to know how the secret had escaped. "Find the one who betrayed me," he commanded, his voice echoing through the grand hall.

Donal, upon hearing the news, felt his heart sink. He had done as the druid suggested, and still, the secret had found its way into the world. He feared that his life, once spared, might now be forfeit. Yet, deep within him, he knew that the truth was no longer his to keep. The winds had carried it far beyond his reach, and there was no calling it back.

Thus, the stage was set for King Labhraidh to confront not just his people, but the truth he had worked so hard to conceal. And as the reeds sang their unyielding song, the kingdom held its breath, waiting for the king's response.

The court was alive with whispers. News of the reeds' strange song had reached every corner of the kingdom, and now the courtiers buzzed with anticipation, their curiosity burning brighter than their fear of the king. Rumors flew faster than sparrows in a storm. Some laughed, finding humor in the tale of their mighty ruler hiding such an odd secret. Others whispered cautiously, wondering how King Labhraidh Loingseach (Lahv-reeh Ling-shock) would react to the revelation.

In the great hall, Labhraidh's fury simmered as he sat upon his throne, his crown seeming heavier than ever before. "Bring the barber to me," he commanded, his voice low and dangerous. The guards hesitated—word of the reeds had already reached their ears. They, too, wondered if the secret had truly been betrayed or if something greater was at work.

When Donal was brought before the king, his knees buckled under the weight of his fear. He fell to the cold marble floor, trembling, unable to meet the king's gaze. "My lord," Donal stammered, "I swore I would not speak your secret, and I have kept my oath. I told no soul. It was the earth—it carries voices we do not understand."

Labhraidh glared at the young barber, his anger like a storm cloud threatening to burst. Yet, as he looked down at Donal, so frail and sincere, something within him began to shift. The king's gaze softened as he realized the futility of his rage. The truth was out— not by betrayal, but by the whims of nature itself. Could he truly fault Donal for what the earth had sung to the wind?

The next morning, the court was summoned to the grand hall.

Nobles, advisors, servants, and villagers packed into the space, their faces tense with expectation. At the head of the hall sat Labhraidh, his crown glinting in the sunlight that streamed through the tall windows. He rose slowly, commanding silence without a single word.

"My people," Labhraidh began, his voice steady but heavy with emotion, "you have heard the reeds. You have heard the truth they carry. For many years, I have hidden something from you, fearing your judgment, fearing your laughter. But today, I will hide no longer."

The room fell deathly quiet as Labhraidh reached up and removed his crown. Gasps rippled through the crowd as the king revealed his donkey's ears, tall and unmistakable. His hands trembled as he placed the crown on the throne beside him, exposing his greatest vulnerability to all who stood before him.

"I was born with these ears," Labhraidh said. "I have spent my life ashamed of them, believing they made me unworthy of your respect, your love, your trust. But I see now that my fear was my own burden to bear—and that burden is mine no longer."

For a moment, the hall remained silent, the weight of the revelation hanging heavy in the air. Then, to Labhraidh's surprise, a ripple of laughter broke through the crowd. But it was not cruel or mocking. It was light, warm, and full of relief. One of the courtiers stepped forward and bowed deeply. "My king," he said with a smile, "you have always been a fair and just ruler. Why should a pair of ears change that?"

Another voice joined in. "If anything, it suits you, my lord. After all, it takes a wise ear to hear the needs of a kingdom." Laughter filled the hall, and Labhraidh felt the weight he had carried for so long begin to lift. For the first time, he allowed himself to smile.

From that day forward, King Labhraidh wore his crown lightly, no longer using it to hide. The people of Éire (Ay-rah) embraced him for who he was, his ears becoming a symbol of his humanity rather than his shame. The reeds, now silent, stood tall in the field as a reminder of the king's journey—a journey from fear to acceptance, and from secrecy to truth.

In the days following King Labhraidh's revelation, the people of his court, and indeed all of Éire, began to view their ruler with newfound admiration. The once-murmured whispers about his mysterious behavior transformed into stories shared around hearths and firesides. But these stories carried a new tone: they were not tales of fear or mockery but of wisdom and redemption.

Sin é

King Labhraidh's journey from shame to acceptance became a lesson for all who heard it. The king, once consumed by the need to hide his ears, had learned that truth, though daunting, was far less a burden than the secrecy that had weighed upon him for years. His donkey's ears, a source of personal anguish, became a symbol of humility and courage.

The humor woven into Labhraidh's tale gave it a special place in Irish lore. Unlike the tragic fates of warriors like Cú Chulainn or the somber lessons of Macha's curse, Labhraidh's story balanced its emotional depth with lightness. The singing reeds and the king's vulnerability invited laughter not at Labhraidh's expense but at the shared human experience of insecurity. It reminded the people that even a king could falter and that dignity was not in perfection but in the grace of embracing one's own imperfections.

Irish storytelling, with its deep well of tragedy and heroism, often turned to humor as a salve for the wounds of hardship. Tales like Labhraidh's showed the resilience of the Irish spirit—a willingness to laugh in the face of life's trials, to find joy even in vulnerability, and to cherish the lessons of humility and honesty.

For generations, the story of King Labhraidh Loingseach was told and retold. Children giggled at the idea of a king with donkey's ears, while adults found solace in the deeper meaning of his journey. Farmers and villagers often visited the field where the reeds once sang, running their fingers over the tall grasses and marveling at the idea that nature itself had carried the truth into the world.

In time, Labhraidh's tale became a parable of acceptance. It taught that to hide one's flaws was to give them power, but to reveal them was to take that power back. It celebrated the strength found in honesty, the resilience of the human spirit, and the healing balm of humor. And in every court, village, and cottage across the land, it reminded the people of Éire that even the most formidable rulers are, at heart, only human.

CHAPTER 18

OISÍN IN TÍR NA NÓG

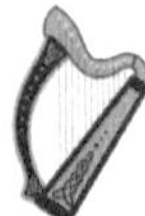

The sun hung low in the sky, casting a golden light over the rolling green hills of Éire, where the Fianna (Fee-ah-nah) rode in pursuit of deer through the dense, shadowy woods. Among them was Oisín (Uh-sheen), son of the legendary Fionn MacCumhaill (Fee-uhn Mac-Coo-ill). Known as a great poet and warrior, Oisín was as swift with his words as he was with his sword, embodying the strength and heart of his father's renowned band of heroes.

As the Fianna rested by a crystal-clear stream, their laughter echoing through the trees, a strange silence suddenly fell over the land. Birds ceased their songs, and even the gentle rustling of the leaves seemed to pause. From the distant horizon, a figure appeared, riding atop a white horse that seemed to glide over the earth without disturbing it.

The woman was radiant, her hair a cascade of gold that shimmered in the light. Her gown sparkled like the sea, and her eyes held the depth of countless lifetimes. She was Niamh (Nee-uv), daughter of the king of Tír na nÓg (Teer-na Nohg), the land of eternal youth.

As she approached, the Fianna stood frozen in awe, their hands instinctively gripping their weapons, though none dared raise them. Niamh's voice, soft yet commanding, broke the stillness. "I have traveled far, seeking the one called Oisín, son of Fionn," she said, her gaze settling on him. "Come with me to Tír na nÓg, where no sorrow touches the heart, and no time withers the soul."

Oisín stepped forward, captivated by her beauty and the promise of adventure. "Lady, I am honored by your invitation, but my place is here, among the Fianna," he said, though his words faltered under the weight of her enchanting presence.

Niamh smiled, her eyes glimmering with a mixture of warmth and mystery. "Oisín, you have been chosen not by me alone, but by the fate woven into your very being. Tír na nÓg awaits you, a realm where the burdens of this world cannot follow. Come with me, and I shall show you wonders beyond imagination."

The Fianna murmured amongst themselves, some urging Oisín to stay, others marveling at the prospect of the Otherworld. Fionn himself stepped forward, his brow furrowed with concern. "My son," he said, his voice steady but heavy with emotion, "you must follow your heart, but know that the path you choose may not allow you to return."

Oisín looked to his father and his comrades, then back to Niamh. The pull of the Otherworld was too strong to resist. With a solemn nod, he embraced his father and bid farewell to the Fianna, who stood in silence as he mounted Niamh's white horse. The creature's hooves, light as air, carried them swiftly across the land toward the distant horizon.

As the Fianna watched their companion disappear, the air stirred again with life, but their hearts were heavy. Oisín was no longer of their world. His journey into the unknown had begun.

The white horse moved as if it were weightless, its hooves skimming the waves as though they were solid ground. Beneath them, the sea shimmered like molten silver, reflecting the endless expanse of a twilight sky. Oisín (Uh-sheen) clung tightly to Niamh (Nee-uv), his mind torn between the wonder of the journey and the faint ache of leaving Éire behind.

As the shores of Ireland grew distant, Oisín turned his head for one last look at his homeland. The green hills and familiar woods he had roamed with the Fianna (Fee-ah-nah) seemed to glow in the fading light. A pang of sadness gripped him, but it was softened by Niamh's voice. "Do not grieve for what you leave behind," she said gently, as if sensing his thoughts. "Ahead lies a realm where joy knows no end and time itself bends to our will."

The journey was unlike anything Oisín had ever known. The sea stretched endlessly, its colors shifting from silver to sapphire and back again. The air was filled with a soft, melodic hum, as though the very waves were singing. They passed islands where eternal spring reigned: trees heavy with golden fruit, blossoms glowing softly in the twilight, and rivers that sparkled like diamonds. On one such island, Oisín glimpsed deer as white as snow grazing peacefully beside shimmering pools. Their eyes met his briefly, and he felt a curious sense of calm.

But the voyage was not without peril. At one point, the waters darkened, and the gentle hum of the sea turned to a low, menacing rumble. From the depths emerged a creature of legend—a sea serpent, its scales gleaming like obsidian and its eyes burning with otherworldly fire. It coiled around their path, barring their way with a hiss that shook the air.

Oisín leapt from the horse's back, his hand instinctively gripping his sword. Niamh's voice rang out, calm but firm. "This is a test, Oisín. Tír na nÓg (Teer-na Nohg) will not yield to the faint of heart."

With a steady resolve, Oisín faced the beast. The serpent lunged, but Oisín's movements were swift and precise. His sword flashed in the dim light, striking true as he evaded the creature's jaws. With a final, piercing cry, the serpent sank back into the depths, leaving the waters calm once more.

Niamh smiled, her gaze warm with approval. "You are as brave as the stories say," she said. "Tír na nÓg will welcome such courage."

As they continued, the air grew softer, imbued with the scent of flowers and the sound of distant harps. The horizon ahead seemed to shimmer, as though the sea itself were giving way to something entirely new. Niamh turned to Oisín, her voice filled with quiet pride. "We are near now. This is Tír na nÓg (Teer-na Nohg), the land of eternal youth, where no shadow can darken your heart, and no sorrow can touch your soul."

Oisín's heart quickened as the mist parted, revealing a land unlike any he had ever imagined—a place of golden light, endless beauty, and the promise of a timeless joy. The journey was complete, and yet it felt as though it had only just begun.

Tír na nÓg, the land of eternal youth, unfolded before Oisín (Uh-sheen) like a dream made real. Rolling green hills stretched endlessly beneath a sky painted with golden hues, as though the sun and stars had agreed to share their light. Palaces of shimmering crystal and gold rose from the earth, their towers reaching gracefully toward the heavens. Rivers sparkled with waters as clear as glass, winding through fields of eternal bloom where flowers swayed gently to a melody carried on the wind.

Oisín and Niamh (Nee-uv) moved through this paradise as if they had always belonged. Their days were filled with feasts in grand halls, where music from harps and flutes created an atmosphere of endless celebration. The air itself seemed lighter, imbued with a magic that made every step effortless and every breath refreshing. Time stood still, and no shadow of sorrow or age touched their lives.

In this otherworldly realm, Oisín's mortal worries melted away. He hunted alongside Niamh, chasing otherworldly beasts that vanished into puffs of golden mist when caught. He learned to tame magical creatures with a mere whisper and participated in contests of skill and strength that defied the laws of the mortal world. Yet for all its wonders, Tír na nÓg's beauty carried a strange stillness, as if the land itself existed in a perpetual dream.

One evening, while wandering the verdant hills alone, Oisín heard a haunting melody carried on the breeze. It was a song unlike any he had heard in Tír na nÓg, with notes that stirred memories of Ireland—its forests, its laughter, and the voices of the Fianna (Fee-ah-nah). He closed his eyes and saw his father, Fionn MacCumhaill (Fee-uhn Mac-Coo-ill), standing by the fire, recounting tales of their adventures. The vision filled Oisín with a bittersweet longing that he could not shake.

Though Niamh noticed the change in Oisín, she said nothing at first, hoping that the beauty of their shared life would soothe his restless heart. But Oisín could not hide his growing unease. As much as he loved Niamh and the paradise they shared, the pull of Éire, his homeland, grew stronger with each passing day. He longed to see the green hills of Ireland once more, to hear the voices of his companions, and to know what had become of the Fianna.

One night, as they sat by a stream that shimmered with colors of the rainbow, Oisín spoke at last. "Niamh," he said, his voice heavy with emotion, "this land is everything one could dream of, and my heart is full with the love we share. But I cannot shake the longing to see my father, my friends, my home. Allow me to return to Ireland, even if only for a short while."

Niamh's face clouded with worry. "Oisín," she said softly, "you do not understand the passage of time in Tír na nÓg. Though it feels as if only days have passed, many years may have gone by in your world. If you must go, promise me this: do not set foot on the soil of Ireland. Stay upon your horse, for to touch the earth is to be bound by it once more."

Oisín nodded, unaware of the gravity of her words. The longing in his heart overpowered any caution. He promised to heed her warning, yet a shadow seemed to pass over Niamh's radiant features as she prepared to send him back. With a kiss that lingered like the memory of a dream, she bid him farewell. Oisín mounted the white horse once more, setting his eyes on the horizon where Ireland awaited, unaware of the trials that lay ahead.

Oisín rode the white horse across the waves, the sea parting before them as if in deference to the power of Tír na nÓg (Teer-na Nohg). Niamh's words echoed in his mind: "Do not set foot on the soil of Ireland." He held the reins tightly, his heart a blend of excitement and unease. As the outline of Éire (Ay-rah) appeared on the horizon, a rush of longing overtook him, the green hills and distant cliffs stirring memories of home.

But as the horse carried him onto Ireland's shores, Oisín felt an unfamiliar chill in the air. The land seemed quieter, subdued, as if it no longer bore the spirit of the Fianna (Fee-ah-nah). He rode through forests where he had once hunted with his father, Fionn MacCumhaill (Fee-uhn Mac-Coo-ill), but the trees now stood taller and denser, untouched by the hands of men. The paths were overgrown, the sounds of laughter and song replaced by an eerie stillness.

Oisín's first destination was the great stronghold where the Fianna had gathered in days of old. He remembered it as a place of celebration, its halls alive with the clash of swords, the telling of tales, and the warmth of camaraderie. But when he arrived, his heart sank. The stronghold was no more—its walls had crumbled, overtaken by moss and ivy. Only ruins remained, silent witnesses to the passage of time.

He called out, his voice ringing with desperation. "Fionn! Oscar! Conán! Is there no one left who remembers the Fianna?"

Only the wind answered, carrying the faint rustle of leaves. Oisín's chest tightened as he dismounted briefly to examine the ruins, careful to step only on the stone foundation. Each step deepened his sorrow, for he knew now that the world he had left behind was gone.

As he rode into a nearby village, his presence caused a stir. Children pointed in awe, and elders murmured among themselves. Oisín asked after Fionn and the Fianna, but the villagers stared at him in disbelief. "The Fianna?" an old man said, shaking his head. "You speak of legends, stranger. They lived long before our time."

Another elder stepped forward, his eyes narrowing as he regarded Oisín. "You look like the paintings of Oisín, son of Fionn," he said cautiously. "But that cannot be. He vanished into the mists of Tír na nÓg centuries ago."

The words struck Oisín like a blow. *Centuries.* It was true—his time in Tír na nÓg, though it had felt brief, had spanned ages in Ireland. The faces of the villagers, their strange accents and mannerisms, all confirmed what he dreaded. The world he knew had moved on without him. He was no longer a part of it.

One of the villagers approached cautiously, offering Oisín bread and water. "Your name is still spoken, warrior," she said kindly. "The tales of the Fianna inspire us, even now. But they are only stories to us—fables of a time long past."

Oisín nodded numbly, his appetite gone. As he mounted the horse once more, the weight of loss pressed heavily on him. He was a stranger in his own land, a living relic of a bygone era. The joy of seeing Ireland again was overshadowed by the realization that he was alone, his companions and kin gone, their voices reduced to echoes in the annals of legend.

Yet even in his sorrow, Oisín felt a duty to understand the Ireland that had risen in the place of his own. He resolved to ride further, to see what had become of the land he once called home, clinging to the faint hope that he might yet find some trace of the Fianna's spirit.

The sun hung low in the sky as Oisín rode through a quiet valley, its hills dotted with small clusters of villagers working in the fields. His heart still ached for the Ireland he had known, but the sight of these people, toiling with purpose, stirred something within him—a faint connection to the spirit of his homeland.

As he passed, a group of men caught his attention. They were struggling to move a massive stone, their faces red with effort and their voices rising in frustration. Oisín halted his horse and called out, "What burdens you so, my friends?"

The men looked up, startled by the warrior astride the magnificent white steed. One of them, an older man with trembling hands, stepped forward. "It's this cursed stone," he said, panting. "We need it moved to complete the wall, but none of us has the strength."

Oisín's gaze fell on the stone, and a flicker of the old warrior pride stirred within him. Though his heart was heavy, his body still carried the strength of Tír na nÓg (Teer-na Nohg). "Step aside," he said. "I will move it for you."

The villagers murmured among themselves, uncertain but hopeful. Oisín grasped the stone, his muscles rippling with the supernatural strength that had once made him a hero of the Fianna (Fee-ah-nah). Slowly, he lifted the stone, his knees bending under its weight.

But as he shifted his grip, Oisín leaned too far. His foot slipped, and before he could catch himself, he fell from the horse. The moment his body touched the earth of Ireland, the spell of eternal youth shattered.

A gasp rippled through the crowd as the transformation began. Oisín's youthful form withered before their eyes. His broad shoulders stooped, his skin wrinkled, and his dark hair turned white as snow. His eyes, once sharp and full of fire, now carried the weight of centuries.

The villagers rushed to his side, their awe mingled with pity. "What sorcery is this?" one whispered. Another knelt beside Oisín, her voice trembling with concern. "Are you well, stranger? What has happened to you?"

Oisín, now frail and weathered, looked up at them with a weak smile. "I am Oisín, son of Fionn MacCumhaill (Fee-uhn Mac-Coo-ill)," he said, his voice rasping with age. "I have returned from Tír na nÓg, the land of eternal youth, to find the Ireland I loved long gone."

The villagers exchanged astonished glances. Many had heard the tales of the Fianna but had never imagined they might meet one of its heroes. They carried Oisín to a nearby hut, where they laid him gently on a bed of straw and brought him water.

As the sun set, Oisín began to recount his story. He spoke of the Fianna's legendary feats, of his father Fionn's wisdom, and of the bond that had once united them all. He described the wonders of Tír na nÓg and his love for Niamh, whose beauty and kindness still lingered in his memory like a dream.

The villagers listened in rapt silence, their imaginations alight with visions of the past. For them, Oisín's tale was more than a story—it was a bridge to a time of heroes and magic, a glimpse into the Ireland of legend.

As Oisín's voice grew fainter, he gazed out the window at the stars beginning to appear. Though his body was frail, his heart was at peace. "I have lived a life of wonder," he said softly. "Though I grieve for what I have lost, I am grateful for what I have seen."

In the quiet of the night, Oisín closed his eyes for the final time. The villagers sat in solemn respect, vowing to keep his story alive. From that day forward, the tale of Oisín in Tír na nÓg would be told and retold, a reminder of Ireland's heroic past and the eternal pull of home.

The story of Oisín (Uh-sheen) and his journey to Tír na nÓg (Teer-na Nohg) lived on long after his passing, carried by the villagers who had witnessed his final days. Around hearths and in great halls, bards wove his tale into songs and poems, ensuring that his extraordinary life would never be forgotten. Oisín's name became a bridge between the mortal and supernatural worlds, his experiences offering a glimpse into Ireland's deep connection to the Otherworld.

Sin é

Through Oisín's story, listeners found both inspiration and caution. His time in Tír na nÓg symbolized the Irish longing for beauty, immortality, and a heroic past—a realm untouched by sorrow, where the seasons never changed, and happiness seemed eternal. Yet, his return to Ireland revealed the cost of such a dream. The world he had left behind had aged without him, and his reunion with his homeland came at the price of isolation and loss. The tale reminded all who heard it of life's impermanence and the importance of cherishing the present.

For the villagers who had tended to Oisín in his final hours, his story was not merely a legend; it was a legacy they felt compelled to preserve. They spoke of his love for Niamh (Nee-uv), the beauty of Tír na nÓg, and the indomitable spirit of the Fianna, whose deeds now seemed like echoes from a distant age. To them, Oisín was not just a hero—he was a living link to a time when Ireland's hills and forests were filled with warriors, magic, and the music of bards.

One young bard, captivated by Oisín's tale, took it upon himself to spread the story far and wide. With his harp in hand, he traveled across Éire (Ay-rah), singing of the warrior-poet who had ventured to the land of eternal youth and returned with a story that transcended time. His songs stirred the hearts of those who listened, inspiring a renewed pride in Ireland's heritage and the enduring spirit of its people.

As centuries passed, the story of Oisín in Tír na nÓg became one of the most beloved in Irish mythology. It resonated with themes of loyalty, love, and the bittersweet nature of longing. For many, it was a tale of choices—the pull between the mortal world and the allure of the Otherworld, between the comforts of the present and the dreams of what could be.

Even today, Oisín's journey continues to capture the imagination, reminding us that while the Otherworld may promise perfection, it's still in the imperfections of mortal life—the fleeting moments of love, laughter, and connection—that true meaning is found. The legend of Oisín and Tír na nÓg endures, and it's a testament to Ireland's rich mythology and its timeless exploration of the human heart.

CHAPTER 19

STORY OF SAINT BRIGID

In the heart of Kildare (Kill-dahr), a perpetual flame burned brightly, its light reaching beyond the monastery walls to illuminate the lives of all who came near. This was no ordinary fire—it was the sacred flame of Saint Brigid (Bree-gid), a symbol of compassion, faith, and the enduring spirit of Ireland. It burned as a testament to the woman who had become one of the most beloved figures in Irish history, a saint who carried the wisdom of the old ways into the new light of Christianity.

Brigid's life began in a time of change, when the druids still walked the forests, invoking the gods of the land, and Christianity was spreading its message of salvation and love. She was a bridge between these two worlds, embodying the values of both traditions: the generosity and connection to nature that defined Ireland's pagan heritage, and the compassion and humility central to Christian teachings. To the people, Brigid was more than a saint—she was a source of hope, her actions reflecting the best of their shared humanity.

Even as a child, Brigid's kindness and boundless generosity marked her as extraordinary. Born to a nobleman and a slave woman, her life could have been one of privilege or hardship, but she chose a different path entirely. Legends say that as a child, she gave away her family's food and possessions to the poor, her heart so full of love for others that she could not bear to see anyone in need. When reprimanded for her actions, Brigid would only smile and say, "The more we share, the more we have."

Her connection to the divine seemed innate, as though she carried within her a spark of the sacred flame that would later define her life. Her name echoed that of the Celtic goddess Brigid, the goddess of poetry, healing, and fire, whose spirit seemed to live on in the young girl. This connection was no coincidence—it was as though Brigid's life was destined to unite the spiritual traditions of Ireland, blending the reverence for nature with the Christian call to love and service.

As Brigid grew, her reputation for kindness and miraculous acts spread. It was said that she could turn water into ale, multiply food to feed the hungry, and heal the sick with a single touch. But it was not her miracles alone that endeared her to the people—it was her unwavering humility and her dedication to the poor and marginalized. In a world often marked by inequality and suffering, Brigid's light was a beacon of hope.

Her journey led her to Kildare, where she founded a monastery that would become a sanctuary for those in need. Under her care, Kildare flourished, not just as a place of worship but as a center of learning, healing, and compassion. It was here that Brigid's flame was kindled—a fire that would burn for centuries, tended by her followers as a symbol of the divine presence in the world.

The story of Saint Brigid is more than just the tale of a saint; it is a reflection of Ireland's soul. Through her life, we see the beauty of a culture that values hospitality, generosity, and the sacred bond between humanity and the divine. In Brigid's flame, we see the enduring light of a spirit that continues to inspire, reminding us that even in times of great change, compassion and love are the eternal fires that guide us home.

Brigid's story begins in the year 451 AD, in the heart of Ireland. She was born to Dubhthach (Duv-ahk), a powerful nobleman, and Brocca (Bruck-ah), a Pictish slave woman. From the moment of her birth, Brigid's life was marked by divine intervention and extraordinary events. It is said that as an infant, she refused to consume the milk of impurity, drinking only from a cow that was blessed, a sign that her life would be dedicated to the sacred and the pure.

Her mixed lineage—noble and enslaved—made Brigid a child of two worlds. She embodied the humility of the downtrodden and the leadership of the elite, a blend that would shape her destiny. Even as a young girl, her compassion for others was evident. One tale recounts how she gave away her father's sword to a beggar, moved by his need more than the sword's value. Furious, her father confronted her, but Brigid's response, full of conviction and innocence, silenced him: "How could I refuse Christ in disguise?"

Brigid's early life was closely tied to nature. She spent her childhood wandering the green hills and fields, where she felt an innate connection to the land and its creatures. Animals seemed to sense her kindness, and it was said that she could calm even the most restless beasts with a gentle touch. Her generosity extended not only to people but to the world around her, nurturing a bond with the natural world that mirrored Ireland's deep reverence for the land.

Her acts of kindness became legendary. In one story, Brigid was tasked with churning butter for her household. When she finished, she divided the butter into four parts: three for the poor and one for her family. Miraculously, the butter never ran out, no matter how much she gave away. Tales like these spread far and wide, cementing her reputation as a girl destined for greatness, one who seemed to carry the divine spark within her.

What made Brigid's story even more remarkable was her connection to the Celtic goddess Brigid, a figure of immense importance in Ireland's pagan tradition. The goddess Brigid was associated with poetry, healing, and smithcraft, embodying inspiration, creativity, and transformation. These same qualities would come to define Saint Brigid, creating a seamless blend of pagan and Christian traditions. For the Irish people, Saint Brigid became a bridge between two worlds, uniting their ancient beliefs with the new faith spreading across the land.

The parallels were undeniable: just as the goddess Brigid was celebrated at Imbolc (Im-bolk), the festival of spring and renewal, Saint Brigid's feast day, February 1st, marked a time of hope and new beginnings. Through her life and actions, Brigid transformed not only the lives of those she touched but also the cultural and spiritual identity of Ireland.

Brigid's birth and early years laid the foundation for her extraordinary life. From the moment she entered the world, she carried a divine purpose, her every action reflecting the ideals of compassion, generosity, and a deep connection to the sacred. Her story reminds us that greatness is not defined by wealth or status but by the kindness we show and the lives we touch along the way.

As Brigid grew into adulthood, her acts of kindness and compassion blossomed into miracles that would define her ministry. Wherever she went, the poor, the sick, and the forgotten flocked to her, drawn by her reputation as a healer and protector. Her life became a tapestry of extraordinary events, each one reflecting her deep connection to both the divine and the natural world.

One of the most beloved stories tells of a leper who approached Brigid, asking for food. Finding nothing left to give, Brigid removed her cloak and handed it to him, her generosity knowing no bounds. As the leper walked away, the cloak miraculously transformed into a shimmering golden fabric. Tales like these spread across Ireland, cementing her status as a saint in the hearts of the people.

Brigid's miracles extended beyond acts of charity. She was said to have the power to bless the land itself, ensuring bountiful harvests and healthy livestock. In one account, she prayed over a field struck by famine, and the land flourished with crops overnight. In another, she turned water into ale to ensure there was enough for a gathering of monks, a miraculous act that embodied both her practicality and her sense of joy. To those who witnessed her works, it was clear that Brigid carried the divine within her, a reflection of both the Christian God and the enduring spirit of the goddess Brigid.

Her ministry found its heart in Kildare (Kill-dahr), the place where Brigid's legacy would shine brightest. She established a monastery on the site of an ancient pagan shrine dedicated to the goddess Brigid, creating a sanctuary that honored both the old ways and the new faith. At Kildare, Brigid kindled a sacred flame, a fire that would burn perpetually in her honor. The flame, tended by her nuns, symbolized the light of compassion and the enduring presence of the divine in the world.

Under Brigid's guidance, Kildare flourished as a center of learning, spirituality, and compassion. Scholars and pilgrims came from far and wide, seeking her wisdom and the solace of the sacred flame. But Kildare was more than a place of worship—it was a haven for the poor and the needy. Brigid opened the monastery's doors to all who sought help, ensuring that no one was turned away. She transformed the site into a living embodiment of her values, where generosity and kindness were as abundant as the light of the flame.

Despite her growing influence, Brigid remained humble, dedicating her life to those in need. She was often found working alongside her nuns, tending the sick, feeding the hungry, and offering solace to the suffering. To Brigid, every act of kindness was a reflection of divine love, and she lived her life as a servant of that love. Her humility and compassion made her not just a saint but a symbol of hope, inspiring generations to follow her example.

Sin é

Brigid's miracles and ministry encapsulate the heart of her story: a life dedicated to healing, giving, and transforming the world around her. Through her acts, she bridged the gap between the physical and the spiritual, the old and the new, and it left an indelible mark on Ireland and its people. Her flame continues to burn, not just in Kildare but in the hearts of those who carry her legacy of compassion and love.

Brigid's story is unique in Irish tradition, as she stands at the crossroads of pagan and Christian beliefs, embodying the qualities of both saint and goddess. This duality is not a contradiction but a testament to the seamless blending of two spiritual traditions during a pivotal moment in Ireland's history. Saint Brigid inherited the attributes of the Celtic goddess Brigid, creating a figure who resonated deeply with a people navigating the transition from ancient customs to Christian teachings.

The Celtic goddess Brigid was revered as a deity of poetry, healing, and smithcraft—domains of creativity, transformation, and protection. She was also a guardian of fertility and the hearth, her sacred flame symbolizing life's sustaining power. These attributes were woven into the life of Saint Brigid, whose actions reflected the goddess's essence in tangible ways. Just as the goddess Brigid was celebrated at Imbolc (Im-bolk), the festival marking the arrival of spring, Saint Brigid's feast day on February 1st became a celebration of renewal, hope, and light.

Central to both traditions is the symbolism of fire. For the goddess Brigid, fire was a source of inspiration, purification, and divine connection, seen in the flames of the forge and the light of the hearth. For Saint Brigid, fire became a sacred presence, represented by the perpetual flame at Kildare. This flame, tended by her nuns, was a bridge between the pagan reverence for elemental forces and the Christian concept of divine light. It united the physical and spiritual realms, embodying inspiration, warmth, and the eternal presence of the sacred.

Brigid's dual identity reflects the coexistence of pagan and Christian practices in early Ireland. As the island embraced Christianity, it did not abandon its ancestral beliefs but rather wove them into the fabric of the new faith. Brigid's story is a testament to this cultural synthesis. She became a unifying figure, her life embodying values cherished in both traditions: compassion, generosity, and a deep connection to the land and its people.

In her dual role, Brigid served as a mediator between worlds. She brought together the old and the new, the earthly and the divine, offering her people a symbol of continuity during a time of change. Her story reminds us that transformation does not always mean erasure; it can mean adaptation and growth, as traditions evolve to meet the needs of a changing world.

This duality of Brigid—saint and goddess, Christian and pagan—is what makes her one of Ireland's most enduring figures. She is a flame that continues to burn brightly, illuminating a path of compassion, creativity, and unity. Her life is a reflection of Ireland itself, a land where the old and the new find harmony, and where the spirit of renewal and resilience shines through every story.

Saint Brigid's feast day inherited the themes of renewal, fertility, and hope, reflecting the eternal cycle of life and the promise of brighter days after the darkness of winter. This connection between the saint and the goddess is particularly evident in the customs surrounding her feast. One of the most enduring traditions is the weaving of the Brigid's Cross, a simple yet powerful symbol crafted from rushes. Families would hang these crosses above their doors or hearths, believing they would protect their homes from harm and bring blessings for the year ahead. The act of weaving the cross, often accompanied by storytelling and prayers, continues to unite communities, keeping Brigid's spirit alive in both ritual and memory.

Brigid's sacred flame, rekindled in modern times at Kildare, is another testament to her enduring legacy. The flame burns as a symbol of peace, compassion, and unity, qualities that define her story and inspire those who seek to follow her example. Pilgrims from across the world visit Kildare to honor Brigid, drawn by her dual role as a saint and a symbol of Ireland's spiritual heritage.

Her influence extends beyond religious boundaries, as she represents universal values that resonate across cultures. Brigid's compassion for the poor, her generosity, and her ability to bridge divides—whether between pagan and Christian traditions or between the earthly and the divine—make her a timeless figure of hope and renewal. She is not only a saint of the past but a guide for the present, reminding us of the power of kindness and the importance of nurturing both the land and the spirit.

In Ireland and far beyond its shores, Brigid remains a source of inspiration. Her life and legacy embody the resilience and adaptability of Irish culture, where ancient traditions find new life in modern practices. Whether through the soft glow of her sacred flame, the protective power of her cross, or the enduring celebration of her feast day, Saint Brigid continues to light the way, reminding us of the enduring strength of compassion, renewal, and the unity of all things.

Saint Brigid's story emphasizes values of compassion, generosity, and the harmonious blending of traditions. Her life and legacy reflect a profound cultural emphasis on hospitality and care for the less fortunate. In Irish society, these virtues were more than personal qualities; they were essential elements of community life. Brigid's acts of kindness—whether multiplying food for the hungry, healing the sick, or providing shelter to the poor—represent an ideal of selflessness that remains central to Irish identity.

One of the most compelling aspects of Brigid's story is its illustration of the peaceful transition from paganism to Christianity in Ireland. As a figure who embodies traits of both the Celtic goddess Brigid and the Christian saint, she stands as a symbol of continuity during a time of cultural evolution. This blending of traditions is evident in her association with fire, fertility, and renewal—qualities celebrated in both pagan and Christian contexts. By bridging these spiritual worlds, Brigid offers a model of integration rather than division, demonstrating how old beliefs can find new expression within emerging faiths.

Central to Brigid's legacy is the sacred fire, a powerful symbol in both Celtic and Christian traditions. For the Celts, fire represented purification, inspiration, and the sustaining energy of life. Brigid's perpetual flame at Kildare continues this tradition, serving as a beacon of faith and divine presence. It embodies the light of hope, the warmth of compassion, and the enduring power of spiritual connection. In a broader sense, the flame is a reminder of the human spirit's resilience and the enduring strength of cultural heritage.

CHAPTER 20

HARP OF DAGDA

The Dagda (Dahg-dah), the "Good God" of the Tuatha Dé Danann (Too-ah-hah Day Dan-an), was unlike any other figure in Irish mythology. He was a giant of a man, known for his immense strength, boundless wisdom, and an ever-present air of abundance. The Dagda was both a warrior and a guardian; he wielded a club that could kill with one end and restore life with the other, and a cauldron that never ran empty. Yet among all his treasures, it was his harp that stood out as the most extraordinary.

Carved from sacred oak and strung with enchanted silver strings, the harp was more than an instrument—it was a vessel of power. This was no ordinary harp, for it held within it the magic of the natural world. Its melodies could stir joy in the weariest of hearts, bring warriors to tears with sorrow, or lull an entire battlefield into a peaceful sleep. The Dagda's harp was not merely an object; it was an extension of his soul, a symbol of the balance he sought to bring to the world.

The harp rested in the Dagda's hall, a place of gathering for the Tuatha Dé Danann, where its music filled the air with a sense of harmony. But its role went far beyond entertainment. In times of war, its notes could inspire armies, turn the tide of battle, or even bring a temporary truce. In times of peace, it brought solace, uniting the Tuatha Dé Danann in celebration or mourning, as the need arose.

Yet, as powerful as the harp was, it was also coveted. Its magic, tied to the heart of Ireland's mystical heritage, was a source of wonder—and envy. The Dagda, ever vigilant, knew the harp was not just a treasure but a responsibility. To wield it meant to honor the balance between strength and compassion, joy and sorrow, the mortal and the divine.

This is the story of the Dagda and his harp: a tale of music, power, and the unbreakable connection between myth, melody, and the spirit of Ireland.

Long before the Dagda's harp became the stuff of legend, it was forged in the heart of magic itself. Some say it was the Dagda who carved the harp with his own hands, working tirelessly under the light of the moon. Others whisper that it was a gift from the aos sí (ays shee), the mystical beings who dwelled in the Otherworld, bestowed upon the Dagda as a token of trust between the mortal and supernatural realms. Whatever its origins, all agree that the harp was no ordinary creation.

The instrument was carved from the sacred oak of an ancient forest, a tree believed to hold the wisdom of the ages. Its surface gleamed with a rich, dark sheen, etched with intricate runes that shimmered faintly in the light. Each rune represented a force of nature—wind, fire, water, and earth—binding the harp to the natural world and the elemental balance the Dagda sought to maintain. The strings, spun from enchanted silver, were said to hum with their own faint melody, a sound only the Dagda could hear.

The harp's powers were as extraordinary as its craftsmanship. With a single stroke of its strings, the Dagda could summon emotions that ran deeper than words. A triumphant melody could fill warriors with unshakable courage, while a mournful tune could bring tears to even the hardest hearts. And when a soothing lullaby was played, it was said that all who heard it—even armies locked in the heat of battle—would fall into a peaceful slumber. The harp was more than an instrument; it was a living force, a vessel for harmony and transformation.

The harp's magic was not merely for grand displays of power; it also symbolized balance. To the Dagda, it represented the need for joy and sorrow, strength and gentleness, life and death. It was an extension of his role as the "Good God," a figure who nurtured as much as he protected, who celebrated as much as he mourned.

In its beauty and power, the harp became an icon not just of the Dagda but of the Tuatha Dé Danann. It was revered as a symbol of Ireland itself—a land rich in emotion, music, and the unyielding interplay between the mortal and mystical worlds. This harp would soon become the centerpiece of a tale that intertwined battle, loss, and the enduring magic of music.

The harp's powers were not confined to the serenity of courts or the solace of quiet evenings. In times of strife, it became a weapon as formidable as any blade, and its role in the battle against the Fomorians (Foh-mor-ee-ans) cemented its place in legend.

The Fomorians were beings of chaos, towering and twisted, thriving on destruction and imbalance. In their envy of the Tuatha Dé Danann (Too-ah-hah Day Dan-an), they sought to steal not just their lands but also the sources of their strength. During a moonless night, under the cover of a storm conjured by their dark sorcerers, the Fomorians raided the Dagda's stronghold. Amid the chaos, they seized the harp, carrying it away as a trophy, their guttural laughter echoing through the halls.

The Tuatha Dé Danann awoke to a profound loss. Without the harp, the balance of their forces seemed to waver. The harp was more than an artifact—it was the heart of their people, a source of unity and morale. Grief and fury mingled in their hearts as the Dagda, with Lugh (Loo), the shining warrior, and Ogma (Ohg-mah), the champion of eloquence and strength, vowed to reclaim what was stolen.

Guided by the whispers of the aos sí, the Dagda and his companions tracked the Fomorians to a shadowy fortress at the edge of the sea. The fortress pulsed with dark magic, and the

Fomorians had gathered to gloat over their prize. The harp, propped in a corner of the great hall, seemed dulled, its strings silent under the weight of the Fomorians' malevolent energy.

The Dagda, undeterred, stepped forward, his booming voice carrying across the stormy winds. He raised his hand and began to chant in the ancient tongue of the Tuatha Dé Danann. The runes on the harp's frame began to shimmer faintly, then brightly, as the magic awakened within it. The harp trembled, responding to the Dagda's call, and then, as if possessed by its own will, it broke free from its captors.

The harp soared through the air, strings vibrating with an unearthly hum. The melody it played struck terror into the Fomorians, freezing them where they stood. The haunting tune reverberated through the hall, and the once-ferocious beings cowered, some falling to their knees, unable to bear the sound. For those who dared to resist, the harp's music shifted, summoning a crushing sorrow that drained their will to fight.

The harp flew into the Dagda's hands, its strings singing with triumph. He played a single, powerful chord, and the remaining Fomorians fled into the night, their spirits shattered. The Tuatha Dé Danann stood victorious, their unity restored by the return of the harp.

As the storm cleared, the Dagda placed the harp in the center of their camp. He played a soft, soothing tune, and his people gathered around, their fears eased and their strength renewed. The harp had not only been reclaimed—it had proven its role as both a weapon and a healer, a reminder of the power of music to shape the course of destiny.

The harp was more than an instrument in the Dagda's hands—it was an extension of his power, a reflection of his wisdom, and a tool of profound influence. Its music held sway over the hearts and minds of all who heard it. In moments of joy, its melodies lifted spirits, binding the Tuatha Dé Danann together in celebration. It became a beacon of unity, reminding them of their shared purpose and the beauty of their land. During times of sorrow, the harp's mournful notes resonated through the halls of their gatherings, a poignant lament for warriors lost in battle. Each string seemed to carry the weight of their sacrifices, turning grief into a collective strength that fortified their resolve.

The harp's magic extended beyond emotion, reaching into the very fabric of life. Its soothing tones could lull even the fiercest of foes into a deep, unbroken slumber. Many battles turned in the Tuatha Dé Danann's favor because of the Dagda's mastery of the harp's calming melodies, granting his people the upper hand without unnecessary bloodshed. This ability to wield both strength and mercy made the Dagda a leader unlike any other—a figure who could balance the raw force of his people with the compassion that defined their essence.

Whether summoning joy, sorrow, or peace, the harp was a symbol of balance, a reminder that power must be tempered with understanding. It resonated with the natural rhythms of the world, echoing the Dagda's own philosophy. Under his guidance, the harp was more than a weapon or a tool; it was a bridge between the physical and the spiritual, a conduit for the shared experiences of his people. Through its music, the Dagda taught the Tuatha Dé Danann that true leadership was not only about wielding strength but about understanding the hearts of those you lead. The harp's melodies lingered long after its notes faded and left a legacy of harmony that would echo through the ages.

Sin é

The harp, once wielded by the Dagda to inspire, mourn, and protect, transcended its mythic origins to become a symbol of Ireland itself. Its story, woven into the fabric of the Tuatha Dé Danann's struggles and triumphs, spoke to the resilience of the Irish spirit. The harp's melodies, capable of stirring emotions as vast as joy, sorrow, and peace, mirrored the depth of Ireland's cultural soul. Over time, its significance expanded beyond the

Dagda's hands, taking root in the hearts of the people as a reminder of their strength and creativity.

In the centuries that followed, the harp became a cornerstone of Irish tradition. It appeared not only in songs and stories but also as a symbol of sovereignty and unity. Just as the Dagda's harp brought his people together in times of trial, it now represented the enduring connection between Ireland's past and its future. Its strings, vibrating with ancient magic, echoed the rhythms of the land—the waves crashing along the coasts, the wind sweeping across the green hills, and the voices of a people bound by their shared history.

The harp's prominence grew alongside Ireland's evolving identity. It found a place in traditional music, where its tones told stories as vivid and poignant as those of the Dagda himself. It became a visual emblem, gracing coins, flags, and national seals, symbolizing not just artistic beauty but the enduring resilience of a culture that had weathered countless storms. For the Irish, the harp was more than an instrument; it was a legacy, a bridge between the mythical and the real, the ancient and the present.

Even today, the harp remains a powerful emblem of Ireland's identity. Its strings carry not only music but a memory—a memory of a land that values its roots, honors its creativity, and cherishes the connection between its people and the natural world. The Dagda's harp may have begun as a tool of divine power, but its true magic lies in its ability to resonate across time, uniting generations through its story and song.

The legacy of the Dagda's harp lives on as a testament to the power of music in Irish mythology and culture. In the hands of the Dagda, the harp was more than an instrument; it was a bridge between realms, a tool that connected the divine and mortal, the natural and supernatural, the emotional and the physical. Its ability to summon joy, sorrow, and sleep was a reminder of music's transformative power—how it could inspire courage, mourn the lost, and bring solace in the darkest times.

Through its story, the harp became a reflection of Ireland's cultural essence. Its melodies resonated with the struggles and triumphs of the Tuatha Dé Danann, symbolizing their strength and unity. It was not only a weapon in battle but a balm for the soul; it embodied the belief that music is as vital as the sword in sustaining a people's spirit. This duality—of power and healing, of strength and vulnerability—is woven into the fabric of Irish identity, and the harp became a symbol of this balance.

As the harp's tale passed from the realm of myth into the traditions of Ireland, it gained an even greater significance. It became a unifying symbol of the island's rich cultural heritage, appearing in music, art, and national emblems. To this day, the harp is a proud emblem of Ireland, a reminder of the land's enduring creativity and resilience. Its strings, once plucked by a god, now vibrate in the hands of musicians, storytellers, and artists who keep its magic alive.

The story of the Dagda's harp carries a timeless message: music transcends boundaries. It has the power to heal wounds, inspire unity, and preserve memories across generations. Just as the Dagda used his harp to protect and guide his people, the melodies it represents continue to echo through time, reminding us of the unbroken connection between Ireland's mythical past and its vibrant present. Through the harp, the spirit of the Dagda and his people endures, a song that will never fade.

PRONUNCIATION GUIDE

áilleacht (aw-lokt): beautiful

aghaidh (ah-giv): face

Áine (Awn-ya): the Fairy Queen of Munster, associated with beauty, magic, and the protection of the land, capable of both benevolence and vengeance

Amergin (Ah-mur-gin): Leader of the Milesians, who was a warrior, a poet, and a druid

amhráin (ow-rawn): songs

Aos Sí (Ays shee): supernatural beings or fairies in Irish mythology, guardians of the natural and mystical forces, often linked to the Otherworld

Aodh (ee, fire): son of Lir

Aoife (ee-fah): Lir's jealous wife

aontacht (ayn-tacht): unity

arán (ah-rawn): bread

arán donn (ah-rawn dunn): brown bread

Ardan (Ard-awn) and Ainle (An-leh): loyal brothers of Naoise, aiding in Deirdre's escape

áthas (aw-hass): happiness

Baile Átha Cliath (Bah-lah Aw-ha Kleeh-ah): Dublin, the Viking stronghold and site of the Battle of Clontarf

Ball Seirce (Bawl Share-kah): the "love spot," a magical mark on Diarmuid's face that made him irresistible to women

Balor (Bah-lur): Fomorian leader with a deadly laser eye, symbolizing chaos and destruction

banshee (bahn-shee): spirit

Bean Sí (Ban-shee): banshee, a harbinger of death in Irish folklore whose mournful wail foretells the passing of a loved one

barróg (bar-ohg): embrace

beannacht (ban-ockt): blessing

bia (bee-ah): food

Bodhmall (Bow-vawl): Cumhall's sister, a wise druidess

Bradán Feasa (Brah-dawn Fassa): salmon of knowledge, a mystical fish that consumed nine sacred hazelnuts, granting it all the wisdom of the world. It was foretold that whoever ate the salmon would inherit its knowledge

Bres (Brehss): a half-Fomorian ruler of the Tuatha Dé Danann who favored the Fomorians

Brian Boru (Bree-an Boh-roo): high king of Ireland and leader in the Battle of Clontarf

bród (brohd): pride

brón (brohn): sorrow

buíoch (bwee-ock): grateful

caillteanas (kahl-cheh-nass): loss

cairdeas (kar-jass): kindness or affection

camán (kah-mawn): hurling stick

caoineadh (kwee-nah): keening, the traditional Irish practice of mourning the dead with sorrowful, vocal wailing

caora (kay-rah): berries

carbad (kar-bahd): chariot

cath (hah): battle, central to warrior life in Irish mythology

catha (kah-hah): battles

ceárta (kyar-ta): forge

ceo (kyo): mist

ceol (kyohl): song

cineáltas (kin-all-tas): kindness

ciontacht (kint-acht): guilt

claíomh (klee-uv): sword

Claíomh Solais (Klee-uv Soh-lish): the Sword of Light, a weapon symbolizing justice and kingship

clann (klawn): family

clanna (klawn-ah): tribes or families, foundational to Irish society

cliste (klish-teh): clever

cloig (klog): church bells, symbolizing freedom or release

cluiche iomána (kluh-ka ih-moh-nah): a hurling match

cnoca (knock-ah): hills

Conn (kahn, chief): youngest son of Lir

Connacht (Kawn-oct): a land often at odds with Ulster

King Conchobar (Kawn-kho-bar): king of Ulster in the Ulster Cycle, depicted as a good king

cosaint (cuss-int): protection

craiceann (krak-enn): skin

crainn (krah-n): trees

Craobh Rua (Kreev Roo-ah): Red Branch of warriors from Emain Macha, Ulster, under King Conchobar

cruatán (kroo-ah-tawn): trials

Cú Chulainn (Coo Hull-un): the central hero of the Táin Bó Cúailnge, renowned for his bravery, supernatural strength, and loyalty to Ulster

cúl (kool): goal in a hurling game

Culann (Coo-lawn): the renowned blacksmith of Ulster

cumha (koo-ah): sorrow

Cumhall (Coo-ill): father of Fionn MacCumhaill, a fearless leader and champion of his people, whose life ended in battle before Fionn's birth

Dagda (Dahg-dah): the "good god" of the Tuatha Dé Danann, symbolizing wisdom, strength, and abundance daideo (dah-djo): grandfather

daracha (dah-rah-kah): oak trees

Dian Cécht (Dee-ahn Kay-acht): healer of the Tuatha Dé Danann, symbolizing renewal

Diarmuid Ua Duibhne (Deer-mwid Oo Duv-nah): the noble warrior of the Fianna who sacrifices everything for love

dídean (dee-jun): shelter

dílseacht (deel-shakt): loyalty

dóchas (doh-khass): hope

Donn Cúailnge (Dun Koo-ul-nyuh): the brown bull of Cooley, the prized animal at the center of Queen Medb's ambitious raid

draíocht (dree-ocht): magic that weaves through the myths of Ireland

draíocht dorcha (dree-ocht dur-uh-ka): dark magic

droichid (drik-id): bridges

dúiche (doo-hah): territory, such as the dúiche of Ulster

dúiche (doo-hah): homeland

dún (doon): stronghold

dúshláin (doo-shlaw-in): trials

éad (ay-ed): envy

eagla (ah-glah): fear

eagna (ag-nah): wisdom

ealaí (al-uh-ee): swans

éanacha (ay-nah-kah): birds

Éire (Ay-rah): Ireland, central to many Irish myths and legends

Emain Macha (Eh-mawn Mah-kha): the seat of King Conchobar, central in the Ulster Cycle

fáinne geal an lae (fawn-yeh gyal an lay): dawn

fáithe (fah-ha): seers

fáilte (fahl-teh): welcome

feall (fyal): betrayal

féar (fay-er): grass

fearg (farr-ug): anger or wrath

féasta (fay-sta): feast

féiniúlacht (fayn-yoo-lacht): identity

Fer Baeth (Fair Bah-hah): a warrior from Connacht (Kawn-oct), a land often at odds with Ulster, had crossed into its borders, threatening the peace; infamous for his brute strength, cunning tactics, and merciless nature in battle.

Ferdiad (Fair-dee-ah): a warrior and close friend of Cú Chulainn, tragically forced to fight him in the epic's most poignant duel

Fiachra (fee-uh-krah, raven): son of Lir

Fianna (Fee-ah-nah): legendary Ulster warriors led by Fionn MacCumhaill, known for their bravery, loyalty, and service to the High King of Ireland

Fiannaíocht (Fee-ah-nee-ucht): Fenian Cycle

file (fil-eh): poet

Finegas (Fin-eh-gass): a revered poet and seer who was known throughout Ireland for his vast knowledge and devotion to the pursuit of wisdom

fíodóireacht (fee-oh-door-acht): fabric

Fionn MacCumhaill (Fee-uhn Mac-Coo-ill): the aging leader of the Fianna, whose pursuit of Diarmuid and Gráinne drives their story

Fionnuala (Fyun-oo-lah, white shoulder): daughter or Lir; the eldest sibling in the tale of the Children of Lir, known for her wisdom and resilience

fiosracht (fis-rokht): curiosity

Fir Uladh (fir ul-ah): Men of Ulster

fírinne (fee-reh-neh): truth

Fomorians (Foh-mor-ee-ans): a race of dark giants led by the fearsome Balor (Bah-lur), whose deadly eye symbolized chaos and destruction; enemies of the Tuatha Dé Danann

fuinneamh (fwin-yiv): energy

ga (gah): spear

Gáe Bulg (Gayee bulg): means belly spear, Cú Chulainn's spear

Gaeilge (Gwel-gah): Irish language

gaoth (gwee): wind

gé (gay): goose

geal (gyal): bright

geis (gaysh): a magical obligation or taboo that binds an individual to fulfill a specific task, often driving conflict in Irish tales.

geasa (gas-uh): magical obligations, plural

Go n-éirí an bóthar leat (Guh nye-ree on boh-har lat): "May the road rise to meet you"

Goll MacMorna (Gull Mock-Moor-nah): leader of the Fianna (Fee-ah-nah), Ireland's most elite band of warriors in the Salmon of Knowledge tale

grá (graw): love

grán (grawn): grain

Gráinne (Graw-nya): the strong-willed heroine of the story who defies societal expectations to follow her heart.

grian (gree-un): sun

halla (hall-ah): hall

Imbolc (Im-bolk): the festival of spring and renewal, Saint Brigid's feast day, February 1st, marked a time of hope and new beginnings

iomaíocht (ih-mee-acht): competition

íonacht (ee-nacht): purity

Kildare (Kill-dahr): the location of Saint Brigid's monastery and the sacred flame that symbolizes her legacy

Knockainey (Knock-aw-nee): the mythical home of Áine, a sacred hill where the veil between the mortal and supernatural worlds is thin

Labhraidh Loingseach (Lahv-reeh Ling-shock): a wise and fair king from Irish mythology, known for his hidden donkey's ears

Láeg (Layg): Cú Chulainn's childhood friend who served as his loyal charioteer láidir (law-jeer): strong

lámh (lahv): hand

laoch (lay-uck): hero, embodying courage and virtue in Irish myths

laochra (lay-uck-rah): band of heroes or warriors

leanaí (lah-nye): children

Lia Fáil (Lee-ah Fawl): the Stone of Destiny, symbolizing rightful kingship

Líath Lúachra (Lee-ah Loo-uh-krah): a fierce warrior woman who helped raise Fionn MacCumhaill

lios (liss): fairy fort or mound, believed to be an entrance to the Otherworld

Lir (Leer): a king and sea god who is a prominent figure of the Tuatha Dé Danann; father of the four children, Fionnuala, Aodh, Fiachra, and Conn, in the Children of Lir tale

loch (lock): lake

locha (lock-ah): lakes

Lugh (Loo): a hero of the Tuatha Dé Danann, representing the harvest, light, skill, and craftsmanship

Lugh Lámhfhada (Loo Lahv-ah-dah): Lugh of the Long Arm

lúth (loo): agility

machairí (mah-kah-ree): meadows

machnamh (mock-niv): thoughtfulness

madra faire (mah-drah fwar-eh): guard dog

madra rua (mah-drah roo-ah): fox

maidin (mah-jin): morning

maidineacha ceoiche (mah-jin-ah-kah kyo-ih-kheh): misty mornings

maithiúnas (mah-hoo-nas): forgiveness

meangadh (mang-ah): smile

Medb (Mayv): the ambitious and cunning queen of Connacht, whose desire for power and possession of the bull drives the events of the Táin Bó Cúailnge

míorúilt (meer-oolt): miracle

misneach (mish-nakh): courage

mná na réalta (muh-nah nah rayl-ta): "woman of the stars"

Moytura (Moy-choo-rah): as in the Battle of Moytura, a sacred plain where the Tuatha Dé Danann and Fomorians battled

muintir (mwin-cheer): family

Muirne (Mur-neh): the mother of Fionn MacCumhaill

Murchad (Mur-kah): the son of Brian Boru and a key warrior in the Battle of Clontarf

Naoise (Nee-sha): a brave warrior and Deirdre's true love, central to her tragic tale

neamhbhriste (nyav-vris-the): unbreakable

néalta (nayl-tah): clouds

neart (nyart): strength

Ní neart go cur le chéile (Nee nart guh kur leh keh-lah): "There is no strength without unity," a proverb reflecting the values of teamwork and leadership.

Niamh (Nee-uv): the daughter of Manannán mac Lir, the sea god, and a princess of Tír na nÓg (Teer-na Nohg), the Land of Eternal Youth.

Norse (Nor-sh): Vikings, influential settlers and invaders in Irish history

Nuada (Noo-ah-dah): leader of the Tuatha Dé Danann, representing resilience and honor

oilithreacht (ull-ih-racht): pilgrimage

oireachtas (ur-ok-tas): assembly

Oisín (Uh-sheen): a poet-warrior of the Fianna, known for his journey to Tír na nÓg and his longing for his homeland

ollamh (uh-lahv): poet or learned person, holding high status in Irish society

onóir (un-ore): honor

plean (plan): plan

radharc (rah-yark): scenery

Réicshe Uladh (Rayk-sheh Ull-ah): Ulster Cycle; one of the great cycles of Irish mythology.

réalt (ray-alt): star

rí (ree): king

Ríastrad (Ree-uh-strahd): the "warp-spasm," a supernatural transformation that grants Cú Chulainn immense power and an otherworldly appearance during battle

ríocht (ree-uhkt): kingdom

sagart (sah-gart): priest

sagairt (sah-gart): priests

saol (sayl): life

saoradh (seer-uh): freedom

scéalta (shkayl-tah): story

scéalaithe (shkay-lah-heh): storytellers

scil (skil): skill

seanchas (shan-khas): folklore

séipéal (shay-peel): chapel

seoid draíochta (show-id dree-ocht-ah): magical charm

Sétanta (Shay-tan-tah): Cú Chulainn's name as a youthful boy before he became a legend

Sídhe (Shee): fairy mounds, believed to be homes of the Aos Sí

Sin é (Shin ay): That's it, The End

síol (shee-uhl): seed

siombail (shim-bill): symbol

siúl (shool): walk

sleá (shlah): spear

sliotar (shlit-er): hurling ball

sneachta (shnak-ta): snow

solas (soh-lass): light

srutháin (sruh-hawn): streams

stoirm (stur-im): storms

strainséir (stran-shayr): outsider

suaimhneas (soo-iv-ness): peace or calmness

tailte (tahl-the): lands

Táin Bó Cúailnge (Tawn Boh Koo-ul-nyuh): "The Cattle Raid of Cooley," the title of the epic recounting Medb's raid and Cú Chulainn's heroic defense

talamh (tall-uv): land, earth, or soil

Tara (Tar-ah): the seat of the High Kings of Ireland

tinte (chin-the): fires

tinteán (chin-chawn): hearth or fireside

tír (teer): a land, country, or region

Tír na nÓg (Teer nah nohg): the Land of Eternal Youth in Irish mythology, a paradise where time stands still

tonnta (tuhn-tah): waves

trua (true-ah): pity or tragedy

tuath (too-ah): countryside

Tuatha Dé Danann (Too-ah day Dah-nan): The godlike beings of Irish mythology, embodying magic, wisdom, and strength who were guardians of Ireland before the arrival of the Milesians

uaigneas (oo-ig-ness): solitude or loneliness

uisce (ish-ka): water

Ulaidh (Ul-uh, Ulster): Ulaidh was a Gaelic over-kingdom in north-eastern Ireland during the Middle Ages made up of a confederation of dynastic groups. It is from them that the province of Ulster derives its name.

urnaí (ur-nee): prayer

www.ingramcontent.com/pod-product-compliance
Lightning Source LLC
Chambersburg PA
CBHW021348150726
47989CB00005B/2159